CAMPUS COUNTERSPACES

CAMPUS COUNTERSPACES

Black and Latinx Students' Search for Community at Historically White Universities

Micere Keels

CORNELL UNIVERSITY PRESS ITHACA AND LONDON

First published 2019 by Cornell University Press

Library of Congress Cataloging-in-Publication Data
Names: Keels, Micere, author.
Title: Campus counterspaces : Black and Latinx students' search for community at historically white universities / Micere Keels.
Description: Ithaca : Cornell University Press, 2019. | Includes bibliographical references and index.
Identifiers: LCCN 2019019613 (print) | LCCN 2019022247 (ebook) | ISBN 9781501746888 (cloth) | ISBN 9781501747908 (pbk.)
Subjects: LCSH: African American college students—Attitudes. | Hispanic American college students—Attitudes. | African Americans—Race identity. | Hispanic Americans—Ethnic identity. | Group identity—United States. | College student orientation—United States.
Classification: LCC LC2781.7 .K44 2019 (print) | LCC LC2781.7 (ebook) | DDC 378.1/982—dc23
LC record available at https://lccn.loc.gov/2019019613
LC ebook record available at https://lccn.loc.gov/2019022247

ISBN 9781501746895 (pdf)
ISBN 9781501746901 (epub/mobi)

For Davu

Dedicated to the mothers who incubated me with their words: Corinth Lewis, bell hooks, Maya Angelou, Sonia Sanchez, Nikki Giovanni, Harriet Tubman, Toni Morrison, Zora Neale Hurston, Lorraine Hansberry, Tsitsi Dangarembga, and so many more.

Contents

Acknowledgments

I am deeply indebted to all the students who repeatedly completed surveys and interviews. This book would not be possible without their willingness to offer up the details of their college and other life experiences. This research and writing could not have been conducted without the generous funding and developmental support of the William T. Grant Foundation. I am thankful for the undergraduate and graduate students who worked with me during various stages of data collection and analysis.

I am grateful for my editor Frances Benson, who championed my goal of writing an academic book that would appeal to nonacademic audiences and pushed me at each step to write with clarity and "grace." Rachelle Winkle-Wagner generously went well beyond her role as a reviewer to provide insightful comments and suggestions that strengthened the depth of ideas presented in the final manuscript. To Barbara Ray, I thank you for quickly and enthusiastically editing this book from top to bottom with an eye toward making it engaging for a nonacademic audience.

I am mutually indebted to Gina Samuels, Rachel Jean-Baptiste, Adrienne Brown, and many others for creating an intellectually and emotionally sustaining campus counterspace.

I am thankful for Vivian Gadsden and Vivian Tseng, who gifted me with their sight: where I saw barriers they saw opportunities; where I saw dead ends they saw around corners.

CAMPUS COUNTERSPACES

INTRODUCTION

It Doesn't Have to Be Race-Ethnicity to Be about Race-Ethnicity

The costs of college extend far beyond the financial costs of attendance. There are opportunity costs in the form of forgone employment, and psychosocial costs in the form of stress, depression, and anxiety. These financial, forgone opportunity, and psychosocial costs disproportionately accrue to students from historically marginalized groups. This is because the costs are greatest for students who need to juggle both school and paid employment, are experiencing financial distress, do not see themselves reflected in the larger student body and faculty, are less integrated into campus life, and experience a cultural gap between their precollege and college contexts. Understanding these and other psychosocial costs is of increasing importance because researchers have established that ability, academic preparation, and financial resources explain only part of the variation in college persistence.[1]

In an effort to improve our understanding of the psychosocial factors that affect minority student persistence, I have been tracking a cohort of approximately five hundred Black and Latinx college freshmen who enrolled in fall 2013. My initial thought was to write a book about financial distress—the effect of inadequate financial resources on campus belonging and commitment to educational goals, as well as heightened doubts about whether college will pay off. However, many researchers have soundly made the case for how the escalating financial cost of college and convoluted financial aid policies fail students.[2] Instead, I focused on how the "college for all" narrative fails students by indiscriminately pushing many to enroll in colleges with very low graduation rates just for the satisfaction and relief of being counted among the college-going population. But that plan, too, was swept aside after being inundated with news articles skeptical of minority students' "imagined" campus microaggressions and mischaracterizations of their desire for safe spaces as self-infantilizing. Those for and against safe spaces are miles apart in their perception of oppression in America. Popular debates position on one side White Americans, 69 percent of whom believe that Black Americans are now treated the same as White Americans, and on the other side Black Americans, 59 percent of whom believe that Black Americans continue to be treated worse than White Americans.[3]

News articles describing historically marginalized students as "fragile and perpetually vulnerable to victimization," as George F. Will put it in the *Washington Post* in October 2016, contrasted sharply with what I was hearing in my annual interviews with seventy Black and Latinx students. None of my students' voices were represented among the victimized students portrayed in these news articles and op-eds. None of the students in my study were asking to be "protected" from new ideas. Instead, as reflected in the statements of one Latinx female student, they relished exposure to new ideas: "I just love having—which I've never had before—being able to sit down with [students] and discussing social issues or political issues and really intellectual conversations that I've never been exposed to before, and for them to enlighten me with new information. I love that." However, these students were asking for access to counterspaces—safe spaces that simultaneously validate and critique one's interconnected self and group identity—that would enable radical growth. Radical growth can be understood as the development of ideas and narratives that challenge dominant representations of and notions about their marginalized identities. It is these needs and opportunities for radical growth that I explore in this book.

The interviews also revealed that many Black and Latinx students were unaware of their need for identity-affirming counterspaces. Students like Marcela, a Latinx female student who personifies resilience. Because of housing instability, she attended three high schools but still graduated on time with a 3.5 grade point average, and scored in the ninety-fifth percentile of the ACT test. However, despite obtaining a "free ride" to a selective private liberal arts university, she left halfway through the second quarter of her first year.

Unlike most of the Black and Latinx students in my study, Marcela expressed that she had no social adjustment and no financial challenges: "I'm multiracial, but I mostly identify really as Hispanic, and I never felt out of place, I never felt uncomfortable speaking to anyone else, so with racial diversity and LGBTQ, even that, everything. Totally tolerant. Everyone's easygoing and fun. Classes were awesome, and the professors were amazing. And the coursework was just fun to do."

Unlike most, her transition to college meant an increase in financial resources, and she enjoyed the accompanying sense of independence: "It was nice to feel like [I was paying my way] through my financial aid or scholarships, 'cause ever since

I was fourteen I've been living with different people, and I've always been dependent on someone, only being able to contribute a really small amount." Unlike most college students, Marcela did not struggle with suddenly being out from under parental monitoring. Her mother had a debilitating brain tumor when she was age ten. "I haven't been living with parents for a lot of years now, since the beginning of high school. Through all of high school I was completely in control of my time, when I did my homework, and things like that." But what did trip her up was the newness of the experience. Like most students, she struggled adjusting to the new academic expectations, and her struggles were compounded by the lack of a rigorous college preparatory curriculum in high school. "I had never done anything like that before. I never had to write a paper above three to four pages, and all of a sudden I had to write papers that were like ten pages. I also expected, I did so well in high school that I expected to just be doing the exact same way in college, and it's really discouraging. . . . [In high school] I wouldn't sleep to get whole assignments done the night before. So in college I had those same habits. And that just didn't work at all for college."

Unlike students with college-educated parents, Marcela had no one to assure her that her struggles were a normal part of the transition. She had no one to offer strategies for managing the workload or encourage her to access campus supports. Her mother was the first and only member of her immediate and extended family to obtain a college degree; however, her mother's poor health left Marcela unsupported in the college transition:

> I called a cousin of mine, I can't remember if he even finished college or not, he's never had a real career and things like that. He's much older than me, so I called him and kind of was like wondering. I was kind of like, "I don't know what I'm doing. I feel like this is not working. What do I do? Should I just forge my own path?" All this stuff. He kind of just told me, "Just do whatever you want, cuz; it's not a big deal, no one's gonna die. You're not a bad person." Those are very nice things to say. But it's not like he told me "No, stick with it. Don't give up." You know, he didn't say those types of things.

This brings us to one of several moments during the interview where it was clear that, through glimpses into her friends' experiences, Marcela knew that there was insider knowledge she did not have access to. She contrasted her family's advice with the advice received from her best college friend, who had college-educated parents: "[My] friend encouraged me to try and stay because she told me about how she also felt feelings of dropping out, but she talked to her mom, and her mom told her all these [other] things."

Leaving college early is not confined to only first-generation college students. I have several friends and acquaintances with advanced degrees, and have heard stories of others, who have called their children home partway through the first year upon realizing that the ship was sinking fast. Each case involved skilled negotiations with the school to ensure that grants and scholarships would still be in place when the children returned. Unlike the children of my friends and acquaintances, Marcela was unable to pick up where she left off. She has since restarted at a community college and no longer has any grants or scholarships.

During the months after leaving college, Marcela struggled to find a job and learned many lessons that cemented her decision to return to college. Key among them was a personalized understanding of why she needed a college degree.

> What I realize now is that I really can't help anyone in my family, because that was another reason why I dropped out. My mom was gonna be homeless, and so I went to work to help her pay her rent for a couple of months. But I couldn't really do it for that long, because part-time minimum wage doesn't pay for rent. I just realized I can't accomplish any of my goals without college. I'm very undeveloped in critical thinking and different things. I'm undereducated and ignorant about so many things. How can I contextualize the issues of today and try to find solutions if I don't understand why they're there in the first place! So I realized, I just need to go to college for the education itself; and in order to make more money to accomplish some of those other goals I need to have a degree, because that's what employers want to see too.

These lessons now form the ideological buoys supporting her second attempt.

I begin with Marcela, a student who did not express any direct racial-ethnic identity challenges during the transition to college, because even though Latinx and Black students' college-going identity challenges are often deeply connected to their sense of themselves as Black or Latinx students, many of these challenges are not directly about their racial-ethnic identity. Instead, many of their college-going identity challenges result from structural racism—an intergenerational system in which public policies, institutional practices, cultural representations, and other norms work to perpetuate racial-ethnic inequity.[4] In this system, Marcela was able to feel free of interpersonal discrimination and still experience systemic inequities in her academic and other college-relevant identities.

So what's race-ethnicity got to do with it? Many of the identity challenges that Latinx and Black students experience result from how race-ethnicity increases the likelihood that they are also first-generation college students; that they attended high schools that did not offer a rigorous college preparatory curriculum; that they have to work for pay to afford college; that they cannot be carefree students and must help support the families they left behind; and that they must contend with many other nontraditional college student challenges.

The aim of this book is to challenge the status quo, which is that despite the proliferation of diversity initiatives, the "overriding assumption is that the dominant White [middle- and upper-class] culture through which the university environment functions is working and requires no adjustment."[5] Furthermore, because universities claim to be non-oppressive spaces, the dominant narrative is that any racial-ethnic inequalities result from supposed non-racial, non-ethnic factors such as income and academic preparation. However, universities fail to connect these supposed non-racial, non-ethnic factors to the historical oppression and continued discrimination of historically subjugated racial-ethnic groups. Consequently, most diversity policies revolve around tolerance—the acceptance of an allowable amount of variation—and aim to help historically marginalized students adjust in ways that leave the institution's culture largely unchallenged and unchanged.

Throughout this book, you will encounter descriptions that make the invisible visible by the highlighting of experiences of cultural "deviants"—students who fall outside normative assumptions of who college students should be. This is because normative cultural expectations are most visible when they conflict with the experiences of cultural deviants.

The book unfolds as follows.

In chapter 1, I present the problem and briefly describe the data used to gain insight into how challenges to Black and Latinx students' college-going identity threaten their persistence.

In chapter 2, I lay out the argument for shifting social identities from the margin to the center of how universities engage with students from historically marginalized groups. I do this by showing that even when minority students intentionally attempt to "move beyond" their social identities and embody a humanist identity, they are regularly tripped up by how they are identified by others, and by the psychic energy they must expend to deny, to themselves, their experiences of prejudice. A colleague of mine likens this to "to standing in the rain while attempting to deny that one is getting wet."

Each subsequent chapter examines a particular social identity or intersection of identities and explores how it is experienced, understood, internalized, rejected, or reorganized during the transition and adjustment to college life. Each chapter also examines how various aspects of the campus context affect the stereotypes, roles, and academic risks and supports that are associated with a given social identity. As expected, some social identities are affirmed at historically White colleges and universities and are associated with feelings of inclusion and an unquestioned embrace of the institution, while other identities are rendered inferior or invisible and are associated with feelings of exclusion and resistance of the institution. In counterspaces, identities that are rendered inferior or invisible in the larger campus culture are explored, critiqued, and deepened, and sometimes claimed for the first time.

Chapter 3, coauthored with Resney Gugwor, delves into how financial distress is associated with how students make sense of the "opportunity" to attend college. Many of the financially distressed students believed they had to attend college to secure their economic futures but doubted that obtaining their degree would ensure financial stability. Their experiences illustrate the large role that one's relative financial position plays in identity and sense of belonging on campus.

Chapter 4, coauthored with Ja'Dell Davis, provides an intersectional perspective on gendered racial-ethnic identities (a gender identity that is racialized and a racial-ethnic identity that is gendered), with a focus on experiences of intellectual invalidation. Black women were the most likely to report these alienating campus experiences, and many responded with identity-protection coping strategies that led them to disconnect from campus life or limit their engagement to activities that affirmed their gendered racial-ethnic identity.

Chapter 5, coauthored with Elan Hope, provides insight into how Black and Latinx students navigated their identity as activists during a period in American history when social media documentation of racially-ethnically motivated violence made it impossible to pretend that America had entered a post-racial state of consciousness. There was little variation in how these students felt about police brutality and the targeting of Latinx deportation; almost all were disturbed, most were outraged. However, there was variation in the public visibility of their response and engagement with activism.

Chapter 6, coauthored with Carly Offidani-Bertrand, turns to the role of racial-ethnic identity-based campus organizations in helping or hindering students to manage feelings of being othered. Students' perspectives on being othered ranged from feeling that their peers appreciated their differences to feeling stereotyped as the sole representative of their group. The extent to which they had counterspaces helped them process those feelings and celebrate their differences as diversity.

Chapter 7, coauthored with Gabriel Velez, illustrates the diverse social identities that are developed in racial-ethnic, identity-based campus organizations. Students listed race-ethnicity as the focus of their initial attraction to these organizations. However, they came to embed themselves in these organizations because the organizations also developed other aspects of their identities, such as their professional, political, and academic identities. This chapter also highlights students who explicitly sought to embed themselves in organizations and clubs that were not connected with their racial-ethnic identity.

Chapter 8, coauthored with Hilary Tackie and Elan Hope, takes up the issue of how and where commuter students, students who do not have access to peer support through living on campus, locate their sense of campus belonging. When students lack a "place" on campus, they are more likely to adopt a functional ("I go to school") identity rather than an all-encompassing ("I am a student") identity. We show how this status is both an identification and an identity.

Chapter 9, coauthored with Emily Lyons, considers the processes of constructing an academic identity for first-generation students. This chapter discusses challenges to building an academic identity among first-generation college students, both for those whose parents are unambiguously supportive of their child's college attendance and those who are ambivalent. Parent ambivalence was particularly salient for first-generation, Latinx women with immigrant parents.

Chapter 10, coauthored with Tasneem Mandviwala, examines how the intersection of students' race-ethnicity and gender is associated with their motivational orientation toward college. Students' motivational orientations were evident in their reasons for going to college and in their adjustment struggles during the first year. This chapter focuses on how Latinx men's motivational orientations can either align them with or place them at odds with their institutions' dominant cultural orientation.

In the concluding chapter, I take a step back to examine the bigger picture and suggest ways that colleges and universities could achieve greater integration by attending to difference. Latinx and Black students' college-going identity challenges are often created through institutional action and inaction, and can be resolved through institutional action.

A methodological appendix is provided for those who want deeper insight into how the data were collected, coded, and analyzed.

But first I present simple definitions for a few key terms. *Black* is used as a racial-ethnic category to refer to a wide range of ethnic groups of African descent. *Latinx* is used as a gender-neutral racial-ethnic category to refer to a wide range of ethnic groups of Hispanic and Latin American descent. *White* is used as a racial-ethnic category to refer to a wide range of ethnic groups of European descent. Also, it is important to explicitly discuss how the racialization of Latinx people in the United States leads to our hyphenation of "race-ethnicity" throughout this book. Latinxs in the United States, unless they can visually, linguistically, and culturally pass as White, are members of a racialized group.[6] Individuals identified as Latinx are essentialized as having one pan-ethnic culture that is placed low in the American status hierarchy and are thus racialized as a non-White group.

Throughout this book the term *historically* rather than *predominantly* White college and university is used because it is about much more than the demographic composition of these institutions that make them hostile places for historically underrepresented students.[7] It is as Patricia Hill Collins has written, the "sedimented or past-in-present [discriminatory] formations where unquestioned ideologies create understandings that appear to be the natural and inevitable."[8] Historically White colleges and universities are the focus of my research because only about 8 percent of Black and 13 percent of Latinx students attend minority-serving colleges and universities.[9]

All names of students, universities, campus organizations, and other proper names are pseudonyms. Identifying aspects such as number of siblings, major, campus job, and parents' occupations have been modified in ways that maintain the accuracy of the narrative while also preserving anonymity.

The pseudonyms for the historically White colleges and universities are "Rural StateU" for a large (somewhat intimidatingly large), rural, flagship state school; "Urban StateU" for a midsize, highly ranked, state school located near the center of Chicago; "Suburban StateU" for a midsize, state-funded, research university located in a distant suburb of Chicago; and "Urban PrivateU-North" and "Urban PrivateU-South" for two liberal arts private colleges in Chicago. Although I do not identify the school of attendance, small details such as rural, urban, or suburban location, the level of minority enrollment, and students' own descriptions of their schools often make each student's institution easily identifiable. This further emphasizes the need to adjust specific details about certain cases to ensure that students remain anonymous. As shown in figure 1 below, the full extent to which Black and Latinx students, particularly men, are a marginalized presence on their campuses can only be seen when looked at in relation to the full undergraduate student body.

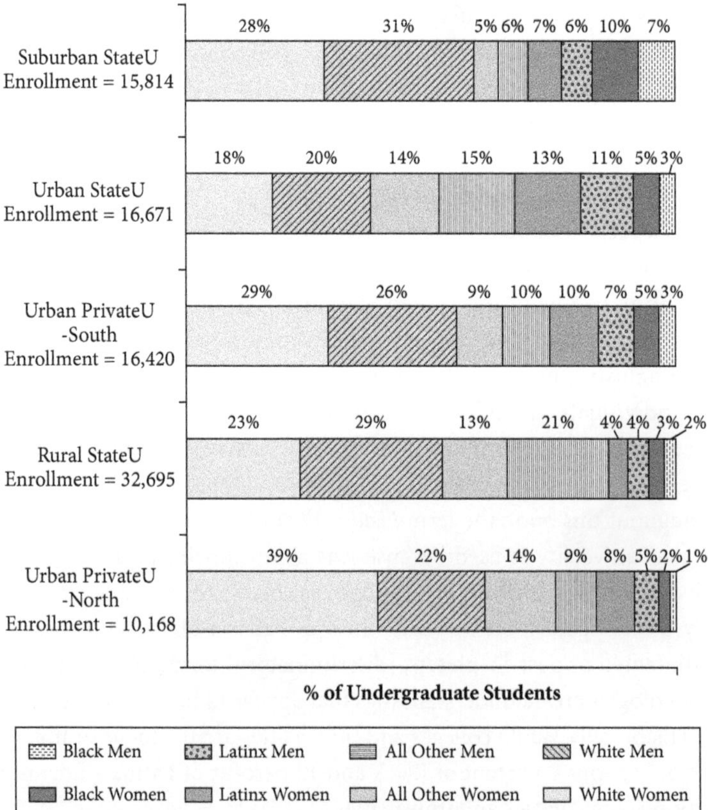

1

OUTLINING THE PROBLEM

It is important to quantify the racialization of college access and success at the outset because, as Tanya Golash-Boza notes, "race scholars have to start with empirical questions about why things are the way they are and push forward theoretical understandings that help us to explicate and end racial oppression."[1] The goal is to highlight what have become long-standing normative expectations about the racialized aspects of degree attainment that continue to be perceived from the vantage point of individual rather than institutional failings.

Obtaining a college degree is now the principal route to upward mobility in the United States, and because there continue to be large racial-ethnic disparities in degree attainment, inequality continues to grow.[2] The benefits are clear and undeniable. In 2016, the median income among full-time workers with a bachelor's degree was approximately $60,112. It was only $35,984 for high school graduates with no college degree employed full-time.[3] Also clear and undeniable is that access to the benefits associated with obtaining a college degree is racialized: 15 percent of Latinx, 23 percent of Black, and 36 percent of White adults have a college degree.[4]

It is not that Latinx and Black youth have not internalized the message that they should go to college—they have. From 1996 to 2012, college enrollment increased by 240 percent among Latinx youth and 72 percent among Black youth, compared to only 12 percent among White youth.[5] Efforts aimed at expanding access to postsecondary institutions have succeeded in creating college enrollments that are more diverse than ever before. However, most historically underrepresented students continue to leave without a degree. Specifically, about

60 percent of Black and 47 percent of Latinx college students will not obtain their degree, compared to 37 percent of White college students.[6] This low likelihood of degree attainment means that enrolling in college can be damaging for the futures of too many Black and Latinx youth.

Enrolling but not finishing can be damaging because the expansion in college access has occurred alongside increasing costs and decreasing sources of grant aid. Today, the average student receives less financial support than four decades ago.[7] In 1975, the average Pell Grant covered approximately 84 percent of published tuition and fees, but by 2017 it covered only 37 percent for four-year public institutions and 11 percent for four-year private, nonprofit institutions.[8] Essentially, tuition increases have outpaced grant aid, and "aid" increasingly comes in the form of loans. In 1980, approximately 66 percent of all federal financial aid was in the form of grants, and 33 percent was in the form of loans. By 2003 the fractions had flipped, and only 23 percent was in the form of grants, and 68 percent was in the form of loans.

This shift toward loan debt is detrimental to the likelihood that students will persist to graduation. Higher rates of grant aid are associated with increased likelihood of graduation, whereas higher rates of loan aid are associated with the opposite.[9] Racial-ethnic differences in borrowing are striking. Approximately 43 percent of Black and 30 percent of Latinx students, but only 25 percent of White students have more than $30,500 in student debt after four to six years in college.[10]

Expanding access while increasing costs without also attending to increasing the likelihood that students will graduate means that not only is college financially riskier but that increasing numbers of low-income and low-wealth students, who are disproportionately Black and Latinx, are exposed to that risk.[11] James Rosenbaum and colleagues were among the first to call attention to the fact that given the reliance of low-income students on loans, broadening college access could further disadvantage those students if attention were not paid to increasing their graduation rates.[12] This warning has not been heeded. Enrollment has increased faster among low-income students than among high-income students, but graduation rates have increased faster among high-income than among low-income students.[13]

Consequently, the downside of the successful push toward "college for all" is that access to a degree becomes access to student debt without also providing the supports necessary to increase the likelihood that historically underrepresented students graduate.[14] Because Black students take on the most debt, they have been hurt the most by a system that has prioritized broadening enrollment over increasing persistence.[15] If we are to continue promoting college as *the* way to enter or stay in the middle class, we must do a better job of creating differentiated institutional structures that facilitate persistence.

Framework for Identity-Conscious Supports

This book orients colleges and universities toward the broad category of identity-conscious supports and, within this category, campus counterspaces as one identity-affirming support that can facilitate the college success of students from historically marginalized groups. Counterspaces are those "exclusionary" spaces where those of a similar social identity gather to validate and critique their experiences with the larger institution. Identity-conscious supports consider how social group memberships differentiate students' precollege and college-going experiences, and then provide supports accordingly. There is increasing evidence that identity-conscious supports can help bridge historically marginalized students' transition to and success at historically White colleges and universities.[16] Advocates of identity-conscious supports take seriously the research showing that social group membership gaps remain even after accounting for academic preparation and intellectual abilities, and then actively work to identify social identity factors that could differentially privilege subgroups of students.[17]

One example of identity-conscious supports is the importance for science, technology, engineering, and math (STEM) departments to intentionally highlight scientific discoveries made by minorities as a way of increasing minority student persistence.[18] Intentionality is needed to counterbalance the implicit messages sent by what minority students call the "wall of White men"—hallways lined with photographs and paintings celebrating the university's great thinkers. Not seeing one's group represented in the institution's cultural artifacts and faculty communicates information about the institution's social hierarchy. This implicit hierarchy intrudes on marginalized students' ability to align their social identities with their academic identity—how they perceive themselves as students at that institution—by continually reminding them of their outsider status.[19]

Throughout this book, identity-affirming counterspaces are discussed in ways that highlight how they help counteract this outsider status—how facilitating formal and informal "exclusionary" spaces enables universities to create the conditions that facilitate historically marginalized students' inclusion and integration into the broader campus community. Students who experience stereotyping, discrimination, and alienation appear to feel a greater sense of institutional connectedness when they participate in campus counterspaces.[20] When administrators actively facilitate counterspaces, these spaces become institutionalized mechanisms that enable marginalized students to support each other in establishing a sense of campus belonging and academic self-confidence.

Inequality at the Starting Gate

The findings reported in this book come from the ongoing Minority College Cohort Study (MCCS), a longitudinal investigation of a cohort of Black and Latinx freshmen who enrolled in college in fall 2013. The MCCS is a sample of 533 academically prepared students: they had an average high school GPA of 3.5, 77 percent had taken at least one advanced placement course, and their average ACT score was in the seventy-fifth percentile of national ACT ranking. This is also a sample of educationally motivated students: 88 percent were certain they would complete their bachelor's degree, and 63 percent were certain they would go on to complete a graduate or professional degree. Because this sample of students is academically prepared and educationally motivated, I can shift the focus to factors other than academic abilities in examining their transition and adjustment. Even with this shift, however, there is no escaping the substantial racial-ethnic differences in the K–12 educational resources to which students were exposed, resources such as curricular offerings, academic rigor, discursive teaching styles, and instructional technology.[21] These differences guarantee racial-ethnic gaps in the extent to which students are prepared for both the content of the college curriculum and the instructional style of most faculty.

Once students get to college, these K–12 inequalities are magnified by institutionalized inequalities on campus. As noted by Vijay Pendakur, a director of college diversity programs, "higher education is currently structured in a way that produces significantly lower outcomes for students of color, low-income college students, and first-generation students."[22] One of those structural inequalities is the extent to which students have college-educated family members who can provide supports that increase their likelihood of succeeding in college. These supports include cultural support (advice on norms and expectations of the social and academic culture of the institution), informational support (advice on how to seek out formal and informal resources and opportunities), and instrumental support (advice on study strategies and acquiring content knowledge for specific courses).[23] This means that Black and Latinx students are more dependent on their institutions for "insider knowledge" about how to navigate college successfully.

However, under the current identity-neutral framework used by most postsecondary institutions, generalized issues such as selecting courses, engaging in cocurricular activities, and adjusting to dorm life are delivered with universal programming. Such identity-neutral programming keeps hidden much of the taken-for-granted cultural knowledge of institutions, knowledge that propagates socio-structural inequalities among students precisely because colleges operate according to many unwritten codes of middle- and upper-class cultural norms.[24] Consider, for example, an identity-neutral first-year orientation. The orientation would likely not include discussions about the institution's norms regarding independence versus interdependence. Students in American universities are expected to be individually motivated, to learn independently, and to develop strong independent voices and ideas.[25] Students who do not subscribe to this cultural norm are often unknowingly in cultural conflict with what is expected of them.

As Nicole Stephens and colleagues illustrate, these cultural conflicts are often connected to students' social class backgrounds.[26] They show that first-generation students had a high likelihood of being in cultural conflict with the implicit expectations of historically White colleges and universities. First-generation students were less likely to endorse independent motives for attending college, such as exploring their potential and expanding their knowledge of the world, and more likely to endorse interdependent motives, such as helping their family and being a role model for their community. This cultural mismatch was associated with lower grades, even after accounting for SAT scores. They then showed how a manipulation of university orientation materials to represent the university culture as interdependent (about learning and working together with others) eliminated a performance gap between first- and continuing-generation students.

The Inescapable Nature of American Racialization

One can almost matter-of-factly state that class identity matters in the college transition in relation to the argument that one must make for the continued attention to students' racial-ethnic identities. The arguments foregrounded in this book are in direct opposition to arguments that students should bring only their academic selves to college, leaving behind attachments to their social identities.[27] Suspicions of attachments to racial-ethnic and other marginalized identities are based on the White American belief that the ideal identity is a humanist identity that is free of group allegiances.[28] The argument is that people who prioritize rational reasoning over subjective preferences are able to "maturely" reason about issues without regard for how it would affect the interests and advancement of members of their gender, race-ethnicity, socioeconomic status, or any other social allegiance.[29] Arguments for adopting a humanist identity are motivated by the assumption that Whites have shed their European identities and associated tribal allegiances. This, however, belies the fact that European customs and values permeate all aspects of American society, and therefore makes the humanist identity a colonized identity in which the price of inclusion is erasure through assimilation.

As Linda Alcoff argues, the push for minority individuals to adopt a humanist identity free of attachment to social groups occurs only when identity is mistakenly essentialized and conceptualized as singular—that there is only one way to be a member of a given social group, and that it is stable across historical time and across social contexts. A more informed understanding of social identities is that they are simply points *from which* to see; "How could there be reason without sight, without a starting place, without some background from which critical questions are intelligible?" she asks.[30]

In this sense, one's racial-ethnic identity is not an immature attachment that individuals must attempt to leave behind, but instead an inescapable perspective from which one makes sense of the social world. This inescapability is evident in the Black Lives Matter movement and in the effects of the Trump presidential campaign's vilification of Latinx and other minority groups. In August 2015, the second year after the students in my study enrolled in college, they were asked about their personal experiences with Black Lives Matter and Donald Trump's messages. Their responses revealed that media messages and events tied to these issues could only be interpreted through students' understanding of themselves as racialized beings.

One Black female student expressed these feelings in response to being asked, "Tell me about the most stressful experience you've had in relation to the increased tension about race and immigration in the US over the past year."

> The most stressful would be just learning about what's going on in the world and stuff like that and all of the Black kids getting killed right now. And, like when we have, like, some type of demonstration on campus, and how White people didn't actually join in with us, more made fun of us and stuff like that. So I guess that would be kind of stressful. I guess my tension would be like, if I'm reading it and then just seeing it play out on the news and how it's always going in favor [of] the White person and then being surround[ed] mostly [by] White people in my school who are ignorant to the cause, so it's just a little frustrating. Because stuff doesn't work in our favor and then being on a predominately White campus where you just have to be aware just in case something happens to you or one of your friends. So, yeah, it's just stressful thinking like what if this could happen to me or what if this could happen to one of my friends?

In response to the same question, a Latinx female student said,

> Depending on what news channel you turn on or what you read, like, there can be really nasty, hurtful comments. Both my parents are immigrants. They're now US citizens, but they came here as illegal immigrants, and my husband, he's also undocumented, he's here legally in the

> US through the Dream Act . . ., so it's definitely a personal issue for me. I've never heard anything negative in person. It is upsetting.

Even for students who did not have any direct personal experiences with either of these issues, public debates associated with race-ethnicity—their race-ethnicity in particular—maintained a permanent presence, just below the surface, ready to activate their racial-ethnic identity. This hyperawareness was evident in a Black male student's response to being asked to describe any personal experiences he had had with police or immigration authorities. "I personally haven't had any bad encounters with the police or anything," he said. "Of course, I see everything that goes on in the news and stuff. . . . Just makes you more aware, like you can just think to yourself, it can happen anywhere, you know? . . . It's not necessarily you look at yourself as a target, 'cause you Black and young, but it's not really far from that at the same time. Just, I feel like it's definitely different for minorities, you know?"

Black Lives Matter and Trump's presidential campaign are only two of numerous sociohistorical events that make it impossible for Black and Latinx students to bring only their academic selves to college. American society does not allow these students to be anything other than Black college students and Latinx college students. Therefore, thoughtful examination of how their racial-ethnic and associated social identities differentiate their transition to and success in college can only improve the actions universities take to facilitate their persistence.

Safe Spaces versus Counterspaces

When I began this project, "safe spaces" and "counterspaces" were interchangeable terms for places where people with a common social identity came together and collectively provided protection from and resistance to social, political, and institutional oppression. However, by 2015, the concept of a safe space had been completely co-opted and reframed as infantilizing, discriminatory spaces that go against what some have come to redefine as the core mission of institutions of higher learning—exposing students to a combative clash of viewpoints that challenge one's beliefs. That sentiment was never clearer than in Judith Shulevitz's *New York Times* op-ed in March of that year, "In College and Hiding from Scary Ideas."

Many of those who argue against safe spaces make patriarchal arguments that consider only the prototypical college student whose development is not placed at risk by engaging in a combative exchange of ideas in intellectual discussions that, at times, personally implicate that student's social identity. This prototypical student is White, male, middle or upper class, and has been validated in educational institutions and in broader societal representations throughout his life. In sharp contrast, many historically marginalized students come to college with a lifetime of negative interactions with those in positions of power in educational spaces. Those experiences are not erased upon entering college, freeing students to engage equally in an "unregulated exchange of ideas," as Matthew Pratt Guterl put it in his *Inside Higher Ed* op-ed on August 29, 2016.

Arguments against safe spaces are often based on ahistorical assertions that colleges and universities are post-oppression of all kinds—post-racial, post-gender, post–sexual identity, post–religious affiliation—because, currently, there are few if any laws that directly disadvantage historically marginalized students. However, history is embedded within people's social identities and is integral to their understanding of societal hierarchies. Post-oppression claims that criticize safe spaces also deny the continued existence and significance of microaggressions—brief and commonplace verbal, behavioral, and environmental indignities that communicate hostile, derogatory, or negative racial-ethnic slights and insults, be they intentional or unintentional.[31]

My own experiences may help reveal the fallacy that American institutions of higher learning are post-oppression. I experienced my first microaggression as a faculty member my second week on campus, when I was still dressing in my best outfits. When I started at the University of Chicago in 2004, my department was in a lovely converted historical house. Because I had a forty-five-minute commute, I left home early to avoid traffic. As I walked to my building on a largely deserted street early in the morning, I recognized a young White woman who was the project manager for one of my colleagues. She was walking toward me on the sidewalk. I smiled, but she did not smile back. I shrugged it off and proceeded to follow her up the path to the door. When she reached the door, she turned quickly, braced her back against the door, clutched her purse to her chest, and breathlessly stated that I would have to come back later because "we don't let people in this early." It took a second to register that although we had been formally introduced and she had seen me passing in the hallway at least a few times, and I was wearing one of my best outfits, in that moment, she was unable to recognize me as anything other than a threat. I then did what I had long ago learned to do: smile and allay her fears. I reminded her that I am the new faculty member (the only non-White faculty member) in the department, showed her my keys, and soothed her feelings of embarrassment. I then kept my day moving; this was not the first and would not be the last time that my blackness would override everything else. Did I mention that I was wearing one of my best outfits?

I experienced my most recent microaggression in April 2016, a few months before I began this book. Again, I got to campus early (note to self: maybe I should stop getting to campus early). I stopped at the Grounds of Being, the Divinity School's student-run coffee shop, and as I was pouring my coffee, I heard "my niggas . . . and my niggas . . ." coming from a Drake song playing loudly over the sound system. The volume itself was an issue that early in the morning, but what disturbed me was the unexpected jolt of hearing those words in an institution that is not "down with niggas." I was the only Black person in the coffee shop; all others were White, except for one Asian individual.

I told the student behind the counter that "I'm going to need you to change that song." At first, she was bewildered by my request but quickly recovered and looked at me with incredulity. I repeated my request with a little more intensity, at which time the other White female student behind the counter asked what was happening. Once informed by the first student, she turned to me and firmly stated, "We don't make judgments here. We play all music." Again, I repeated my request with enough intensity that the first student quickly changed the song. She then attempted to chastise me for my judgmental intellectual immaturity. At that point I could have provided some information about who I was and engaged her in an intellectual discussion of the issue. Instead, I chose to tick the Grounds of Being off as one more place on campus to avoid.

Though in both of those interactions I was the higher-status individual based on my achieved status at the university, American society granted each of those White women, at birth, an ascribed status that supersedes credentialed status. However, what my achieved status and years of developing adaptive coping skills do afford me is the ability to prevent microaggressive experiences from derailing my day. Historically marginalized students need safe spaces to develop those affordances—perceptions of the world that determine their possibilities for action.

Those who oppose safe spaces make empirically false arguments that fail to understand the experiences of minority college students. Minority college students have more diverse friendship networks than majority students, learn from faculty who do not represent their backgrounds, and attempt to obtain support from administrators who lack an experiential understanding of the families and communities the students grew up in.[32] In other words, minority students navigate unequal power relations in almost all aspects of their college experiences. Safe spaces, then, can be thought of as providing respite and restoration, enabling minority students to continue engaging in the "clash of ideas." As noted by Morton Schapiro, Northwestern University's president, in a January 2016 *Washington Post* op-ed, "students don't fully embrace uncomfortable learning unless they are themselves comfortable."

It is clear to me that those arguing against the need for identity-affirming counterspaces do not understand the identity-based challenges that marginalized students encounter—the constant reminders of the aspects of their social identities that prevent them from equal membership in the larger student body, the toll of the psychological and emotional "energy and resources [they devote] to understanding and responding to involuntarily being positioned as a [marginalized] subject."[33]

The co-opting of safe spaces has placed marginalized students in a defensive position. Their request for identity-affirming supports such as safe spaces now threatens their academic identity when safe spaces are described as antithetical to college student development. Many news articles and op-eds have stuck to polemic arguments that position students as either intellectually and emotionally sophisticated enough to engage ideologies that challenge their own or too intellectually and emotionally immature to tolerate ideological diversity.

In contrast to these polemic arguments, Alison Cook-Sather, a professor at Bryn Mawr College, describes how being introduced to the concept of "brave spaces" illuminated her misunderstanding of what marginalized students are requesting.[34] She had previously understood safe spaces as contexts that precluded the possibility of intellectual challenge, discomfort, and risk, not places for students to take intellectual risks. However, once introduced to the concept of brave spaces, a concept used in the literatures of critical race, Latinx critical, intersectional, social justice, and Black feminists, she realized safe spaces' rightful place on college campuses.

Essentially, safe spaces are brave spaces. Because people who create formal and informal safe spaces see themselves in each other, they enter a collective commitment to ensuring that each other's humanity will not be invalidated during discussions and debates. Safe spaces thereby enable marginalized students to be brave in their critique of themselves and their group in ways they cannot in contexts where they must defend the very validity of that group membership.

Because of the distorting and co-opting of "safe spaces," I am discarding that term and advocating for *counterspaces*. Counterspaces are "revolutionary settings embedded within larger settings and contexts. That is, they are pockets of resistance that may, to one extent or another, disrupt the dominant narrative of the larger setting and context."[35] This means that, yes, counterspaces are designed exclusively for individuals from marginalized groups, but they can welcome individuals from advantaged groups, so long as those individuals adhere to the goal of supporting adaptive responding. *Adaptive responding* is the constellation of emotional, psychological, and behavioral capacities that enable marginalized individuals to cope with and resist oppression, thereby exhibiting resilience. In counterspaces, college students wrestle with radical ideas, develop self-narratives that challenge stereotypes, share instrumental knowledge about the rights of marginalized individuals, and experience growth along numerous other dimensions that can only occur when students are challenged by like-minded peers.[36]

The idea that one can be challenged by like-minded peers is where many reflexive objectors of counterspaces get stuck. A counterspace filled with Black and Latinx college students may have as a common denominator individuals with direct experiences with oppression and marginalization in educational spaces. Beyond this, however, all bets are off with regard to a universal set of experiences, attitudes, or beliefs. Because, in such a counterspace, individuals do not have to debate the existence of marginalization and oppression, they are freed to move on to deeper, more radical discussions.

A large body of social and psychological research on identity undergird the varied presentations of formal and informal counterspaces discussed throughout this book; counterspaces can be ideational, relational, and/or physical spaces, and have academic, social, cultural, and/or political goals. I lean on the work of Na'ilah Suad Nasir and others who draw our attention to the cultural aspects of educational institutions and learning that occurs therein—taken-for-granted social practices and expectations that can place marginalized students' social identities in conflict with their educational identity.[37] I stand on the work that Beverly Tatum and others have done to unpack the reasons why youth of a given racial-ethnic group often gather in particular physical spaces within educational contexts, and place this phenomenon within a framework of normative identity development.[38] Lastly, I borrow from the work of Daniel Solorzano and others who use critical race frameworks to show how counterspaces provide marginalized students with sites of resistance that enable them to name, critique, and counter stereotypical understandings of their group.[39]

Grounding Our Understandings in a Critical Examination of Students' Experiences

Because most college administrators and professors did not grow up in Black, Latinx, or socioeconomically disadvantaged households, they lack the depth of understanding necessary to develop identity-affirming supports. Given the brief and perfunctory nature of most social interactions, it is almost impossible to understand the perspectives of those with background and status characteristics that are markedly different from one's own. Only by digging deep into students' experiences of their college campuses can we understand the positions of marginalized and underrepresented students in relation to the culture and structure of the institution.

Critical race theories enable this examination by foregrounding in all aspects of the research process race-ethnicity, racism, and discrimination.[40] These theories center race-ethnicity as a salient social category that is used to identify individuals as belonging to distinct, hierarchically organized groups, and through processes of social interaction, race-ethnicity becomes internalized as identity.[41] Critical race theories further clarify that it is because race is a social concept (embedded in hierarchical interpersonal interactions) rather than a physiological concept (genetically distinct and biologically measurable), that it maintains its significance in the face of evidence disconfirming its biological reality. Latinx critical theories push past the Black-White binary and articulate discrimination as a salient part of the Latinx American experience.[42] Latinx critical frameworks theorize issues such as language, immigration, culture, identity, and phenotype that are distinct in Latinxs' experiences of oppression, identification, and identity in the United States.[43] By situating this research within critical race and Latinx critical theories, I am able to privilege college-going Black and Latinx students' experiential knowledge as legitimate without the need to ground them in direct comparisons to students of other racial-ethnic groups.

In subsequent chapters, my coauthors and I attempt to unpack many of the assumptions about who college students should be, whether race-ethnicity should be integral to their academic identity, and how they should relate to institutions of higher learning. In discussing our findings, when there are no differences between Black and Latinx students we discuss them as a group. We will also highlight differences among Latinx students and among Black students because gender, class background, parent education, political identity, acculturation, and numerous other social identities matter. Critical race and Latinx critical theories foreground *intersectionality*, which is the understanding that key status characteristics such as race-ethnicity, gender, national origin, class, and sexuality are indivisible in understanding people's experiences of the social world. Latinx, immigrant, queer, lower-income college women experience campus differently from Latinx, American, heterosexual, middle-income college women.[44] As Na'ilah Suad Nasir discusses in her book, *Racialized Identities: Race and Achievement among African American Youth*, knowing a student's racial-ethnic identity and identification tells us important but never enough information.

To guard against the human tendency toward abstracting simple patterns and simplistic explanations, we excerpt a broad range of students' voices throughout this book. Each chapter attempts to ensure that no one student's experiences dominate (except chapter 2) and provides enough information about each student to ensure they are not flattened into one-dimensional caricatures of themselves. Some chapters could only be written by providing the arc of students' experiences over their first-year transition. For those chapters, we detail the experiences of three to four students who represent the full range of the larger sample. Other chapters are more thematic and include excerpts from many students' experiences to ensure that the diverse ways that a singular issue was experienced and understood are richly presented.

I take seriously Chimamanda Ngozi Adichie's admonishments regarding the danger of a single story. "The single story creates stereotypes, and the problem with stereotypes is not that they are untrue, but that they are incomplete. They make one story become the only story."[45] Complex understandings can emerge by sharing the differences as well as similarities in how several Black and Latinx students experience the transition to historically White colleges and universities. Also included are the narratives of students who dispute the need for counterspaces that affirm their racial-ethnic identity, or believe that their racial-ethnic identity is best affirmed in racially-ethnically heterogeneous counterspaces. Presenting one unified argument in favor of counterspaces runs the risk of making them an oppressive expectation for Black and Latinx students who choose to locate their campus home elsewhere.

My coauthors and I analyzed a considerable amount of data in writing this book. Although the first-year transition is highlighted, at the writing of this book we had interviewed seventy students for three consecutive summers and invited the larger sample of 533 students to complete seven waves of online surveys. The narratives presented here illustrate much of what we have learned about how students' social identities are associated with their transition to college. We focus on students' narratives because identities are essentially the compilation of the stories we tell to say who we are, and the stories we tell about who our people are. On rare occasions we bring in findings from the larger survey sample.

A Brief Summary of the Minority College Cohort Study

We recruited students from five historically White colleges and universities in the Midwest: 24 percent were recruited from two urban private institutions; 35 percent were recruited from an urban public institution; 28 percent were recruited from a rural public institution; and 13 percent were recruited from a suburban public institution. The sample is ethnically diverse. Latinx students specified their belonging to a diverse range of ethnic national origin groups, such as

Mexican, Puerto Rican, South American, and Cuban. Black students specified their belonging to a diverse range of ethnic, national origin groups, such as Haitian, Nigerian, African, African American, and Caribbean. The majority of Latinx students self-identified as Mexican American (68 percent), and the majority of Black students identified as African American (84 percent).

All participants were first-time freshmen who had recently graduated from high school. The students came from more than 255 different high schools. All were enrolled as full-time students and were, on average, age eighteen at enrollment.[46] The overwhelming majority (90 percent) were in-state students, and most attended high schools in the Chicago metropolitan area. The majority (60 percent) were first-generation college students, where neither parent has a four-year degree. Latinx students were particularly disadvantaged with regard to parent education; 28 percent of Latinx students' parents did not have a high school diploma or GED, compared to only 5 percent of Black students' parents.

The summer after their first year in college, we randomly selected seventy students after stratifying the sample by race-ethnicity, gender, and level of financial distress reported on the survey. A team of three male and three female Latinx and Black interviewers completed in-person interviews, or phone interviews with a small number of students who were out of state at the time. By the time of the interviews, participants had completed three online surveys during the course of the first year. During the interviews, students reflected on the process of deciding to go and applying to college, their experiences regarding the transition and adjustment to college, their financial struggles in paying for college, and how their family supported them along the way. Students talked about their social and academic challenges and about the people they turned to for support. Lastly, they talked about their immediate plans for getting through college and their career aspirations.

A research team of eleven scholars, representing a diverse range of racial-ethnic groups, class backgrounds, and immigration histories collectively coded and analyzed the interviews to ensure that no one voice or perspective biased data interpretation. Much of this collective feedback was aimed at keeping one another open to unexamined patterns and explanations for observed patterns. This involved suggesting alternative strategies for comparing and contrasting cases, alternative and additional ideas for the coding the text, and concepts and theoretical frames from allied disciplines. Through a collective and iterative process, we created a master list of codes. All transcripts were first coded by a randomly chosen primary coder and then a randomly chosen secondary coder. Subsets of team members then delved into more detailed sub-coding based on the focus of each chapter.

2

THE IMPOSSIBILITY OF A COLOR-BLIND IDENTITY

Shifting Social Identities from the Margin to the Center of Our Understanding of How Historically Marginalized Students Experience Campus Life

Some individuals use identity to refer to a core sense of self, composed of valued personal characteristics such as goals, personality style, intellectual abilities, and other private opinions of one's self.[1] This core sense of self is believed to be stable across contexts. Others use identity to refer to the roles people play in society, such as student, employee, athlete, and sibling.[2] As expected, one's identity roles are contextual. Identity can also refer to the social groups with which one identifies, such as gender, race-ethnicity, national origin, and social class.[3] It is this latter definition that is the focus of this book. Although this chapter focuses on racial-ethnic identity, much of what is discussed would be true of other marginalized social identities.

To some extent, simple demographics predestine particular American racial-ethnic groups to be minorities on college campuses, but the marginalization that Black and Latinx students experience is an institutionally constructed phenomenon. To be minoritized is to be a member of a group that is both less in number and has less power and more stigma than other groups. Karolyn Tyson argues that it is the combination of being both in the demographic minority and negatively stereotyped—having to interact with peers and professors who hold racialized stereotypes about academic potential—that leads Black and Latinx students in historically White colleges and universities to experience marginalization in ways that implicate both their racial-ethnic and academic identities.[4]

Throughout this book, *identity* is used to refer to both identity (the way we see ourselves), and *identification* (the way others see us). These internal and external aspects of identity cannot be separated or interchanged. Simply matching the characteristics of a particular racial-ethnic, socioeconomic, gender, or other social group is not enough to determine whether and in which contexts an individual will *claim* that social identity. For example, there were times during the interviews when Julissa clearly identified as Black and liked being identified as one of the "Black representatives on campus." This occurred when she discussed her leadership roles in the predominantly White campus organizations. However, she also actively rejected being seen as just another member of the "Black community" on campus, a community that she stereotyped as "entitled," "not inclusive," "[without] school spirit," and low achieving. This one social identity—Black American—is associated with different stereotypes, roles, and opportunities, depending on the context in which it is evoked.

Julissa claims her Black identity in contexts when she is the rare Black member of a campus leadership organization because in those contexts it comes with stereotypes of "Black exceptionalism"—White validation of a Black person whose success is held up as atypical of the Black collective. However, this is a fragile Black identity that must continually be defended, because as soon as she exits spaces in which she is identified as exceptional, she returns to being just another Black student on campus.

> With the fact that I don't [wear my hair natural] and I wear glasses, and the clothes that I do wear are kind of conservative, and not really out there, I really think a lot of people feel safe. And I'm just really basing this on my college experience of people literally saying, "Oh well, I don't really see you as you being a Black person." . . . I really think they just view Black people, especially Black women, by what they wear and how they [do their hair].

The challenge is that buying into Black exceptionalism legitimizes respectability politics—the extent to which the success of Black individuals hinges on their ability to distinguish themselves in socially respectable, nonthreatening ways.[5]

The Transition to Historically White Colleges and Universities

The transition to college is accompanied by a considerable number of stressors, such as adapting to new classwork expectations, creating new social networks, managing independence, and identifying career pathways. Racial-ethnic minority students have the added burden of navigating racialized interpersonal stressors in their interactions with peers, faculty, and administrators. We usually focus on racialized stressors that come from intergroup interactions, and particularly interactions between White Americans and members of minority groups.[6] However, racialized stressors can also occur among peers of one's own group in the form of identity insults such as the "acting White" accusation.[7] Santiago, a Latinx male student attending Suburban StateU, had this experience of being called out for "betraying" his culture because the peer group he related to most was not of his racial-ethnic origin.

> I did get a lot of bash for not having Mexican friends, as others had. But, honestly, at my high school, I had a lot of Mexican friends. But I really do get along with Black people, White people. . . . I was open to anyone. . . . What had happened was, the Hispanic fraternity on campus, they were really the ones first semester showing me around, and I loved it, I was really committed to them. But . . . I didn't talk to many of the younger guys. Younger guys came in with the mentality that they were different, they were from the real Chicago, the areas in Chicago that aren't too good. I come from a suburb, and they didn't understand it. . . . I never got name-called or anything, but there was a few comments made like, "Oh, so you joined the White fraternity." But, I really paid no attention.

This means that minority students navigate both intragroup and intergroup racialized stressors, which tax their cognitive, emotional, and physiological energies and undermine their ability to focus on academics. The result is that race-ethnicity continues to matter in determining student success in college. Compounding this stress is that minority students are often placed in the position of feeling it necessary to prove that race-ethnicity continues to matter in these supposedly post-racial college contexts. Despite the beliefs of many faculty and administrators, research contradicts the idea that intellectualism is enough to overcome long-held prejudices. Toon Kuppens and Russell Spears show that as people gain education, their explicit, deliberative racial-ethnic biases decline substantially, but not their implicit, intuitive biases.[8] Kuppens and Spears conclude that individuals with higher levels of education are more likely to "genuinely endorse racial equality, but nevertheless carry spontaneous negative evaluations of, or associations about Blacks."[9] This "unintentional" discrimination is as consequential as intentional discrimination.[10]

I have seen firsthand the indignant response among faculty when I argue that race-ethnicity continues to matter. They quickly claim that they judge only ideas, not the cultural frame of a particular idea, and they definitely do not judge the social status of the individual presenting a particular idea. Such statements reflect the belief that if one does not personally engage in blatant and overt acts of discrimination, then race-ethnicity is not an issue, at least not within one's sphere of influence.[11] This need to call discrimination and racism things of the past was evident in claims that Barack Obama's elections was proof that the United States had arrived at a post-racial state of consciousness. Ironically, the years immediately after this claim evidenced an increase in racist events.[12] What has lingered from post-racial arguments is the idea that foregrounding race-ethnicity perpetuates racism, the argument being that if we want racism to disappear, we must first ignore the existence of race-ethnicity.

Instead, I argue that ignoring the existence of race-ethnicity reduces a significant aspect of people's lived experiences as meaningless and denies the profound effect that it has on their sense of self. This denies racialized students—students marked by stigmatized embodied characteristics such as skin tone, hair texture, language, and accent—opportunities for critical discourse aimed at reorganizing existing racial-ethnic stereotypes, and it denies them opportunities to create new, transformative understandings of race-ethnicity.

Racialization of the American College Campus

Racialization can be thought of as a relational process, a combination of dynamic social and psychological processes, that places people into distinct racial groups and then becomes internalized as identity.[13] This perspective is in keeping with the belief that race has no biological basis and is instead made real and consequential through social positioning. Critical race theorists like Bonilla Silva argue that it is because race is a social concept that is embedded in hierarchical interpersonal interaction, rather than a physiological concept that is genetically distinct and biologically measurable, that it has maintained its significance in the face of evidence against its biological reality.[14]

During orientation week, most incoming racial-ethnic minority students are shocked to realize just how few of them there are on campus, particularly for students who attended diverse high schools. Sharon, a Black, female, first-year student at Rural StateU who attended a diverse high school (36 percent Latinx, 28 percent Black, and 25 percent White), was surprised to realize that she was not going to have the same mix of friends as in high school. Rural StateU's campus was only 5 percent Black and 8 percent Latinx.

> I didn't know that when I moved there. I thought it was evenly dispersed, but, it's not. . . . It was very new because I was used to Bolivar high school kids. Very evenly dispersed. There was not more of anyone at Bolivar. That's really, really diverse. [In high school] I had Asian friends, Black friends, White friends. At [Rural StateU] you can probably have a [few] White friends, but they were . . . like really rich, rich

> White people. Instead of the kind of settled [White] people that I know. I hang out with more Black people now than I did when I was in high school.

Many students had experiences similar to Sharon's. Several also noted how White students frequently assumed they were lower class, which added yet another barrier to building diverse peer networks.

Today, historically White colleges and universities have a student body that is, on average, about 9 percent Black and 13 percent Latinx. Even so, more than one-third of Latinx and Black students attend colleges that are less than 4 percent Black or Latinx[15]—institutions where they are often the lone representative of their group in class, in the dining hall, on the floor of their dorm, and in the clubs they join. Being such a small fraction of the student body is itself a racial-ethnic identity challenge and a challenge to one's sense of belonging at the institution.[16] Racial-ethnic minority students also quickly notice that they are not well represented—and sometimes even completely absent—among the faculty. That said, it is about much more than lack of representation among the students, faculty, and staff. Racialization is about social positioning; Black and Latinx individuals are often overrepresented among the service staff, so much so that students report being mistaken for service staff when not displaying clear markers of their student status. Latinx and Black students also move through campuses filled with named buildings, murals, statues, and portraits celebrating those who amassed their wealth by colonizing and oppressing their ancestors and ancestral lands. It should come as no surprise, then, that research consistently shows that Black and Latinx students continue to experience racial-ethnic microaggressions and feelings of isolation on campus.[17]

Julissa's Story

In 1928, Zora Neale Hurston wrote, "I feel most [Black] when I am thrown against a sharp White background. . . . I feel my race." In 2018, that description still captures Julissa's experiences at Rural StateU. In fact, much of what research tells us about the significance of racial-ethnic identity for marginalized youth navigating White spaces is evident in Julissa's story.[18] We will see that Rural StateU structured false choices between her academic identity and her Black identity, and false choices between inclusion in the Black community and inclusion in the broader campus community.

Julissa is an only child to working-class parents who had her later in life. She was motivated by their sacrifices to ensure her bright future, such as how hard they labored to move out of a dangerous Chicago neighborhood to a more stable northern suburb. "Things got a little too rough for me, I would say, growing up," she said. "You know, living in a house where you see people constantly running down the side of your house being chased by law enforcement." Moving to the suburbs and enrolling in a science and technology magnet high school gave her access to educational opportunities and a college-going peer group that paved her pathway to college. In particular, seeing her classmates struggle during high school, "and then signing up to struggle again [for] four [more] years kinda motivated me to go to college and ultimately end up at [Rural StateU] with them. So I guess, you know, that peer support group kind of steered me in the right direction."

Research tells us that peer support for college can be more important than an individual student's record of academic achievements.[19] In Julissa's case, her parents' belief that education was the way to ensure a brighter future, coupled with her own desire for a better future, formed the base of her drive to go to college.

> I wanted to go to college because no one in my family ever went to college. Seeing how much my parents have struggled to bring me up in a nice community, providing me with resources, and putting the right people in my life to get me where I am today. So my main reasons for going to college were not to struggle like my parents, or anybody else who kind of struggles on a daily basis, you know, who didn't go to college. I knew then that I wanted a career, not a job.

This belief that college is *the* way to a better financial future, coupled with the awareness that job loss, foreclosure, and bankruptcy left her parents struggling, propelled Julissa's unceasing drive to both get in and find a way to pay for college. Knowing there would be little financial support, she took it on herself. "Imagine doing sixty-one different applications with two or three different essay prompts," she said. But it paid off. She received "a lot of scholarships," and college was fully funded. She was also able to send her parents a couple hundred dollars each month to help with their rent.

But the demands of college coursework were still a shock. "I started struggling around maybe the fifth week of my first semester," she told us. "Physics was really difficult, all this new stuff that I was seeing for the first time." But she "kinda hung on" and entered "senior year, with senior standing." Her ability to hang on was in part the result of her suburban high school with its college preparatory curriculum, and a residential summer research program at one of the state universities that she gained access to through her high school.

What Julissa's high school did not prepare her for were the ways that the racial-ethnic stratification in academic achievement create false identity choices for high-achieving Black and Latinx students.[20] The initial dearth of Black students in her STEM major was made worse by higher attrition among some Black and Latinx students. By her senior year, she said, "I noticed I was the only African

American student in my classes." It became clear to her that the university was a "weed-out" school. In an August 2016 op-ed in the *Observer*, professor Sarah Cate Baker referred to "the math-science death march" that undergraduates must survive to major in a STEM field. Such courses persist because many faculty believe that they weed out the students who are not well prepared or who lack the ability to succeed in that major. Weed-out courses are also based on the belief that there is a bell curve of academic talent, and that grading on the curve provides the competition necessary to weed out less able students.

These beliefs are filled with structural and cultural misassumptions. One structural misassumption is that all students have similar K–12 academic opportunities for developing their underlying talents. One cultural misassumption is that all students are similarly motivated by competitive versus cooperative classroom contexts. Countering these misassumptions is a growing body of research showing that collaborative and interactive classrooms help level the uneven playing field.[21] They also increase engagement with and retention of academic content, and increase minority student retention in STEM majors.[22]

This "weeding out" of students from STEM courses, a disproportionate number of them Black students, and the segregated nature of all aspects of campus life, including study groups, left Julissa academically isolated. "So now I'm the only African American in [the class]. It is kind of like a weakness, because the study groups are segregated a little. But, you know, I still work through it though."

The attrition also reinforced stereotypes and biases that manifested in professors' interactions with her. When asked if she ever received any advice that was bad or not helpful, Julissa mentioned the low expectations of her. "Just a lot of professors who see a Black student in this large physics lecture and it's just [they] tell you, you might not be able to get a certain score on that exam." Those messages, she said, made her second guess why she was in college and whether the major was really what she wanted to do. "So just a lot of negative advice when it came to academics," she said.

These and other marginalizing experiences created an institutionally constructed need for her to choose between her racial-ethnic and academic identities. This false choice dogged her entire college career, created waves of self-doubt, and created social struggles that were much more challenging than any of her academic struggles.

It Didn't Have to Be This Way

When Julissa applied to Rural StateU, she assumed the university created and offered racially-ethnically themed housing for minority students. Such housing is one of many types of living-learning housing options for students who share common objectives or interests and who actively express an interest in sharing a common living environment. However, Rural StateU's "unplanned" housing segregation is in sharp contrast to deliberately created racially-ethnically themed housing, which is generally a small number of dorms or floors within a larger dorm that celebrate a particular cultural history. Living in carefully planned themed housing has been associated with higher feelings of campus belonging and higher graduation rates.[23] But as Julissa only later discovered, the university's housing policy did not offer themed housing and instead fostered segregation and promoted stereotypes.

Julissa was assigned to housing on the "Black side of campus," which ultimately led to a disconnect between how she perceived herself and what she believed was the Black versus White student identity on campus. "On the Black side of campus," she said, "things didn't look as beautiful. The [White] side, you see a total difference in student motivation, their preparedness, resources offered to them. They had nicer dorms, nicer facilities and resources." Interestingly, she associated individual attributes such as "motivation" and "preparedness" with institutional attributes such as "resources offered to them." She also placed those individual attributes first, as if the motivation and preparedness of White students preceded the institution providing the White side of campus with better resources. These perceptions created a rupture between her Black identity and her academic identity when she moved to the White side the next year. Her comments reveal just how much she had internalized racial-ethnic stereotypes: "[Once] I moved to the [White] side of campus sophomore year, I experienced a lot of diversity. Getting to meet people that were motivated, that felt like they weren't only entitled to things but they needed to go out and work for it. Ultimately finding my niche and group of people that motivated me was what made my sophomore year a great experience." As Na'ilah Nasir notes, youth are always searching for ways of understanding who they are, and whenever they are in doubt, culture provides many stereotypes to fill the gap.[24] Julissa was no exception. She internalized and deployed racial-ethnic stereotypes to fill her gaps in understanding of the Black student body from which she distanced herself.

Julissa believed that her hard work and scholarship funding earned her the right to live on the White side. It was the university's fault, she told us, for not making it clear that she could have lived on the White side of campus that first year, "especially since I had that first year paid in full with scholarships." What she did not know was that her scholarship funding was exactly why she ended up on the Black side of campus. Rural StateU uses a first-come, first-served policy for housing. Students who have all their finances in place early have the first pick of dorms. This policy segregates students by income and, because of the racial-ethnic dynamics of American society, also by race-ethnicity. For Julissa, institutional decisions created the division by clustering students requiring financial aid, scholarships, and deferment into particular dorms.

Minority students at the university have long requested this policy be changed. Five years before Julissa enrolled, a minority student group drafted a resolution requesting changes to how first-year undergraduates were placed into housing. The resolution illustrates students' understanding of how housing policies stereotype students associated with each dorm.

> Whereas, [introducing a lottery system] first-year students who are waiting on financial aid, scholarships, and deferment would no longer face an unequal choice in housing assignments, students of low-income and similar racial and ethnic backgrounds would be more evenly distributed in housing, and [other] students would no longer be able to choose their housing based on perceived stereotypes,
> Whereas, this lottery system would encourage more racially and ethnically diverse housing and provide first-year students with a new perspective on diversity at [Rural StateU],
>
> Whereas, this lottery system would have the long-term benefits both of breaking down the stereotypes associated with each housing type, breaking down the stereotypes held by individual students, and encouraging lasting, diverse multicultural communities in housing,[25]

Because Julissa did not know that the Black students were themselves among those asking for greater housing integration, she assumed that the majority of the Black students were not open to "being around different types of people." This unplanned housing segregation is one example of the institutional processes through which some subgroups of students are minoritized.

The Search for Campus Belonging

Although Julissa experienced several instances of structural and interpersonal discrimination, her need for broader campus belonging motivated her to minimize and suppress those experiences. I can only speculate that this must have created substantial internal conflict, because she also describes herself as someone who speaks up about prejudice, as she did when serving as an elected representative on one of the student affairs committees.

> There was a time last year when a lot of the African American football players threw a party at a bar. It was on the main street of campus, and the police saw a lot of Black students in a line trying to get into the bar,

> and they shut it down. Very quick, and brought out mace, and they brought out police dogs. When you see Caucasian or Indian students standing in the same line going to the bar, on the same night, just a different week, you don't really see a lot of action, and a lot of reaction to break up the fun, or break up the community. Bring out dogs and mace on a bunch of college students who weren't doing anything but standing in a line? They weren't blocking the road at all, they weren't acting ignorant, they weren't loud, just standing in a line trying to get to a bar. I kind of addressed [it in my student affairs organization], and they're still working on that, as we speak.

Despite her recognition of and readiness to challenge discrimination and prejudice whenever she saw it in others, she was often blind to her own experiences with discrimination, and blind to her own prejudices or, more aptly, blind to her own internalized racism—conscious or unconscious acceptance of the racist stereotypes and biases of one's racial-ethnic group, and the resulting discriminating, criticizing, fault-finding of oneself and others of one's group.

Julissa's conscious acknowledgment of having experienced individual and institutional discrimination only surfaced at the end of roundabout answers to questions. When asked direct questions about experiences of discrimination, her first response was denial.

> I really haven't had any in the community where [my parents] live, everyone knows me, everyone knows my family, I've worked with the village and with the mayor, so I really don't experience a lot of racial identity type of issues. As well as, on my college campus I really don't experience it at all. I have had one, but that was in freshman year. Other than that, I really haven't experienced that much. I do support the protests that the other Black students do have on campus. I always go to look, to listen to those experiences that they've had, because I haven't had them at all. So I just kinda look to stay connected to the Black community by just listening to the stories and going back and sharing them with different college officials.

The conflict between her need for institutional belonging and experiences with institutionalized racism was evident when discussing a protest during her sophomore year. The protesters' demands, she said, "sparked into African Americans' feeling like they don't have as many resources and opportunities available to them. I totally disagree. I was even more disgusted that campus administrators that classified as African Americans or African felt the same way as students." Do recall that she described, at length, the benefits of moving to the White side of campus.

> [After moving to the White side of campus I was] finally hearing some different resources that other African Americans don't know about, other minorities don't know about. Being able to step outside of the Black community as a whole and be accepted into other communities on campus, ethnic and cultural [communities] on campus . . . really feeling like I belong, which is [Rural StateU's] motto.
>
> I would also say the resources that were offered to me when I moved to [the White] side of campus helped me to perform academically [better] than I did my first year of college. Resources such as the Leadership Development Institute, resources such as having a twenty-four-hour location where you can study within the housing community as opposed to going to the library, where it's really classified as a "zoo" because people go to the library to party. There was really a huge disadvantage [first year] because I didn't know those resources were available to me because of the [Black] side of campus that I lived on.

Her new resources were not just material supports but also informal informational supports.

> Those resources really opened up to me because I had different friends of diversity that would tell me, "Hey, Julissa, you need to be in this. Hey, Julissa, you need to be in that. You're studying pharmacy, you need to be involved with this organization." So all of that opened up to me. That just really helped me kind of steer in the right direction. Meeting the right people, hearing the resources that are available to them, and then sharing those resources with me.

At other times, she noted the relative lack of resources and opportunities in the organizations tasked with serving minority students.

> The office of minority and student affairs really knows me a lot. . . . I liked the opportunities that they had there, but they are very limited, and there aren't as many opportunities [as the organizations that serve White students]. Our African American Cultural Center, the place just really sucks, so that's another aspect that I would kind of give advice to high school students, look for schools that have cultural centers that support you pretty well, cause the cultural center should be like your second home.

Each discriminatory and differential experience was discussed as a discrete event, and she didn't tie them to institutionalized racism. Julissa's need for institutional belonging was so strong that not once in any of the interviews did she connect the improvements she experienced after moving to the White side of campus with Black students' demands for institutional change and redress.

Her perceived conflicts between her institutional identity (who she was as a student at that institution) and her Black student identity (who she was as a Black student at that institution) were so strong that she felt uncomfortable when attending Black student meetings. She felt that Black student organizations were "not inclusive" and consequently were not aligned with the "university's mission to be inclusive." Her identity conflicts become even more apparent when these critical comments are compared against the matter-of-fact tone taken when she discussed observed self-segregating behavior among White students: "When [as a junior] I sit back as a new student orientation adviser and it's the first day, and we take our freshmen to dinner, and they don't really know each other, of course the White males always flock to each other, White females always flock to each other, and it really leaves the minorities [with] a sense that, OK, since they're doing that, we have to, kinda flock to ourselves too."

Julissa's critical view of self-segregation when discussing Black student organizations but more matter-of-fact view of self-segregation among White students aligns with Beverly Tatum's finding that "when a group of Black teens are sitting together in the cafeteria . . . school administrators want to know not only why they are sitting together, but what can be done to prevent it."[26] Like the school administrators, only when focusing on Black students does Julissa see self-segregation as problematic, and also like the school administrators, Julissa misunderstands the role of self-segregation in positive identity development. Research shows that same race-ethnicity peer networks facilitate minority students' adjustment to historically White schools.[27] Such identity-affirming counterspaces allow them to maintain a strong sense of self while striving for school success.[28]

Essentially, her understanding of herself as a successful student who was integrated into the larger campus community was in direct opposition to being embedded in the Black campus community.

> People say you're not Black enough, [because] I'm not really in those Black student organizations. I really enjoy working on a campus level, more so than just a racial or an ethnic level. I'm very involved with the office of inclusion and interracial relations [which at her university was distinct from and had a different mission from the office of minority students]. The one campus organization that I will be joining in the fall to kind of move back into the Black community [for my senior year] is called Women of Purpose and Excellence.

Julissa also lacked critical insight into being the token Black student in the many cocurricular organizations in which she was a member. She was either the first or currently the only Black student in all of her cocurricular activities. Tokenism occurs when individual members of minority communities "are [singled out as] representatives of their social category; they are asked for expert opinions about this category, treated according to the stereotypes about it, and face other problems related to their distinctiveness."[29]

Instead, she expressed pride in being the first or only Black person in the organization and did not see it as an aspect of structural racism. Without being prompted, Julissa repeatedly prefaced discussion of her cocurricular activities by stating her racial-ethnic status in that organization. "Being the first African American to join a predominately Caucasian student organization since the school opened. That was really huge," she said of her membership in the organization for future professional chemical scientists. She was also "the first Black student ever to have an executive board position," and "the only Black person in the student advancement committee in the college of pharmacy. And I'm the only Black person to serve on that executive board as the vice president of college relations." This repeated, unsolicited referencing of her racial-ethnic status in her campus activities illustrates how tokenism is injurious to one's sense of self and creates a false sense of progress.[30]

Julissa's shifting between claiming and denying her Black identity illustrates how the meaning of any given social identity depends on situational cues.[31] In Julissa's eyes, the weeding out of Black students from STEM majors created a need to distance herself from her racial-ethnic identity in academic contexts, but she embraces the token prominence of her racial-ethnic identity when she is the only Black student in the organization.

Internalized Racialism

Julissa uncritically internalized both the positive and negative stereotypes of Black Americans, a process that is termed internalized racialism, and then uncritically deployed them when referencing herself and others.[32] Her reflexive stance throughout each interview was to deny that being connected to the Black community on campus was an important aspect of her sense of self. As she says here, "Now in my junior year of college, my closest friends don't really identify as African American, and there's a mixture of ethnic cultures and diversity within my circle of friends. So campus social life is really awesome!" A closer look at this claim of not having any friends who "really identify as African American" revealed that two of her core group of friends were Black women. What she did not have, however, were Black friends who typified the racial-ethnic stereotypes she had internalized.

> You don't really see that many people from the Black community on [the White] side of campus. Or if you do see 'em, you know, they're hanging out, and usually loud. So I get questions from my peers who

> don't identify as being African American or of African descent, asking me why are Black people so loud? . . . They want to learn more about the culture, but I can't provide them with all of the answers due to my upbringing and the fact that I don't act like the majority.

Her broad-bush stereotyping of unknown Black students reveals how Julissa herself applies tokenism and exceptionalism to the individual members of the Black campus community who were her strongest sources of campus support.

> The school connected me with a very well-known basketball player who graduated from the university. Having the opportunity to talk with her, about the struggles that I face in the Black community, and hearing that she had the same struggle as well, and her guiding me through the right path has been awesome. . . . Oh, [office of minority and student affairs] they were awesome. . . . One of the awesomest RAs in housing is African American, and she's the only African American RA on the White side of campus, so it's really good having her as a mentor. She'll email me and be like, "Hey, I noticed you were looking a little sluggish, can you swing by so that we can chat?"

Julissa again named the Black resident adviser as the person she went to for support her junior year: "For advice about school, I normally go to one of my mentors who is actually a resident director on campus, and I identify with her very well because she is African American."

Despite being supported by Black students, staff, and alumni, when asked about her most negative experiences, each year she cited feeling rejected by and not having a connection to the Black community on campus. This issue dogged her from the start of her first year. "Freshman year was horrible. I thought that [Black students] would be welcoming, but they really weren't."

Being from a predominantly White northern suburb of Chicago, she said, was alienating. Black students from the city or the predominantly Black south suburbs formed cliques that excluded her. Being from "the northern suburbs, where you live in a suburb that is predominantly Caucasian, that you know has houses that look the same on the same block, they really weren't accepted into the African American community."

> I found myself very depressed, and I wasn't as motivated after that fifth week. Being attacked for living in north suburbia. Ultimately being called an "Oreo." They don't accept you due to where you live and the resources and credibility that you have that prepared you for college. And then with people seeing the credentials, and the accomplishments and the achievements that I had, prior to starting my first year of

> college, that totally came as a disadvantage for being welcomed because a lot of people viewed me on a totally higher pedestal than they were, so they totally just gave me the hand wave of, hey, you will never be accepted in the Black community.

It continued to be a problem sophomore year. "I get the 'you're not Black enough,' and I get the examples of you don't hang out with Black people or you don't wear the same clothes that we wear, or you don't go to the same parties that we do, or you don't associate with only Black people." By junior year, she was feeling even more alienated. "I question why people feel the way that they do, why my Black brothers and Black sisters feel as though they should be intimidated by someone who has a lot of connections, who can share so much, so many resources, and so much knowledge." By senior year, she was disconnected. "I can't tell you what's going on in the Black community; I'm not connected," she told us.

By graduation, she was at a loss for how to respond to being asked to give a graduation speech on the journey through campus life as a Black student. In the end, she declined the invitation, "because my experience wasn't really similar to the general experiences of Black students on campus."

Given Julissa's level of involvement with the broader campus community, one might wonder whether her lack of a connection to the Black campus community was indeed a defining aspect of her college life. After all, Julissa was in many ways the person to know on campus: "I'm very well known on campus because I'm always doing a lot of things. So I could be late for class, because everybody's, you know, like 'Hey Julissa,' 'Hey Julissa,' 'Hey Julissa.' And I'm just, like, how do you know me? But it's just friends saying, that's Julissa, who does a lot of things on campus. And they become very interested in that. And they know me through blogging [about courses]." If not for her stated longing for "sisterhood," one would conclude that Julissa's lack of a connection to the Black community on campus was a marginal aspect of her campus life.

> [Sophomore year] I did want to invest time in a [Black] sorority as well. Really start investing in a sorority and getting more support. More so of a sisterhood as well, especially being an only child. . . . The way that I'm thinking is, if I need something in the future, I don't have that sibling that could step up to the plate and offer it for me.
>
> I was really just trying to join the organization for sisterhood, but I really couldn't see those, those women as being future sisters, as well as them making it very difficult for me because of the type of person, and the value that I had on the campus. I think the most stressful part was kinda putting everything aside to try to pledge that sorority.

Being known on campus and visible in several predominantly White organizations did not provide her with the belonging she was searching for.

Institutional structures play a considerable role in determining the extent to which historically marginalized students are integrated into the broader campus community. It appears that at Rural StateU a limited number of Black students were chosen to play leadership roles in several campus-wide organizations and committees. As Julissa noted, this created competition among Black students to fill those roles, and put distance between the few Black students who held those roles and the other Black students on campus. She struggled with the competition, particularly between her and another Black female, because she "took on this very high role to represent the university." Jealousies and accusations emerged, and as a result, "now we don't really communicate as much. It's just a lot of tension between a lot of Black student leaders who are doing awesome things on campus, and who are representing the Black community, when administration pulls in the same five Black faces in meetings."

Julissa was presented with false choices between her racial-ethnic identity and her academic identity, as well as between inclusion in racial-ethnic counterspaces and inclusion in the broader campus community. The very low representation of Black students on campus (about 5 percent) means that their coming together in physical counterspaces is paradoxically highly visible. This intentionality and visibility may be experienced by some Black students as making a very public and political choice to separate one's self from the broader institution. Most universities stop at structural diversity, and most, like Rural StateU, have made only marginal progress in that regard. As will be detailed in the subsequent chapters, the other aspects of diversity that matter are interactional diversity (the quality of intergroup social interactions among peers, faculty, and administration), cocurricular diversity (the social and cultural diversity in the range of clubs, activities, and living arrangements), and curricular diversity (the extent to which underrepresented students can engage academic content that allows for critical examinations of their social identities).[33]

Julissa's experiences illustrate just how profoundly one's identity is shaped by whether a given identity is perceived as being valued in a given context. In her case it was racial-ethnic identity, but the same would be true of any marginalized social identity.[34] She understood the material segregation and unequal distribution of resources on campus, such as the lower-quality housing on the Black side of campus and the minority student office's proportionally lower financial resources and staff, as indicative of Black students' low status on campus. Her first response as a Black student was to question her campus belonging. However, her second response and way of resolving this identity conflict was to separate herself from Black students and then question Black students' campus belonging.[35]

Her experiences also illustrate that people have multiple sources of identity and that there can be conflict among those sources of identity. Minorities are particularly aware of one's shifting self-understandings and shifting self-presentations as the context changes. This shifting is captured by the concept of code switching—linguistic and behavioral changes in the ways people express themselves based on their immediate cultural context.[36] Minority students have a greater burden of being responsive to the various contexts that they traverse across the university, differing contexts that communicate different messages about which aspects of their identities are valued versus stigmatized in a given context. In contrast, White students, particularly White men, are more likely to perceive a high level of contextual stability that results in experiencing consistent identity feedback.[37]

All college students are seeking answers to the following three questions: How are people like me viewed at this institution? How do I want to engage with or distance myself from various subcultures of this institution to protect my sense of self? And ultimately, who am I at this institution? Student development in college is strongly determined by how the institution organizes itself to answer these questions.

3

AN AMBIVALENT EMBRACE

How Financially Distressed Students Make Sense of the Cost of College

With Resney Gugwor

College is expensive. As the following students indicate, many first-generation students are taking a leap of faith that the high cost of the opportunity to go to college will pay off. As one student put it, "I'm gonna continue to get loans because that's the only way that anything will be possible for me. But besides that, I don't know. I haven't really thought it through, because there's nothing that I can really do. I work now, but . . . I don't have a significant amount of money saved up for me to get through the entire year, so I kinda just take it how it goes. Skate by, figure it out when I get there."

Or this student: "[The first year] was a lot of uncertainty, I guess, 'cause I was still not sure how I was going to pay for it. Even the first semester I had to ask my dad to take out money from his retirement fund to pay for my first semester so I could continue to go to school my second semester. That was very troubling, with the uncertainty of all that."

These two students are representative of those who arrived at college in financial distress, students who believed they had to go to college to obtain the future they desired but unsure of how they would pay the cost. Given the debt that many historically marginalized students assume, it is incumbent on their institutions to not add additional social identity–based barriers to success.

In this chapter, we discuss how financial distress itself can become an identity challenge; one's relative financial position plays an outsize role in students' identity construction.[1] Counterspaces for economically marginalized students can help to alleviate this identity challenge. Counterspaces that bring students together around financial issues can reduce the negative identity effects of financial distress by changing their narrative from an individual to a structural framing. Specifically, these spaces can transform the question from "Why don't I have the resources to attend college like more affluent students do?" to "Why is it that despite the societal benefits of having college-educated citizens, I'm asked to mortgage my future for the chance to educate myself into the middle class?"

"College for All," but at What Cost, and on Whose Dime?

Students from lower-income families are less likely to consider college as a space for personal exploration and development and more likely to see college as a way to prevent an undesired future and, for some, to escape an undesired present. This makes "college a tool or instrumental pathway to a better job or career future than what your social origins would dictate."[2] These sentiments dominated the reasons that the first-generation students in our study gave for why they enrolled in college. However, this is not to say that the students do not also value the learning that happens in college. It is simply that they do not have the luxury of setting aside the fact that, for them, college is foremost about getting the degree.

These students are simply reflecting the pragmatic side of the "college for all" expectation—that all can, should, and need to get a college degree. For lower-income students, this expectation has coincided with dramatic increases in the cost of college, and shifts in who bears those costs.[3] When large land grant universities were first created in 1862, the belief was that states should bear much of the costs of college because the economy and society would benefit from an increasingly well-educated public.[4] However, in recent decades, as the financial benefits of degree attainment continue to increase, there has been a shift to emphasizing the individual benefits, and consequently more now believe that the individual should bear the costs of college.

Today, the absolute amount of federal, state, and institutional grant aid has never been higher (totaling more than $238 million annually). However, with more than 10.5 million students enrolled in four-year institutions, and with tuition increasing faster than grant aid, the average student is paying more than ever before.[5] Because Black and Latinx students have a higher likelihood of coming from low-wealth or low-income families, they are particularly susceptible to how financial distress can structure one's college experiences.[6]

We found that one-third of the 533 students in our larger survey were under tremendous financial pressure.[7] These students started college in financial distress. What we focus on in this chapter, however, is the added psychological burden of managing the internal conflict of investing in a degree that they doubted would be worth the cost. As one political science and history major put it, "My biggest fear is that while I'm bending over backwards to pay off my tuition, I won't be as successful as I plan to be in the future." Even those seeking profitable majors were worried; as one economics and marketing major put it, "Sometimes I wonder if college is worth it, because even with a degree, nothing is guaranteed in the current state of the economy. Sometimes I feel like maybe I am just wasting my time, especially when I could instead be learning a useful trade or skill that a college degree doesn't provide."

The high cost of college comes with negative psychological and emotional consequences when one's family is not wealthy enough or when the student is not among the precious few who obtain a full-ride scholarship.[8] The relief of knowing that things are paid for is an obvious benefit, as is the sense of belonging that comes from being able to pay for and participate in campus social activities, as well as the confidence to invest fully in coursework without the fear of having to drop out for financial reasons.[9] Through the first-year experiences of three first-generation students, we detail many of the psychological and emotional aspects of financial distress, including interjecting doubt about whether they are college material and uncertainty about whether college is worth the cost.

Jenni, a Black woman enrolled at Rural StateU, attempted to manage her financial distress by working in both on- and off-campus jobs and by applying for scholarships. Her financial distress was anticipatory; she was concerned with a debt-burdened future, a debt she would never be able to pay off. She applied for as many scholarships as possible to ensure that she would graduate mostly debt free. Too many loans, she knew, might mean dropping out. Her worry was likely fueled by the numerous high-profile news stories with headlines like "For Millions of Millennials: Some College, No Degree, Lots of Debt"; or "College Students' Nightmare: Loan Debt and No Degree."[10]

Dave's financial distress was even more immediate than Jenni's. In his first semester, Dave, a Latinx man enrolled at Suburban StateU, doubted his ability to return to school for the second semester despite loans and working two jobs. He was able to stay because he got "lucky" and had an academic adviser who found a university scholarship for him. Until then, his plan was to rely on contributions from already financially strapped family members and, reluctantly, on loans.

Tanya, a Black woman enrolled at Suburban StateU, learned how important insider cultural information is to success. She realized that many available institutional supports are not simply offered—one must ask for, and, if necessary, demand them to gain access. By the end of the first term of her first year, college costs were threatening to derail Tanya's future. The university advised her to "take a break" and get her finances in order. But she refused. Instead she asked nearly everyone she knew for financial assistance. Her refusal to fail, coupled with her willingness to ask for help, is what kept her in college. This persistence led to interactions with institutional agents who said yes when others had already said no. In addition to the tangible financial support, her experiences taught her what students from higher-income families know—that rules are negotiable.

The (Nonmonetary) Value of Education

For first-generation college students, a college degree itself can be a source of family honor, one that positions them as role models. Dave epitomizes the student whose college motivations are rooted in the desire to make his family proud.

> Being that I come from a family, my dad didn't go to college, my mom, she only got her associate's degree, . . . I just really just wanted to be the example to [my younger brother]. . . . My mother, she raised me practically all on her own, with the help of her family. She was always the one on top of me, always the one pushing me to do sports, and of course she was the one who was on top of me to continue going on to college. She would tell me it was best for me. She would tell me don't do the easy way out and just join the military. Work for things in your life, go to school, get good grades, come out successful, and it will better yourself. And she just stressed how proud she would be.

Tanya's college motivations were also rooted in her family experiences.

> None of my parents have a degree, so I am a first-generation student, but it was just like the way I was raised. And my grandmother, if anything, no matter how bad she treated me, she would drive us to school. I went to a magnet school, and they were really good with the curriculum and the core, ideas on what you wanna do, so I planned to go to college. If I do anything, I need to go into college. Even if I can't get the degree I want, at least to want to have a degree.

While believing that obtaining a degree would bring honor to their lives and to their family, for Dave and Tanya the college degree also took on an additional element of necessity—to make their families proud for the sacrifices made for them to have the opportunity to go to college. Their family's support and encouragement became a source of motivation for them.

The Necessary Credential and the Promise of Desired Future Selves

The "college for all" push has been a fraught debate in the United States.[11] Challengers typically point out that some of the fastest-growing sectors of the economy need specialized vocational training.[12] Nevertheless, for most, a college degree is necessary for a financially stable adulthood. Researchers Jennie Brand and Yu Xie found that the occupational and income benefits of college were most pronounced for students who were among those least likely to go to college, typically low-income and minority students.[13] As they state, "a principal reason for a relatively large economic return experienced by low propensity college-educated workers is that their social position, coming from disadvantaged socioeconomic origins, is marked by substantial disadvantage." In other words, being born into families that have the least, they have the most to gain.

In the absence of a college degree, youth from lower-income families have limited mainstream human, cultural, and social capital they can tap for job leads and career advancement. For students like Jenni, the college degree is a necessary credential. From an early age, she had her eyes set on a degree. "It was just always something that I knew I wanted to do and had to do. . . . It's like nowadays you need a college degree in order to do, like, mostly anything. So I feel like you have to go to college if you want a decent career at least. . . . If I was to graduate [high school] and then just stay [home], I couldn't really think of what I would be doing. So I figured that going to college would be a good alternative."

Tanya had a similar perspective, and the careers to which she aspired all required a college degree. Though Tanya's aspirations were high, she lacked the guidance necessary to chart a smooth course. "By the grace of God, really—like I said, I didn't have any guidance for the most part. I took my classes last minute." That lack of guidance and a clear path would come back to haunt her. She had begun, like many, not knowing what she wanted to do in life. But volunteering at her local park district, where she worked with children with special needs, made something click. "I had a wonderful time with them," she said. She focused on becoming a special education teacher. "But with not having a correct guidance," she said, "I didn't realize, well, if you're gonna do something like that, you have to have the grades and the persistence, and the patience, to do that. . . . I realized, recently, that obviously the way my coursework is right now I probably won't be able to be in the special ed program, so I just recently switched to entry ed." Her reliance on guidance from institutional agents left her academically adrift.

Unlike Jenni and Tanya, Dave did not enroll in college with any specific occupations in mind. All he had was a vague sense that college was necessary for future success. "My main reasons were just the talks about what college can do for someone later on in life," he said.

Loans Are an Anxiety-Filled Solution

The very American notion of limitless possibilities is one reason that the college years are embraced as an important part of the transition to adulthood.[14] The multitude of college courses, resources, and options allows students to imagine any number of futures and explore many different fields.[15] However, the ability to explore, try things out, and find the right fit is not free. And the loans required to do that exploring are a major source of anxiety.

For many students, as in Jenni's case, the constraining effects of some costs occur long before entering college. "At my school we had to apply to ten colleges. . . . [For] some of 'em I got a fee waiver. But then I think it was maybe a few of 'em that I had to just pay for. . . . But it was pretty expensive." Mesmin Destin and Daphna Oyserman show that preadolescents' perceptions about the cost of college can have academic consequences by harming the level of effort that they put into schoolwork. Some secondary school students conclude that "if college seems too expensive, what is the point of homework? Doing homework, studying, staying after school for extra help, and going to the library for extra reading make little sense if all of these are focused on a future that is blocked."[16]

Jenni's financial package covered all of Rural StateU's costs, but a substantial portion of it was loan "aid." So although the costs were covered, Jenni still worried about her financial future. "I'm worried about after I graduate, with the loans and everything. . . . I didn't really want to leave college being in debt. But now that I have loans, it's no way around it, I guess."

To reduce her anticipated future financial distress repaying loans, she fretted over applying for more scholarships during the summer after her first year. She also worked two part-time jobs during the academic year. While the jobs eased some of her financial distress, they introduced other challenges.

> My biggest [time management] challenge was probably finding time to do homework. I was so busy with class, and then I had to work most days. And then trying to go out, and keep up with my friends and everything. So then it was like, I did the homework that I thought was important, but then sometimes I would just skip over reading, like, ah, whatever, it's just reading. So I had a difficult time figuring out when to focus on my homework and everything.

Jenni was stuck: Work more and keep her financial distress to a minimum, or take out more loans and accept the financial anxiety so she could have more time for school and a social life? Jenni's way of thinking is common, and lower-income students are particularly susceptible to the negative psychological effects of student loan debt. Student loan debt beyond $10,000 increases the likelihood of leaving college.[17] In contrast, every $1,000 increase in the amount of aid from a Pell Grant is associated with a 10 percent decrease in the likelihood of leaving college.[18]

Resolving the constraints caused by the rising costs of college will require more thoughtful solutions than simply increasing student access to debt. As Jenni's actions illustrate, even when students technically don't have to work to pay for college because they can obtain enough loan aid to cover their costs, they often want to work because of the anxieties created by mounting debt.

Paying the Cost to Retain (versus Recruit a Replacement)

In an October 2016 *Insider Higher Ed* op-ed, I argued that universities would do well to embrace the understanding that retention is as important, or even more important, than recruitment. A high retention rate is itself a competitive recruitment tool. Furthermore, it is more cost-effective to retain those already enrolled than to invest in recruiting replacements for those who have dropped out. Joe Cuseo, for example, found that retention initiatives are estimated to be three to five times more cost-effective than recruitment initiatives.[19]

Dave is one of those students who comes to mind when you think about how much better it would be if universities put as much effort into retention as they do into recruitment. His financial distress was apparent in our discussions, so much so that he "seriously did not think I was going to return for the second semester." Dave also believed that the university could offer more help if he could just figure out how to ask. The financial aid office, he said, was "sometimes tricky to get around. And they're really tricky to communicate with, because it's really a matter of fact it has to go their way or no way."

Dave ended up taking out an unsubsidized loan and a direct subsidized loan, and his family paid another $5,000 for the first semester. "That was crazy," he said, because "at the time, my mom, she was unemployed, and she didn't have medical insurance." His sisters, brothers, and even his brother-in-law pitched in to help him stay in school. But it was his college counselor in his second semester who "came through for me by my doing my part, getting good grades, and her part, helping me out getting a scholarship mid-semester. She would just tell me, like, if I get good grades . . . she would be able to really stick her neck out for me." With an additional $2,200 from the university, he made it through the second semester, though he still took out approximately $7,000 in loans.

Dave felt that most of the institutional support offered was informational only.

> [Suburban StateU] told me about the loan options, they told me about the Parent PLUS loan option. . . . [The financial aid office] was kind of just an annoyance that went on. It was the fact that I would do what they would tell me, and they would just send me an email saying they needed more information. [They] were really open to helping out. But I really didn't know at first that sometimes they don't want to [help right away].

While both the financial and informational support were helpful, it was not enough to meaningfully reduce his financial distress.

There are only so many hours in a day, and because part-time pay is low, students are either working more than ever before or acquiring more loans than ever before. As recently as two decades ago, students could work one part-time job during school plus a full-time job over the summer and cover most of their college costs. That strategy no longer works.[20] Jenni, Tanya, and Dave were each working two part-time jobs during the academic year, and all three still experienced financial distress.

Self-Certainty in the Face of Uncertainty

Like Dave, Tanya attended Suburban StateU, was financially distressed, and came to the same conclusion—the university hid financial resources and could be more helpful if one could figure out how to gain access. Thanks to her gregarious personality, history of self-advocacy, and dogged determination, she learned how to demand financial resources to keep her aspirations alive.

Tanya is someone who can handle much more than the rest of us and still keep a positive outlook on life.

> I don't really know how to explain who I am—I guess you could say I'm a little quirky. Apparently, I'm very spontaneous, and exuberant in expressions. My first year was actually extremely difficult. I am a foster child. So I was raised by my grandma the majority of my life, and when I turned eighteen my grandma kicked me out, 'cause she couldn't receive any money for me, so I was on my own. That was most of the summer before I was going to [college], and I actually got in contact with some of my older relatives, who let me bounce around through them. And my only role is like I really need to be in school, obviously, because I have nothing else to my name. I have nothing to call my own. So of all schools to contact me, it happened to be [Suburban StateU], and they were like, well, no matter what you got going on, you're still

> welcome to come. So I took them up on that offer, and it was, like, two days before classes started, I had registered a room, meal plan, and all that other stuff on my one card.
>
> I matured, for the most part, on my own. Having a grandmother that was always sick, I took care of her, so I guess it wasn't difficult being on my own. But it was difficult not knowing what to do, seeing as, you know, I'm new to being 110 percent on my own. You know, no one asks me what I'm doing, where I'm going, so it was a little hard balancing being an adult with being responsible sometimes. . . . My motivation to not end up back where I was over the summer after I graduated from my high school kept me focused enough to at least get to class, get the homework in. And my first semester I ended up with 2.5 at the end.

Tanya was also working two jobs during that first year. Just imagine how much better her academic performance would have been if she attended as a "traditional" student.

Tanya's plan for paying for college was common among the first-generation and lower-income students in our study. They enrolled with the belief that financial aid would cover all expenses, and that after signing the aid forms all they would have to worry about was keeping up with the academic demands of college. Tanya learned otherwise:

> I was hoping, they always kept telling me, "Hey, you're an independent, so you'll receive a lot of money." I was hoping the financial aid would cover it. But me being naive and misguided, I actually ended up living in [resident hall], which is the most expensive residential home on campus. And it ended up putting me in debt, like $3,000, with the school. Finally, when I got the two jobs, you know, it was a little bit easier, in some ways. But difficult in other ways. . . . As bad as it [seems], I do weigh my class schedule around my work schedule. Because I have to make sure I'm making money in order to make sure I put food in the house for myself, and [I've sold food stamps] so I can just make sure that the lights stay on.

Despite working two jobs, by winter break Tanya had no more money to continue into her second semester. This is where her personality came in, along with her lack of shame about her financial resources, a perspective that could have benefited all the lower-income students interviewed.

> For winter break, I ended up going back to the city of Chicago and fund raising the money. . . . I was able to talk to someone important at the [university], and she was like, "Well, I'll give you $1,500 if you can come

> up with the rest [of the $3,000 owed]." So that's exactly what I did. . . . and so I ended up having to call like, Jesse Jackson, all types of people in regards to helping me fund my education. Like, so I only have a 2.5 [GPA] my first semester, so you know, it wasn't a lot to go on. But my personality apparently—to some of the people [who] had helped [me] after high school, I didn't realize that they put an award out for me. Next thing you know I came up with $1,500. And I ended up registering for class again, two days before class exactly started.

Many of the other students who experienced financial distress tried to get help through official requests, and when that failed retreated into themselves because of shame. These students used passive coping and simply waited as long as they could, hoping that something would come through. Tanya's history of self-advocacy and her lack of a backup plan pushed all feelings of shame aside.

> It was the most stressful thing ever. Because so many times that I've [been] told, we can't do anything, or you need to get a job, or they would tell me obvious things, or maybe you should take a semester off and go to community college. Obviously. You don't know my circumstances and the situation that I'm in. I have nothing to go back to in order to go to community college. So that's not an option for me. [If] I'm not in school, I'm out of a place to live, I'm out of an education, and I'm out of a job. There's a lot laying on the line with my education.

For Tanya, a no from an institutional agent just meant she had not yet spoken to the right person.

> Let's see, I am horrible with names. I know there's a lady by the name of Francis, she works at the scholarship office. And then there was George. He works in a program. . . . And, if anything, like just random people. I didn't get to meet them, I didn't know them, but it spread by word of mouth. People heard what was going on with me, and they were like, you know, here goes the number. Or here goes, so on and so forth. I'll just take it up. I'll take up the work for it, wing it. And hopefully I'll end up getting [something].

She also learned to not "come off as a complete psycho, crazy madwoman. But let them know, hey, I'm not playing. I need this money. Give it to me, because you have no other option but to give it to me. I will work for it. I will prove you wrong if you think that I don't deserve it." By the end of her first year, she had a deep understanding of just how costly college is for students, especially for students who, like her, are without any family financial means to pay for it.

> It's expensive to be in school. Extremely. And, I always tell students who are calling my workplace [on campus], saying they can't afford it, "You just have to look for it." Because the university has money. . . . It's just they're not gonna let you know. You have to fight for it, you have to dig for it. You have to look for it to receive it. And I ended up learning that. So now I've found the monies and I've made sure I'm staying in school and you can't stop me. I don't care how expensive it gets. I need to stay in school. I have no other options.

Access to financial support should not be a psychologically and emotionally draining survival-of-the-fittest competition that distracts from students' ability to engage in learning.

Counterspaces for Financially Distressed Students

Students' feelings of helplessness about their financial distress exist in the midst of an abundance of financial aid information. A simple Google search for "financial aid" produces a myriad of web links. However, because much of the information does not easily translate into actionable steps, guidance from a knowledgeable institutional agent remains essential. As Alicia Dowd states,

> Certainly, many students realize that financial aid is available and so take advantage of it without interacting with school and college personnel. Most often, these are students with educated parents and siblings who help them form their educational aspirations and choose their path to a bachelor's degree and beyond. First-generation college students and others from families with few financial resources are less likely to realize that financial aid is "for them." Teachers and counselors must therefore act as institutional agents, as advocates for students, and so actively help them negotiate bureaucracies and understand cultural norms of academia and the risks and benefits of borrowing for college.[21]

Given students' stories about the reticence of institutional agents, one viable alternative would be to turn to counterspaces for financially marginalized students. In such spaces, students would be able to connect with and gain valuable insider information from others like Tanya who have figured out how the system works and are willing to share their insights. We infer that no such counterspaces existed on any of the universities in our study because support from peers who were also trying to make ends meet was never mentioned.

Deborah Wornock and Allison Hurst's examination of a failed attempt at student organizing based on social class helps explain why there was no mention of counterspaces in our students' discussions of their financial distress.[22] Wornock and Hurst found that collective organizing was difficult because of lower-income students' invisibility on campus. They are invisible because there are few visible markers of class differences that would enable them to readily identify each other. In addition, lower-income students are often off campus when not in class because they are more likely to live and work off campus. Consequently, even if one found a way to identify the other "poor kids" on campus, time to meet, network, and build the trust needed to start a student organization and provide mutual support is in short supply.

The other barriers to collective organizing center largely on the difficulties of claiming poverty as an identity for one's self. Students struggled with the fact that one's class status is largely seen by others as an individual failure rather than a collective or structural issue. Low-income students' class status is also something that they are actively trying to change or reject by going to college, so it is not an aspect of themselves that they want to claim as part of their personal identity.

Wornock and Hurst conclude that "because of the absurdity" of celebrating one's poverty in the ways one might celebrate one's blackness, colleges must recognize that "organizing around social class identity is fundamentally different from organizing around other identities, such as race or sexual orientation."[23] This means that creating counterspaces for lower-income students requires more thoughtful action than simply adding it to the list of needs met through the diversity or multicultural student affairs office.

4

STRATEGIC DISENGAGEMENT

Preserving One's Academic Identity by Disengaging from Campus Life

With Ja'Dell Davis

If there is one narrative that permeates research and practice on the transition to college, it is that the college campus becomes students' "home away from home." The campus community is believed to be capable of fulfilling students' intellectual, social, and emotional needs. For instance, one of the items in an index measuring successful transition to college and predicting risk for dropping out is the number of times the student returns home for weekend visits. Vincent Tinto and George Kuh have been influential in establishing these campus-wide belonging and engagement perspectives of what matters for student success in college.[1] In this conception, it is not just students' initial goal of completing college that spurs persistence, but also their connection with and commitment to their college institution that jointly determines the likelihood of leaving without a degree.[2]

But some students' embodied characteristics—defining aspects of their physical being—place their college experiences at odds with these theories. We found that Black women, by virtue of their being in a body that is visibly both Black and female, reported experiencing the highest levels of microaggressions.[3] The three Black women profiled in this chapter, Claire, Fiona, and Mercy, entered college with a strong sense of the central role that campus life would play in their present and future selves. They were completely open to embracing campus life. Early in their first year, however, they and many of the other Black women interviewed found it necessary, in order to persist in their education, to strategically separate their academic identity, or how they understand themselves as students, from their institutional identity, or how they understand themselves as students at that institution.

Fiona, a Black woman attending Urban PrivateU-South, rode a wave of nervous excitement and newfound freedom into college life. At the end of the second week of her first year, she and her newly acquainted friends set out in search of that standard weekend college party and landed on frat row. Fiona came to college expecting to make friends with people from different backgrounds, open to what had been advertised as the full college experience, and frat row was to be a central aspect of experiencing difference. But frat row was no more than an extension of most of the spaces on campus—from classes, to the student union, to dorms—dominated by White students. And Fiona quickly learned that she was to be excluded. "The frats weren't Black people, they were White," she told us. "We would go to the parties, and they would be like, Sorry. We're not letting any more people in."

They reasoned away not being let in. Capacity issues and fire hazards, right? It was only when they returned to these fire-code-abiding frat houses a little later that they discovered that White groups of partiers were being allowed in.

> We would be like, "Oh, nah, that's bogus." For real, that's pretty racist. But at the end of the day we just dealt with it.... Overall the interactions between the people, it just depends on who you come across. Some people are more friendly, they don't really care about your skin color. And some people you can tell that it affects how they're about to approach you. Or how they expect you to approach them. So pretty interesting to see and even take in for myself. 'Cause I've always liked to be aware of stuff like that. So I thought it was pretty interesting.

Testing her freedom and responsibility as an emerging adult also meant testing the boundaries of where this self-actualization could take place while in college. Frat parties and other types of predominantly White social gathering spaces were no longer a safe option. Though she "tried to make the best out of it," Fiona weighed the risk of being vulnerable in the face of strangers who may or may not actively reject her because of her skin color, and she chose to establish boundaries. These boundaries delimited where she went for weekend college fun, where and with whom she enjoyed her meals, and from whom she sought critical advice for navigating college.

Claire, a Black woman attending Urban PrivateU-North, headed to the dorm office unsure of why she had been summoned, knowing only that the matter was urgent enough for a meeting. Monique, the Brooklyn-born lead resident adviser, who was also a Black woman, was waiting and instructed Claire to sit. The topic: a stolen Confederate flag. This fraught symbol, often defended as a reference for southern pride, had come to be an integral part of her transition to college. One of the dorm rooms on her hall, occupied by two White men, had a Confederate flag hanging prominently on the door. Both amused and troubled by its presence, Claire had taken a picture of the flag and passively questioned its owners by writing "Flag?" on the dry-erase board that shared the space on their door. She soon came to understand that she was summoned to Monique's office to discuss the flag's disappearance.

Though Clair had tried to go about life as a new college student and mostly ignore this daily reminder of racial-ethnic oppression and backlash against the Civil Rights movement, when the flag went missing she was the first person accused of stealing it. Monique insisted that the flag needed to turn up and, in her position of authority, put on the table the potential for criminal vandalism charges. This broke Claire. She spent the next half hour sobbing in Monique's office, wondering how the disappearance of a Confederate flag was more cause for concern than its presence in the first place.

This was the first week of Claire's first year of college, and it set the terms on which she would negotiate the remainder of her years at Urban PrivateU-North. "That blew me [away]," she said. "That's why I don't like spending time on that campus. It's kind of a hostile environment for people of color and women. It just made me kind of mistrust [the university], I think. I knew that it wasn't gonna be a safe space for anybody and that things weren't gonna be taken seriously. It was really egregious in my eyes."

That Monique was a Black woman, and had placed those White male students' right to free expression over Claire's need to feel safe, contributed to Claire's complete loss of faith in the institution. Unsurprisingly, despite all the college preparation her elite high school provided, she was not prepared to encounter racist symbols on campus. She was also unprepared for the backlash she would receive for questioning the presence of these symbols in an educational context that touts a commitment to diversity and inclusion. The university had made its impression on Claire: This was not a safe place.

Throughout this chapter we will illustrate the benefits and costs of Claire's and Fiona's conscious decisions to disconnect from general college life. Claire's approach was blanket rejection, while Fiona severely narrowed the range of spaces and people that she incorporated into her college experience. Contrary to theories that promote identification with the broad college campus as crucial to both the maintenance of an academic identity and overall persistence, these Black women reveal other ways that marginalized students maintain academic engagement in hostile learning contexts. Claire and Fiona are representative of other Black women in our study who, in response to racial-ethnic discrimination, adjusted their campus participation in ways that allowed them to maintain high levels of ambition and persist in their goal of attaining a college degree. Mercy, whom we introduce later, took a more extreme form of disconnecting.

Her story highlights the role that counterspaces play in making the disconnection from college life sustainable.

Pathways to College

Pop culture images and college websites drive home the idea of what the typical college experience looks like: jovial interactions with peers and professors, participation in campus organizations, and an essential feeling of belonging in and out of the classroom. For the uninitiated, college is envisioned as the ultimate "cosmopolitan canopy." Sociologist Elijah Anderson describes the cosmopolitan canopy as a place where "virtually all racial groups are well represented . . . but not in even proportions. . . . People appear relaxed and are often observed interacting across the color line. . . . This is a calm environment of equivalent, symmetrical relationships—a respite from the streets outside."[4] This is the image that colleges project in their brochures, images that depict just the right ratio of smiling students of various racial-ethnic groups.

College is marketed to minority students as a place where Claire and Fiona should feel safe to explore their interests and discover new passions while enjoying equality among their peers. College will become their respite from the world outside. If the recruiters are to be believed, race-ethnicity and gender should play additive and integrative roles by contributing to campus diversity. But Claire and Fiona found that others responded to their race-ethnicity and gender in subtractive and rejecting ways.

Both Claire and Fiona long desired to attend and do well in college, and each connected her ambitious career goals to obtaining a college degree. However, they traveled different paths on their road into college, and it is in their different paths that we get a sense of the campus experiences that are all too common among Black college women.

Claire did not have to put forth too much effort to get into a college-going mind-set—it was a matter of where, rather than if, she was going to college. Both of Claire's parents had bachelor's degrees, and her father also earned a graduate degree. She went to top-tier schools, and everything up to her senior year of high school explicitly shaped her identity as a future college student. Claire wanted to be a screenwriter and actress, and though no degree was needed for her chosen profession, for Claire college was simply something that everyone in her world does. "I think all my friends are in school. It was just expected that I would go. I don't even know what I would do otherwise."

Like Claire, Fiona had college on her radar long before the average child starts giving it much thought. However, for Fiona the idea and mechanics of the college-going process were not built into her family, peer, and school experiences. Her mom, a single parent, graduated from high school and did not attend college, and her older sister completed only one semester at a nearby community college. Inconsistent support from her high school would be what Fiona relied on for a significant portion of the college preparation process. But her immediate and extended family were fully in her corner, which helped her persevere through the uncertain and often ambiguous process of applying to college.[5]

> I think that was my biggest obstacle. Being a first-generation college student, my mom didn't really know, and my sister didn't know, so I kinda [had] to figure that out for myself. By the time I had balanced the applications and just regular school in general, I was kinda on a crunch time. If I just had a question I would ask my mom, but she tried to guide the best way she could. . . . I mean, I pretty much took the reins while they were just supportive. That's all they really could do.
>
> I have a lot of family staying in [the area]. It's always like, if you're hungry, just come over. Just call me, come over. If you need anything just call me, I don't care what time it is. They definitely played a role in just telling me basic dos and don'ts, just having real deep conversations just about things I might face, and if I am facing this what I should do. Even if I don't, what I can do after that. Just talking with me, just preparing me enough. Just keeping it real and just being real straightforward and honest. That's really all I needed them to do. For everything else schoolwise and stuff, I knew I would have to prepare myself for that. So they were definitely great. I mean, I got a great group of people in my corner.

The differences between Claire's and Fiona's backgrounds generally, and their paths to college specifically, are noteworthy. While the college-going process for Fiona required concerted effort and focus in the midst of limited guidance from home and school, Claire was bolstered early on by knowledgeable parents and highly resourced schools. These differences show up in their perspectives and experiences during the initial transition to college. The social and academic preparation Claire received before college rendered her transition uneventful, for the most part. "It seemed easier than I thought it was gonna be," she admitted. "I guess 'cause I didn't take any math classes or anything, which would've [messed] me up. All the English and all the writing stuff comes pretty naturally to me. And it's all stuff that we worked on a lot in high school."

Fiona, on the other hand, could not hide her jitters and fascination about what college had in store for her:

> I remember when I moved in, that first day, when my family was leaving I was crying. I didn't know anyone. I knew I was gonna be more

> independent at that point, once my family left. The first couple of days I just tried to look at it and embrace everything. Oh, I had fun. It was cool. I was just hanging out all night with people in the dorms and getting up and going to class in the mornings. It was kind of like how the movies portrayed it. So I thought it was pretty great. But at the same time, I was nervous. I guess being so independent, there was no one there to say, "OK, is your homework done, did you eat yet, make sure you're home by such and such time? Do this, do that, make sure you're up in the morning." I guess my biggest fear was, what if I wasn't responsible enough, or if I just messed up somehow. But, I didn't, so I'm cool.

Fiona's transition to the academic expectations of college-level work was also more challenging than it was for Claire.

> My first two quarters, I realized I was taking way too much time with my friends and not enough time doing my actual work. So by the time third quarter came around I had to cut back significantly. 'Cause I realized staying that way, through all this homework, and then getting to class in the morning was killing me, all because I wanted to stay out, hang out. So at first it was an issue, but I got myself in check, and I changed that.

Despite their differences in preparation and expectations for college, Claire and Fiona arrived at similar decisions to disconnect from their campuses. Their experiences with campus exclusion led them to realize that college life would not be the one they saw in TV sitcoms and movies. They learned that their college experience would have to be restructured in ways that would protect their core sense of themselves as Black women and allow them to maintain their educational goals and career ambitions despite their marginalizing experiences on campus. It is this similarity of experiences of prejudice, discrimination, and oppression that prompted them to seek similar strategies for navigating marginalizing terrain.[6]

Education scholars remind us that Claire and Fiona are not alone in their raced and gendered campus encounters. Joanna Williams and Tanya Nichols describe other Black women who experience these types of interactions in college.[7] The Black women they spoke to in historically White universities and community colleges faced peers and adults who assumed that they were criminals, questioned their intelligence, denigrated Black culture, and negatively stereotyped Black women. These identity assaults are not confined to their gender or their race-ethnicity; instead they are in response to their embodied social identity of being both Black and woman.[8]

Taken individually, race-ethnicity and gender are visible identities that carry their own challenges in a society that disadvantages Black people and women. Black women, however, embody both these identities and thus do not experience womanhood the way White women do, or Blackness the way Black men do.[9] Because of commonalities in their lived experiences and the nature of prejudice enacted upon Black women, it is entirely reasonable that Claire and Fiona would recognize when their race-ethnicity and gender impact their everyday interactions on campus. Patricia Hill Collins cautions, however, that common experiences of discrimination do not guarantee common responses, especially because other elements such as class and sexuality add nuance to these experiences.[10] Therefore, the common response we see from Claire and Fiona of consciously disconnecting from their campuses is significant.

Racialized Rejection

Of all the Black and Latinx students interviewed, Black and Latinx women reported experiencing racial-ethnic microaggressions more frequently than their male counterparts by the end of their first year, and Black women more so than Latinx women. These micro- and sometimes macroaggressions communicate that they do not belong, assume criminality, sexualize them, or denigrate their culture as inferior.[11] Such encounters in and out of the classroom are the conditions under which the Black women we interviewed navigated campus belonging.

Claire's reflections show how the classroom was both a welcomed and rigorous space for growth, as well as a site of burdensome racialized social dynamics, especially for students with visible marginalized identities. Claire gained a lot from her courses. "My classes were all really amazing, I will say that. And I got a lot out of them." She enjoyed her professors and the way they taught new ideas. However, she simultaneously loathed interacting with peers in the classroom, dorm, or other social spaces. Her mostly White peers' inexperience with racial-ethnic diversity was glaring.

> Just horrible, all the people sucked. They were just all really dumb, like so dumb. Probably one of the dumbest environments I've ever been in in my life. And not even just on an academic level, on like a life experience level. 'Cause a lot of those kids come in from the suburbs, and they know nothing about anything, and it's just, it was kind of a culture shock for me, honestly. Just as far as the racism, and the homophobia, and all that kind of stuff. I never really experienced that because I always went to schools where we had these diverse populations, and it was always OK to like who you liked, and do what you wanted to do, and do well in school, and that kind of thing. And these kids are just so strange, and they just don't have that kind of cultural experience.

> It is just like a bunch of White kids who don't really understand, well at the very least, the historical aspect of race in America. And at the highest level, race relations in modern times. And they're just thrown into this, it's not even [diverse]; they think it's so diverse. It's like, maybe 90 percent White. OK, that's an exaggeration. But it's a lot of White kids. They're like, "It's so diverse here, I love it, I love the diversity." And you're just like, this is nothing. What are you talking about? And the administration also definitely plays up their diverse aspects. When you go to presentations for the first week or whatever, when they were doing introductions, they would be like, "We have this and we have this, and we're so tolerant of everyone," and blah. It's just so strange. You shouldn't have to do that, you should just [say] we have this, like it's really cool, this culture's pretty cool, you should check it out. Not advertising it. Or bragging about it. Which is definitely something that you find there a lot.

Claire's experiences also highlight how being a biracial queer woman played into the racially gendered encounters she endured on campus and in other areas of her life. The particularly sexual nature of the responses from men highlights the insidious ways in which race-ethnicity and gender interact to create unwelcoming conditions.

> Obviously, there's basic sexism, which is prevalent everywhere, but Black women have a specific brand of racism and sexism combined. All of the racism that I encounter is sexualized, as opposed to expanding into other aspects of my life. In a lot of ways, I can assimilate really well with White people, and, I don't know, it's more like being exotic. So it's hard for people to just make assumptions about me just from my outward appearance. It just makes it so that any problem that has to do with my race is inherently sexualized almost. Or follows with something that sexualizes me. It's hard not to feel like a commodity.

It is apparent that she thinks about how her race-ethnicity and gender operate in her daily interactions, as did the Black women whom education scholar Rachelle Winkle-Wagner interviewed.[12] Black women were conscious of the pressure from their White peers to think, act, and interact in ways based on the assumptions their White peers held about Black womanhood. Winkle-Wagner found that at an important time in their personal development, the sense of self that Black college women were choosing and seeking to enact was overpowered by identities ascribed to them. The imposition of these "unchosen" identities, produced in the everyday interactions of campus life, were experienced as a daily negotiation and renegotiation of the self. Claire similarly could not choose the range of raced and gendered assumptions that others imposed on her during campus interactions. She would, however, come to exercise choice in whether those interactions would take place at all.

Fiona, too, struggled with identity. She took at face value what the brochures professed about the opportunities a college experience offered, including forming meaningful friendships with people different from herself. However, that meant opening herself up for racialized rejection.

> I did random roommates, just 'cause I thought that would be pretty cool. I figured maybe there was a possibility that one of the people I room with [would] end up being a good, long-term friend of mine. But I lived with two White girls who clearly had not really experienced—it's possible they didn't have a lot of Black friends. And I wasn't in the room much. When I was, it kind of felt awkward. 'Cause I felt like they didn't know how to interact with me. I did actually try my best to make the best out of it. You know, go in and talk to them, see how their day was, make sure they were comfortable. I didn't want them to feel uncomfortable at all.

Fiona struggled to articulate that distinct yet ephemeral sense of being othered in the intimate environment of dorm life.[13] Fiona's roommate difficulties, like those experienced by many of her Black peers, had a dynamic in which racial-ethnic prejudices won out against best intentions. Tamara Towles-Schwen and Russell Fazio's psychological study of randomly assigned interracial roommate pairings found that even when the White roommates were motivated to behave in a nonprejudiced manner, their negative implicit racial-ethnic biases resulted in behavioral consequences that led to poor roommate relationships.[14]

The academic and social spaces on campus also signaled to Fiona that she was expected to be accommodating at the expense of her own comfort, as the following interaction with public safety officers made clear.

> Our campus police officers often like to, I don't wanna say target, but if they can find a reason to mess with you, it seems like they do that sometimes. I'll have times where I'm on campus and I just randomly get asked to show my student ID. And that's not a policy whatsoever that you have to carry your ID on you at all times when you're on campus. You actually don't need your ID for anything. . . . I'm like, OK, I'll show you my ID just so you can leave me alone. But I know what this is. . . . Sometimes if we're having an event on campus where it's like free food and games and T-shirts, I'll constantly get asked if I'm a student first

> before I'm allowed to get food. But it'll be like three White people ahead of me, and that question never gets asked.
>
> The last time I got asked to show my ID was probably last week. I was cutting through the Student Center to go to the train, and public safety was in there, and he stopped me. At first, I had my headphones in so I didn't hear him saying, "Excuse me, Miss." Then he tapped me on my shoulder, and I turned around, and he just asked to see my student ID. So I showed him, and, you know, he took my ID, stared it for a while like the picture wasn't gonna match. And then he just gave it back and said, "OK. Thank you." I just didn't want any more problems, and I had somewhere to be, so I just showed him my ID and walked off. I felt bothered. I felt like, can he just leave me alone so I can go ahead about my business like I'm trying to do? And I felt irritated also because I didn't know why he was asking me for my ID. He never stated why he needed to see it. . . . Just leave me alone. I'm not bothering you, so please don't bother me.

Amid the heightened awareness of police misconduct toward marginalized groups, the experiences of Black women have largely been excluded. Legal scholar Kimberlé Crenshaw underscores the importance of intersectionality as media coverage and protests center on Black male victims. In a recent TED talk, she asked the audience to respond to the names of victims of police violence that they recognized.[15] Overwhelmingly, the audience members knew the names of Black men, but not those of the Black women who were victims of the same types of violence. Assuming that the issues Black women face will be addressed by focusing on Black people or on women in general constitutes what Crenshaw calls a "trickle-down approach" to social justice that serves to further marginalize Black women.

Intersectional understandings of misconduct among public safety officers are urgent for Fiona and other Black women who have been made to feel unprotected by the very people who are entrusted and paid to ensure their safety. In light of this and other invalidating experiences in multiple campus contexts, Fiona began to make protective choices, carving her own micro-community out of the larger college campus.

Because most incoming minority students buy into the idea that college campuses are cosmopolitan spaces, their initial openness exposes them to an identity-disaffirming process of disillusionment. The roommate situation was something Fiona would have appreciated a heads-up about, especially when she learned that this specific racialized brand of roommate conflict was common among her Black peers. Claire was groomed for college contexts and still was unprepared for the severity of her racialized encounters across campus. The college campus was not a respite from the world outside. College was, in reality, more like the world outside than popular images, recruitment materials, and administrators led them to believe.

To cope with the hostile racial-ethnic climate on campus, Claire and Fiona moved toward a strategy of disengagement from general campus life. This strategy shows up for other Black women we interviewed and in other researchers' accounts of Black women's raced and gendered experiences on college campuses. Psychologist Jioni Lewis and her colleagues explored the ways that Black women coped with subtle gendered racism and explained Black women's strategy of disengagement with campus life as a self-protective response.[16] Disengagement involved desensitizing themselves to the severity of the experience and seeking to escape such interactions. They found that Black women employed disengagement strategies more often than engagement strategies, such as getting involved in peer education and advocacy on campus.[17] In addition, the more frequently Black women experienced gendered racism on campus, the more they turned to disengagement strategies to cope, which in turn led to more psychological stress.

Lewis and her colleagues found that, overall, disengagement was not an adaptive active coping strategy, and was instead an unhealthy passive coping strategy that led individuals to internalize gendered racism, to self-blame, and to turn to drugs and alcohol. We come to a different conclusion. We see Claire's and Fiona's disengagements as healthy coping because their active move away from general campus life was matched with a move toward counterspaces. These counterspaces held an important place in counteracting the negative effects of needing to disengage from campus life.

Making Space

In addressing raced and gendered discrimination on college campuses, working toward institutional change is a worthwhile goal. But waiting for campus conditions to change is not realistic for students who must sustain their sense of self in an environment that daily contests their very presence on campus. Claire and Fiona chose different ways to disconnect from campus. Claire chose complete detachment, while Fiona made strategic decisions on how and with whom to engage. These women acted on their own behalf, adjusting their college life in ways that made it possible for them to persist in college, despite the hostile campus climate.

By the end of her first year, Claire opted out of campus life completely. Any time spent on campus was for class. Extracurricular activities took place among longtime friends attending nearby schools and close family members. Claire enjoyed this and directly associated her well-being and positive feelings about college with her distance from campus.

> Well [sophomore year] I wasn't living on campus, which was so nice, because I don't want to be anywhere near campus, ever. So that was very nice to just go to classes and then go to work and then go home. That was ideal. . . . I don't really have friends at [school] 'cause my best friend goes to [a nearby university]. She went to high school with me. One of my other really good friends goes to one of the City Colleges, and so I hang out with them. I don't really have to deal with any of the kids at [my college], which is optimal. . . . [Sophomore year] was much better in a lot of ways because . . . I got to kind of limit my campus time, and I wasn't in the dining halls, and I wasn't dorming, and I wasn't dealing with anybody.

She even offers the advice of planning for campus disconnection for students like herself who are preparing to enter historically White colleges and universities.

> Just be yourself, I guess, and find people who are cool with you. Be yourself, and people will support you and everything that you need in order to be happy. Go to a big city, so if you hate your college, you can kind of branch out. I think a lot of kids get stuck—I guess, being specific, students of color get stuck—on whitewashed campuses in the middle of nowhere. I think that's really not advised. I think if you can go to a bigger city, I think that's better. At least in my experience.

Fiona's strategy was to limit her campus interactions to spaces where the small population of Black and other marginalized students hung out. She and her circle of friends managed to carve out their own space where they established their own norms. Fiona was not completely insulated from the effects of negative campus interactions, but the micro-community was there to support her in those times so she could stay on the path toward graduation.

> I got a close group of friends, we just call ourselves the Crew. It wasn't that many Black incoming freshmen, so we all kinda linked up pretty quickly. . . . We really do everything together. We go to [one another's] events and support [one another]. Cause there's not a lot of Black people on campus to begin with, so we gotta support each other.
>
> We have a thing called family dinner where we'll all go to the Student Center, get a table, sit down, just talk, just hang out. Do homework, do whatever, just chill. We're away from our families, so we felt like it was

> important to have dinner and just relax and take a break. So we would notice [an obvious and surprised response from others] when people see this group of Black people, just sitting and hanging out.
>
> That's one thing I like about the people I hang out with at school. Everyone seems to be in it for the long run. . . . We've made plans for our futures already, and we involve each other in it. So like when someone graduates from grad school, we already talked about being there for their graduation and the trip that we're gonna take out of the country after they do so. It's cool to just meet somebody about three years ago but to feel like we're gonna be friends for a lifetime. It's an amazing thing to be able to have.

When these college women found that the conventional social life and peer support in college would not suit them, they sought out counterspaces, what Lori D. Patton describes as "a home away from home, and a haven in a hostile territory."[18] Claire located her college-going counterspaces at universities other than her own. Fiona found in "the Crew" a social and ideological counterspace that helped maintain her envisioned future.

These counterspaces—racially-ethnically homogeneous social interactions—were more than friendship networks. These counterspaces were developed, strengthened, and sustained in deliberate reaction to feeling marginalized in the broader campus community. Claire and Fiona began college with the explicit intention of developing diverse friendship networks, but they found that to persist in predominantly White academic spaces, they had to create Black social spaces.

Disconnecting without Compensatory Supports

We now turn to Mercy, a Black woman attending Suburban StateU, who also detached from the broader campus but who had no counterspace to turn to. The challenges this created highlight how counterspaces can become assets for Black women attending historically White colleges and universities. Like Claire and Fiona, Mercy got the message early on that she needed to go to college. She approached college primarily from the instrumental standpoint of getting a job, but that proverbial "college experience" was not far away from her thoughts about what she wanted from college. "I wanted the whole college experience," she said. "Meeting new friends, learning, obviously, that was always a passion of mine. Originally, I wanted to go to college to start identifying who I was, and I, like, originally I wanted to make my own art club, so that's something still in process. But that was one of the minor reasons why I wanted to go. Just to start a new life and something like that."

Both her parents had graduate degrees and were as supportive as possible, but many of the details of the process were unfamiliar to them, since they had been educated outside the United States. Her nervous excitement and the surge of responsibility she sensed when she first stepped onto campus are reminiscent of Fiona's college transition. Mercy's plan was to be hyper-organized; she placed a lot pressure on herself.

> It was very nerve-racking 'cause I didn't know anybody. It was like high school all over again, so you're like, you're the new kid. But then I realized that I'm not the only new kid. There's a whole bunch of people coming in. I was also really excited because, again, trying to start a whole new life on my own. So it was fun. I remember, first semester I moved into the dorms. It was just a new feel. I didn't know what to expect mostly of college life. And then, I think during second semester, like it all hit me, like, OK, I got bills to pay now, I have responsibilities, more responsibilities. Can't be calling my dad for all these things that didn't work. Like, it's all on me. And then I noticed that I needed to step out of my shell and actually talk to other people.
>
> How did I manage? I just went with it. I try to be organized. They always give agendas at these schools, so I try to fill out my agenda every time. I use my phone a lot for reminders. . . . Actually, ask questions to those who are there to help you. So I found myself a lot in the financial aid center, in the student center to academic adviser centers. I booked a lot of appointments with special people that helped with students like me. I had to push myself a lot.

Early on, Mercy went with the fervor that often comes with new college beginnings—opening herself up to new friendships, attending campus-wide events, connecting with the African student organization, and making plans to bring her passion for art to the campus culture. The art piece was huge for her. She wanted to promote a message that art is relevant in all majors, especially in the hard sciences. In essence, she wanted to create a campus-wide micro-community, a space to break from the pressures. "It would be like having a group of people together who have a strong passion to create. I'd be accepting all majors. . . . So I think like if you're doing math, you can still be in the art club. It's a way of expressing yourself, so I feel like especially in college, you should have a means to express yourself, and [Suburban StateU] doesn't have an art club, so I just wanted that opportunity to share with other people."

Her openness was not reciprocated by the mostly White and male faculty and peers in the chemistry department or those in her pharmacy tech campus job, nor by many that she encountered in the mostly White spaces across campus.

Being the only Black woman prompted her to adjust her behavior and efforts in ways that her peers were not expected to do. Mercy felt she had to respond to the demands on her "unchosen" visible identity rather than being able to simply introduce herself and have people learn about her interests, values, abilities, and work ethic.

> When I'm at work right now, I am the only Black woman on my pharmacy tech job, and my boss is a middle-aged White male, and I know, like, in the beginning I had looks like, "Why is she here?" or, "Oh, let's go easy on her, she's probably not familiar with [this material]. Let's give her busy work and not give her the real work." And I noticed that, but I felt like I had to prove myself a little more in comparison to my cubicle buddy who's also doing similar work. I have to prove myself, that I am capable, I am competent. Establishing my credibility was very, very difficult just because I was a Black woman.
>
> Why should I have to do this? I deserve it just as the next girl, same as me, but because of my color, I don't know, it's hard. You see other people, they look at you like, "Why is she here?" But they don't actually say it to you, you just kind of feel it. So when I walk into a room, I feel judgment. I always feel, like, OK, they don't think that I deserve to be here. It weighs down on you. I just have to be extra precautious with my words, and when I go into the chemistry department I have to prove to them that, hey, I'm not what you think I am—basically, give me the same respect as my peers. Simply because when you walk into a room and you're a Black person, or a Black woman rather, and you're young, you have three stereotypes on you: that you're young, you're Black, and you're a woman. So when you walk into a room with, say, White people, they're gonna say, OK, this girl is gonna be super loud, she's gonna be obnoxious, she's gonna be dumb, we don't want her in our group.

Like Claire and Fiona, Mercy was conscious of the gendered and raced stereotypes that preceded her into her interactions. A critical difference, though, is that the need to prove worthiness was often an internal dialogue for Mercy, without the benefit of a counterspace of peers to provide needed perspective of shared experiences, or the space to deconstruct stereotypical narratives and construct counternarratives.[19]

The need to disprove others' assumptions was all-encompassing and drove Mercy toward isolation. To be sure, preoccupation with college finances made working on campus and maintaining academic standing her priorities, but her particular disconnection from campus life was wrapped up in proving herself as a Black woman in chemistry. By her junior year, Mercy was well aware of the toll such isolation took on her mental health, as well as the missed opportunities to form strong relationships with her peers.

> [Junior year's] been one of my most brutal years as far as academics goes, 'cause I wanted to get good grades and I really lost track of taking care of myself and my mental health in the process. I finally realized that, yeah, I kinda put myself in a situation that I'm not sure I can handle anymore. But as far as studying every night, for seventy-two hours straight, really took a toll on me. I lost friends as a result. I'd be that person who's always reading or on their computer, you know, just studying, and my friends were like, "Hey, you don't have time for me," and thought I didn't care for them because I wasn't putting in hours to them. I would put most of my hours into my work.
>
> [Junior] year was just me, myself, and I, and work, and school. Previous years as a freshman I wanted to find my people more, like open to trying new things. I started my own organization. I was really out there in the campus. But this year it was mostly just me in my room and my computer. It was really sad.
>
> I don't really think I have a strong friendship with anyone on campus. . . . I hate saying that, like, that makes me cringe to say I don't have time for friends. That's not something I would say years before. But it was my harsh reality.

The identity-disaffirming challenge of being a Black woman in a White, male-dominated academic space figured heavily into the intensity of her desire to succeed. However, she soon learned that academic achievements are not enough and that the self cannot be sustained without external social supports.

> I've realized that you go college to learn, but it's more than just getting a GPA. I realize that although your GPA is good, it's very important that you meet people that can come and be there for you. And if you need some help finding a career, then, you know, you have somebody that you can go back to and say, "Hey can you help me." I want to get a good GPA and stuff, but I'm not as concerned as I was during my freshman year for those reasons.

Fiona and Claire's response to being othered was to retreat to spaces filled with people who validated and nurtured them. Mercy's response was to retreat into herself, putting great effort into disproving the negative assumptions about her. Overall, disconnection for these Black women was a response to the gendered racism they experienced, just as Szymanski and Lewis found among the Black women they interviewed. Mercy's strategy, however, isolated her from not only the larger campus, but also from other supportive micro-communities where she could have located her campus core. The differences in how these women disconnected from campus highlight the role of counterspaces in enabling marginalized students to maintain a strong academic identity.

The variation in how each disconnected and what that meant for their persistence and overall well-being expands our understanding of how separating one's academic identity from one's institutional identity can increase the likelihood of persistence when accompanied by a counterspace. Through the lens of traditional theories of college persistence, the responses of Claire and Fiona to campus hostility would be interpreted as a rejection of a formative time in their lives. Instead, the more nuanced picture shows how their decisions to strategically disconnect opened up rich experiences that allowed each to feel competent, accepted, and satisfied when their campuses proved early on to be identity-invalidating spaces. That these young women had successful academic careers despite disconnecting from general campus life pushes us to think beyond generic prescriptions for college success that assume college campuses are cosmopolitan spaces that validate all students equally. Claire, whose college attendance was part of an early childhood path rather than one connected to her screenwriting and acting aspirations, stopped out after her third year and is currently working full-time. Fiona earned a bachelor of arts degree, and Mercy earned a bachelor of science degree within four years.

This chapter again highlights the need to integrate universalist theories of college persistence with a recognition of the diversity of macro-societal oppressions and micro-contextual experiences. Student services administrators can and should reach for theories of student development that identify subgroup differences and the intersectionality of identities.[20]

5

POWER IN THE MIDST OF POWERLESSNESS

Scholar-Activist Identity amid Racially and Ethnically Motivated Violence

With Elan Hope

If the 1960s was the watershed moment of activism and political organizing for racial-ethnic equity and inclusion, 2012–2014 marks the years that a new generation of activists awoke to understand that they would have to bring a new fight to an old battle. As they did in the student-led justice movements of the past, college students today are leading and answering persistent calls for social and political change.[1] In addition to developing their intellectual and occupational selves, college students are also developing their political selves by exploring who they are in relation to the communities around them. They are deciding how they will contribute to the greater community beyond one's self. This is what Heather Malin and colleagues describe as "civic purpose."[2] This long-term commitment to and participation in civic and political actions includes learning about social justice and what can be done to make the world an equitable place for marginalized groups.

For our cohort of students, who entered college in 2013, identity development included understanding a world with the first Black president of the United States. A world with social justice movements like #BlackLivesMatter, which use distributed leadership to challenge systems of racial-ethnic oppression and seek justice for racially and ethnically motivated violence. A world with the Dreamers movement, which unites undocumented immigrant youth who risk themselves to protest anti-immigrant sentiments and advance the stalled conversation on immigration. Because of these societal realities, Black and Latinx college students have to balance academic pursuits with evolving racial-ethnic identity and growing civic purpose. In this chapter, we focus on how identity-based counterspaces and activist campus culture facilitate Latinx and Black students' critical examination of race-ethnicity and racism.

We begin with Cindy, a Latinx female first-generation college student. Cindy was raised primarily by her father in a working-class household. She was the middle child, with an older sister in college and a younger sister in high school. Cindy always had a love for learning and knew since elementary school that she wanted to go to college, an opportunity that neither of her parents had. At her suburban high school, she was one of only a handful of Latinx students. She navigated the college application process on her own, despite her guidance counselor's recommendation to attend a community college. Upon her first visit to Urban PrivateU-North she knew "this is where I'm gonna go." Cindy described her transition to college as "very smooth," marked by engaging classroom experiences, participation in campus organizations, and exposure to people from different cultural backgrounds and lifestyles. For Cindy, social life is about personal growth, which she describes as "developing myself as a human being, becoming aware of what's going on in society, and then helping others do the same." She enjoyed being involved in political activism both on and off campus.

Another of our interviewees, Faith, was also excited to begin college. Faith, the youngest of three, is a Black female first-generation college student. Faith was raised in a two-parent, working-class household. Faith knew in elementary school that she wanted to go to college, and her parents, friends, and a high school guidance counselor supported her through the college application process. Unlike Cindy, Faith described her experience at Urban StateU as a "culture shock." The student population on campus was more racially and ethnically diverse than her majority African American and Latinx high school. Faith was not social during her first year. She struggled with going from being "somebody" in high school to being "nobody in a sea of millions." However, by the end of her sophomore year she had "opened up more to people. I was willing to develop more relationships with others and not be so solitary." While Faith was abreast of the hostile climate surrounding racial-ethnic minorities in the United States, she preferred to avoid high-risk political activism, like protests.

Pathways into College

Both Cindy and Faith came to college with the goal of upward mobility through higher education. As Cindy put it, "I've always loved school, so I knew since the second my parents told me that they didn't go to college that that was something I was gonna do. Since elementary school I knew that was gonna be something for me."

Cindy majored in accounting, and by the end of her first year she had secured an internship with a local accounting firm, with prospects of employment after graduation. She went to college to further her intellectual development. "I love learning and applying that information that I've learned." And, given the financial hardships she experienced growing up, she was motivated to attend college equally for the prospects of upward mobility. "I know how my dad struggles, and I know how he lives paycheck to paycheck and can barely stay above water sometimes. . . . I don't want that for my children, and I don't want that for myself either."

Faith also saw college as a way to obtain higher-paying and more secure job opportunities than her parents had. Neither woman wanted to repeat the family pattern. As Faith put it, "I just felt like if [my mom] had a degree, maybe things would have been easier for her as far as raising her kids. So that was one of the reasons why I definitely wanted to go to school . . . so that I wouldn't have to ever struggle. And I know that that doesn't guarantee anything, because you can get a degree and still kind of have a low-income job. But my main reason, so that I could get a good job."

"I also wanted to go to college for the experience," she continued. "I didn't want to just graduate high school and work at McDonald's. . . . I'm still young now, so I have this opportunity to go out and have fun and learn things, and I feel like knowledge is really important now, so you have to use it." She also felt an obligation, she said. "Obligated because I wanted to make something of myself, so I kind of felt like I had no other choice. I could have done the military or taken a year off, but I felt like this is the time now. And if I don't do it now, then I'll regret it later."

While there are many similarities between Cindy and Faith, they had different pathways into college. Cindy was self-directed as she completed her college applications and chose a college to attend. Her parents provided emotional support, but they could not guide her through the application process. She also received minimal assistance from her high school guidance counselor. Cindy carried this independence and self-advocacy into her first year at Urban PrivateU-North.

Although Faith's parents also did not have college degrees, they had taken some college courses and did not have the challenge of being complete outsiders to higher education, as Cindy's immigrant parents were. Faith noted that "my adviser in high school [helped], my parents helped me, and some of my friends [helped]. [My parents] helped me by finding colleges that they knew that I would be interested in, . . . and they took me on the tours and the trips to see the colleges." Despite the differences in their path into college, both women enrolled with the same level of willingness to intertwine their personal identity with their institutional identity.

Sociopolitical Engagement and Campus Belonging

As they transitioned to college, Cindy and Faith had opportunities to participate in extracurricular activities on campus. Some of those opportunities included civic engagement or other forms of political activism. The sociopolitical development model suggests that youth civic engagement and political activism are predicted, in part, by opportunities to engage.[3] Essentially, give students an opportunity to participate in a cause that resonates with them, and they will. For Cindy, extracurricular activities that included civic engagement and activism were a prominent part of her first-year college experience—and an important counterspace.

> One of the best experiences that I've had was doing service. . . . We have this thing called Noel Nights, where we put together a huge Christmas event . . . and we invite students from inner-city middle schools where it'll probably be their only Christmas. . . . I think that was one of the best experiences: taking around my little student and how excited she was to get one present was just so wonderful.
>
> So this coming year I plan to get involved in what's called Donum, which a student started on campus. It's kind of like every Thursday a bunch of students go on Michigan Avenue [in downtown Chicago], and they prepackage lunches for the homeless. But they don't just go and offer the people the food. They talk to them and build relationships with them. After taking my social problems class and doing my big paper on homelessness, it's something that I really want to get involved in.

Cindy's experiences illustrate that academic courses can function as ideational counterspaces, especially when ideas from class translate into civic action. Andrew Case and Carla Hunter note that ideational counterspaces are created when individuals of different social groups come together for a similar anti-oppression purpose.[4]

Cindy's scholar-activist identity developed through campus student organizations and extracurricular activities. When asked what was her most positive first-year experience, she highlighted social issues: "Probably the events I did with my [social and political activism] organization. I think what keeps me going is people going up to me from different organizations after the event and saying like, wow, my perspective has completely changed, or you know this has inspired me to want to do this, or let's collaborate on something, let's bring an event together." The sense of fulfillment and "having people say thank you, you've inspired me" to her was worth all the work. "There's no price tag on the way that me and the people that put on that event feel."

Opportunities to engage with social justice actions were important for the development of Cindy's scholar-activist identity. She grew in her understandings of structural inequalities and her desire to address injustices through political activism. Participation in social justice works in concert with opportunities to interact with students from diverse backgrounds, and universities implicitly acknowledge this symbiotic relationship. Among college and university mission statements, two of the most prevalent themes are commitment to diversity and institutional and civic service.[5]

These intentional efforts at creating opportunities for interactional diversity are the primary way that Urban PrivateU-North differed from all the other schools in our study. As Cindy said, when the department of multicultural affairs put on an event, "everybody knows it's not just the students of color on campus who are allowed to go. . . . I invite my Caucasian friends all the time, and they don't think twice to come because we know it's OK to interact with the people of different cultures, and they know they're gonna be accepted and not looked at. . . . I like that everyone is willing to accept everybody, and even if they can't resonate or identify with that idea or that religion or that culture, they accept it and embrace it."

As noted in almost every chapter in this book, college students, many of whom are coming from racially-ethnically and socioeconomically segregated high schools, have limited skills for building relationships with others who are "not like me." Research shows that institutions that are intentional in creating opportunities for frequent, meaningful, and sustained interactions across student diversity create campuses with greater tolerance for diverse perspectives and a greater likelihood of not just interracial contact but meaningful interracial friendships.[6] Meaningful opportunities for intergroup interactions, coupled with a campus social justice focus, may make for greater opportunities for coalition building among students and an integrated scholar-activist identity.

For Faith the shift from being a big fish in a small pond to being a little fish in a big pond initially destabilized her sense of self until she was able to find her micro-community on campus. Faith is an avid musician, and her micro-community was with other members of a campus band. "I only play saxophone, oboe, and clarinet at [Urban StateU], and I made my friends there. And musicians are really weird, so I learned that about them."

Band was a time-consuming extracurricular activity that first year, so although she expressed interest in civic activities, Faith had little time to engage with other campus organizations. By sophomore year, however, Faith had become more integrated with the campus community, which improved her overall college experience. "I opened up more to people," she said. "I was willing to develop more relationships with others and not be so solitary and only hang out with people that I knew. I joined a group called Student Activity Board, so that opened up to meeting a lot of people. It helped me to network. I got to meet a lot of famous people actually. . . . And it was sooo fun, it was so much fun. So that's improved my college experience for the better."

Although Faith embraced the racial-ethnic diversity of her campus, her engagement did not yield the same scholar-activist identity that Cindy developed. There is no expectation that all racial-ethnic minority students should or need to develop a scholar-activist identity, but research shows that it facilitates more adaptive coping with racial-ethnic microaggression, discrimination, and injustice.[7]

College Students Are Not Immune to Social Unrest

Paths to scholar-activist identities are varied and can be influenced by students' personal beliefs, by their campus context, and by the larger society that intrudes on their "time away at college." Part of the context for both Cindy and Faith was the public documentation of racially-ethnically motivated violence, including the deaths of Michael Brown, Freddie Gray, Sandra Bland, and Renisha McBride. This social-media-consumed, constant display of racism in America means that Black and Latinx college students are repeatedly reminded of life-threatening structural oppression and opportunities for consciousness-raising and action to combat this oppression.[8] Traditional models of college student development argue that college provides young adults with time and space to free themselves of sociopolitical concerns and embark on individualized self-development.[9] That is rarely true for students from historically marginalized groups, however, and in today's climate, Black and Latinx students do not have the luxury to dissociate from larger sociopolitical issues.

Cindy and Faith describe similar cognitive and emotional responses to issues of racial-ethnic injustice. Cindy was marked by her cousin's death the previous year. Released from jail, he was making attempts to "get his life together," she said. But he would later die in police custody without receiving medical attention. That, to her, was inexcusable. "To me, no one should be [treated that way], I don't care what you did. You should not be refused the right, the possibility of life. And for me I just think how different would it be if he was Caucasian. If he was a White guy. . . . He's of a very dark complexion. So, at first meeting him you would probably think that he's Black, that's how dark-skinned he is."

Social and news media discussions of racially and ethnically motivated violence are not theoretical or an abstraction for students like Cindy. These discussions have very real implications for family, friends, and friends of friends.

Constantly needing to defend her humanity and struggle against racism deepened her convictions on these issues, but it was also mentally and emotionally taxing.

> For me what's most disturbing is having to sit and explain to somebody [that] it is not OK for the result of a woman [Sandra Bland] not putting on her turn-lane signal [is] she's fucking dead, right? That's psychotic.... And it turns out, I had lunch with a very good friend the day before yesterday, and that's the first thing he asked me. How do you, what are your thoughts, what do you think? I sat there and I ranted, right. Just very upset, very angry, and he's like, you know, [she] went to my church.
>
> My other really good friend, who is also part of our organization, was even closer to Sandra Bland, that was a family friend. And it's just like, it's hitting closer and closer to home for me. And it's just scary, because my first thought is all of my close friends, everybody, like they're all African American, and I don't even know what I would do if something happened to them. I'm fearful for their safety and then mine.... It's only gonna get worse, so for me I don't know it's, it's concerning, it's disturbing what's going on. But I do as much as I can to raise awareness to the topic, and when people post ignorant things on my post I sit there and suggest books, talk about how I feel about it and what my rationale is.

By the end of sophomore year Cindy had developed a nuanced articulation of her social justice–oriented civic identity. "You know those are innocent lives that are being taken," she said. "I don't think that just because you don't identify with a race or you don't come from that culture you should be able to brush aside an injustice." Cindy's development illustrates how a university's intentional cultivation of both interactional diversity and opportunities for civic engagement can foster the ability to connect one's future with the futures of others "not like me."

Faith's response to racially and ethnically motivated violence was directly tied to her identity as a Black woman and the implications of being Black in America.

> I wanna say it made me feel angry, but I would say it made me feel small, made me feel like I didn't have much power. And I didn't like that feeling, because I do have power. So I didn't feel like because I'm Black that [power] should be taken away from me because the police don't know how to act. I'm not just gonna say it's the police, because there are some Black people out here not doing right. [But] it seems like the Jim Crow era is coming back. So I wanna say it's something I'm fearful of, because I can't see it all coming back that way, but I wanna say it's something I'm conscious of.

In addition to the daily news about racially-ethnically motivated violence and the stress it brought, Faith had to defend against stereotypes and assumptions about how she should feel or act as a Black person in this sociopolitical climate. When asked about her most stressful experience, she said it was being generalized and stereotyped, "because I'm Black that I am going to feel a certain way about what's going on in the world."

As discussed in chapter 9, social identity threat is when individuals experience or perceive that one or more of their social identities is not valued.[10] When Faith's Black identity was threatened, she responded in ways that deemphasized rather than reinforced that identity. This is in sharp contrast to Cindy, who, because she was embedded in a campus network of justice-oriented peers, responded to identity threats in ways that asserted rather than weakened her Latinx identity. The two women's different coping responses would not have been predicted from the level of structural diversity on their respective campuses. Faith's institution (26 percent Latinx and 8 percent Black) was substantially more demographically diverse than Cindy's (13 percent Latinx and 4 percent Black). However, as Nick Crossley and Joseph Ibrahim note, a "critical mass per se is insufficient for collective action and that a mass only gives rise to collective action where its members are networked."[11] Cindy was immersed in her university's culture of social justice and the many available campus counterspaces. Faith did not describe a similar culture, and while those groups might exist, she was unable or unwilling to engage them, even though her campus was demographically more racially-ethnically diverse.

The Role of Counterspaces in Adaptive Responding to Identity Threats

Differences in precollege life experiences and transitions to college affected how Cindy and Faith responded to racial-ethnic injustice and violence. Cindy learned the importance of self-advocacy on her pathway to college, and Faith had many supporters walk with her on her pathway to college. Cindy immediately embraced the social justice campus environment and found like-minded friends, and Faith struggled to find friends and campus organizations to engage with. Beyond that context, we focus on how their involvement in racial-ethnic counterspaces during their first year on campus set them up to engage versus withdraw when feeling racially-ethnically threatened.

As detailed in chapter 7, minority-focused extracurricular clubs and organizations serve as counterspaces for students on campus, spaces where minority students can develop agency—active resilience, resistance, and circumvention of the psychological consequences of oppression.[12] Students like Cindy locate their campus belonging in these counterspaces, whereas students like Faith eschew these spaces in favor of participating in campus-wide activities. Cindy was involved in several such counterspaces her first year and held a leadership position in at least one of them. "I'm not like super, super active [in] the Latin American Student Organization," she said, "but I like that just because it's a nice place to come and be able to kind of, you know, there has to be a time where you go and talk to people who identify with your culture or know who you are and how your family works, and just like the cultural things you were surrounded by when you grew up." Cindy also joined the Association for Latin Professionals of America as a way to reinforce her goals and plans and remind her that she is not alone in her pursuit, particularly as she strides ahead of her parents and other family members.

> There's a lot of times where, myself included, you know as an underrepresented student or someone who comes from a low-income background, I just sit there and think, . . . should I, can I keep going—like is, is it going to work? [The Association for Latin Professionals of America] . . . brings in individuals who come from that background just to say, You know what? This is possible for you. You can do this. Like, I was once there, and I used this adversity to push forward. So I know that's vital to my hopes and my dreams and my pushing forward.

The social justice programming that is associated with minority student centers is a legacy of previous generations of students who had to become student activists to get such centers instituted on their campuses.[13] In an article that was aptly titled "In Defense of Themselves," Joy Ann Williamson details how Black students needed to protest to initiate and reshape student services that would help ensure their survival at historically White colleges and universities. Because universities conceded minority-focused counterspaces to students in response to their demands for inclusion and equity, these spaces hold the potential, as organizational leadership researchers Garrett Hoffman and Tania Mitchell put it, "to foster student activist movements aimed at changing the structures and systems of exclusion and injustice."[14]

There is important overlap between an institutional culture that reinforces equity and inclusion and institutionally supported student organizations for civic and activist identity development. As Cindy's comments below reveal, her identity as a Latinx woman and her desire to seek racial-ethnic justice are not positioned in opposition to the institutional culture. In fact, her institution's culture propelled Cindy through social justice opportunities in coursework, extracurricular activities, and an overall climate that embraces and encourages students to seek justice on campus and in society at large. "The whole stereotypical college party social scene is not my cup of tea, far from," she said, "so my social life consists of progressing myself, developing myself as an intellectual, as a human being, becoming aware of what's going on in society and then helping others do the same."

She joined the Minority Alliance for Progress Chicago; started off as the event coordinator, bringing in speakers to shed light on "positive things that people of color have done in the past and in the present and can do in the future." The speakers also helped to shed light "on controversial topics that people don't generally sit and have a conversation about over lunch." The group focused on social activism, hearing from a former Black Panther party leader and "a lot of different minority groups from the university to come and just talk about activism as a whole," she said. "I thrive on things like that. I live to further my experiences and further my knowledge on topics like that and also help other individuals be enlightened."

Roderick Watts and colleagues argue that opportunity structures—spaces that offer occasions for youth from marginalized backgrounds to practice leadership and civic skills—are necessary components of sociopolitical development.[15] The relationship between activist identity and opportunity structure is reciprocal. Students like Cindy are initially drawn to activism through racial-ethnic justice organizations because of their growing social-justice-oriented perspectives. Equally, these organizations function as opportunity structures, where students like Cindy can further mature in their understanding of social and political oppression and develop skills that support political activism.

Inspired by the organizations and what she was learning, Cindy was determined to counter anti-Black and other forms of racism, and strive for social justice more broadly through activism and social actions. Black and Latinx issues, she said, were "very similar."

> I mean both populations of people are marginalized and have been oppressed, continue to be oppressed. I mean especially from what's been coming from the mouth of Republican candidate Donald Trump, right? And there's so many people behind him. . . . I feel that there's probably a lot more intensity for the Black community, but I do feel that . . . Latinos, Hispanics, and Blacks but also Middle Eastern people, Native Americans, just anyone really who isn't from European descent, like really struggles to comfortably identify with who they are and be who they are and be able to have validated emotions. So I think that the most amount of power will come from these communities coming together and fighting for each other . . . which is what my organization is trying to do.

Cindy's sense of power comes from becoming part of something larger than what her individual actions could achieve.

In sharp contrast, Faith was not integrated into minority-focused counterspaces on her campus, though, as she said, the "majority of my friends are Black." For Faith, race-ethnicity was a suppressed component of her sense of self, which made campus counterspaces that were created for Black students less appealing.

> Black students on campus seem to be very pro-Black. And not that I'm not, but I don't wanna talk about it all day, I don't wanna have to defend my skin color all day. I don't wanna have to be a part of something that talks about stuff that we done suffered all day. And a lot of Black students at [Urban StateU] do, a lot of Black students are—they question why I'm not in a sorority that's Black, why I'm not in BSU, why I'm not going to the Black parties, why I'm not doing all this stuff. And it's just like, I don't want to. I don't want to limit myself to just that. I don't want my college experience to just [be] about that. If that was the case, then I would have went to an HBCU. I wanted diversity.

In some respects, Faith saw any form of self-segregation as a step back. She would not, she told a friend, walk in the separate graduation held for Black students. When her friend challenged her, saying that Blacks have fought for the ability to do just that, she disagreed.

> I'm like, well, if that's the case, then I wanna do it with people of every race. Don't get me wrong, I think it's a beautiful thing that, you know, they want all of the minorities to walk together.... It's just that I feel like I'm equal to the Whites. The White guy I sit next to, the Asian girl I sit next to, so I wanna graduate with them. 'Cause I wanna show everybody like, yes, I'm Black and I'm just like them, just as smart as them, and I'll walk right along with them at graduation.

Faith exhibits what Robert Sellers and colleagues call the multidimensional nature of racial-ethnic identity.[16] Faith consistently reinforces a high regard for the Black community. At the same time, she does not want blackness to be a central or defining component of her identity. Research finds that Black students for whom race-ethnicity is less central to their identity participate in fewer Black-centered campus organizations.[17] Faith's desire to explore friendships and experiences beyond her racial-ethnic group does not inherently undermine her understanding of systems of racism or her desire to see those systems dismantled. At the same time, she did not have the benefits of a sense of collective identity that counterspaces can nurture—the feeling that one is neither alone nor powerless.

Cindy's and Faith's visceral responses to racially-ethnically motivated violence were the same, but their scholar-activist identities, and distinct paths to those identities, diverged. Cindy was an advocate, for herself in the college application process and then for others in her activism. With the death of her cousin, Cindy had personally experienced the effects of racially-ethnically motivated state-sanctioned violence. Although Faith had no immediately similar experience, she still experienced instances of interpersonal discrimination related to police brutality. Both women displayed critical awareness of racial-ethnic-based injustice. But they differed in the extent to which this critical awareness matured into critical consciousness—the ability to analyze the root structural factors that perpetuate racially and ethnically motivated violence and discrimination and engage an action-based response. Faith stopped at the level of critical awareness.

Faith hesitated at becoming strongly identified with a racial-ethnic-based sociopolitical cause. When Black Lives Matters protests swept the campus, Faith "didn't want to put myself in a position where I could jeopardize my future because they had a lot of, they had the SWAT outside on the campus. They [the protesters] blocked the expressway, and it wasn't that I wasn't in support, I was just tryin' to stay protected." Faith, although critically aware of injustice, was cautious about political activism, particularly the ramifications of high-risk activism for her future.[18]

Cindy, in contrast, was energized by the thought of protesting. She stood out as someone who entered college ready to be engaged. She was highly efficacious, believed that she and her friends could and would make a difference and right the wrongs of systems of injustice. She came to college aware of some of the issues and hungry for more information and involvement in social justice movements. Research has found that those who engage in high-risk activism also have higher racial-ethnic centrality, and adhere to beliefs about the importance of social responsibility to the community.[19] All in all, Cindy and Faith show how students can have similar internal reactions to racial-ethnic oppression but differ in their activist identities and actions because of individual aspects of their developmental histories and embeddedness with identity-affirming supports.

College students all over the world have answered and led many calls for social justice changes, from the 1960s civil rights movement to the Tiananmen Square protests of 1989 to the 2010 Arab Spring. Although university administrators cannot predict the societal issues that will emerge, they can be aware of how various subpopulations of students may be differently affected and inclined to respond.[20] To that end, universities can create campuses that prepare students with skills and worldviews that enable them to critically assess justice, equity, and inclusion, and then make strategic decisions about whether, when, and how to engage in activism, while also advancing their academic careers. As students' awareness of social injustice grows in tandem with their desire to engage in activism to address such injustices, colleges and universities must shoulder the responsibility of supporting student development in alignment with institutional missions that promote civic engagement.[21]

6

IMPORTANCE OF A CRITICAL MASS

Experiencing One's Differences as Valued Diversity Rather Than a Marginalized Threat

With Carly Offidani-Bertrand

Despite glossy university flyers depicting a diverse circle of friends in the library—smiling white, brown, and black faces—minority students often arrive to campus only to realize that their new environment is a very different picture. As detailed in a December 2013 National Public Radio story, "A Campus More Colorful Than Reality: Beware That College Brochure," universities often oversell their diversity. Tim Pippert looked at more than ten thousand images from college brochures, comparing the racial-ethnic breakdown of students in the pictures to the colleges' actual demographics. He found that, overall, the whiter the school, the more diversity depicted in the brochures.[1]

Upon arrival on campus, racial-ethnic minority students find themselves dramatically outnumbered by White students, taught by largely White professors, and learning about White historical figures and artifacts. Because of the segregated nature of American K–12 schooling, this shift into suddenly being racially-ethnically outnumbered can be a significant challenge to campus integration. Mounting feelings of social isolation add an additional layer of stress atop an already difficult transition. Away from home for the first time, many minority students feel culturally lost as they begin their new life as college students. Lourdes, a Latinx woman enrolled at Suburban StateU, where Latinx students were 9 percent of the student body, described how she felt as if she were the lone representative of her group. "I felt like I was the only Hispanic person there, which I know I wasn't, but it felt like it. You wouldn't really see many Hispanic people. And then, I got really homesick, so I hated it even more."

Even on campuses with more diverse student bodies, feelings of social segregation still pervade. Rosa, a Latinx woman enrolled at Urban StateU, where Latinx students were 26 percent of the student body, felt no institutional support in helping her to build friendships across racial-ethnic boundaries.

> I chose [Urban StateU] 'cause it was so diverse . . . but everyone tends to gravitate towards their own cultures or their own race. So that's kind of hard. You do get to meet some other people, but usually you end up being part of your own culture, or your own little clique. So that kind of gets you down, 'cause you wanna meet other people. When you go and see people of a certain race, you get kind of timid and shy, you don't want to approach them 'cause you don't know what to expect, or even though you don't wanna be judgmental, you kinda judge, like, oh, you know, I don't wanna mess with them, or they're gonna think I'm stupid or something.

Research shows that without intentional efforts to facilitate cross racial-ethnic interactions and relationships, universities may succeed at creating structural diversity but fail at facilitating meaningful relationships between students of different racial-ethnic groups.[2] Although most campus cultures seem to resist deep discussions of racial-ethnic differences, at the same time these differences feel inescapable in everyday social interactions. Although students believe it should be possible to move beyond these differences, they continue to be confronted in their daily lives with cultural stereotypes and differences in understandings and expectations.

At historically White colleges and universities, minority students must get over the shock of feeling alone in their difference, while also learning how to cope with microaggressions suggesting that they do not belong. In describing some of her most negative experiences over the last year, Camilla, a Latinx woman attending Urban PrivateU-North, talked of the hurt that minority students feel when they are othered.

> Some of the students were rude, prejudiced I would say. I know sometimes I have an accent, sometimes my words get chopped, or sometimes I say things differently. And I know sometimes they would laugh at it, like a joke, but for me it was "that's not a laughing matter." . . . If you say something wrong, I'm not going to laugh at you even if it was funny. So I take that seriously. That was one of the issues. Sometimes I feel they talk down to me, like they'll be, if you are not at my level I don't talk to you. . . . I know they have made remarks like, "What are you doing here?" And I'm like, "What do you mean I'm doing here? I go to school

> here." Other than that, sometimes they don't say to my face but I hear comments like, go back to your country. This is my country. I was born and raised here.

The students in our study varied widely in how they managed these new experiences and feelings. Some felt positive recognition of their differences, while others felt stereotyped as the sole representative of their group. Regardless, students should not be left to simply cope on their own during this transition. Counterspaces can bring minority students together in large enough numbers to mitigate feelings of being the sole representative of their group on campus.[3]

Positive relationships with faculty and administrators are critical to shaping how students manage their concerns about difference.[4] But many faculty and administrators are often unaware of or insensitive to minority students' transition experiences and needed supports.[5] When those sources of support fail, minority students seek additional support in minority-focused offices and organizations. These counterspaces where they are not othered can provide social and emotional comfort, guidance, and understanding that enable them to process the social aspects of the college transition, as well as provide instrumental information about how to become a successful college student.

Throughout this chapter we will weave back and forth through the transition experiences of eight students. Their stories illustrate many of the common themes that emerged from students' discussions about feeling othered—that is, made to feel out of place or deviant because of aspects of themselves that are identified as different from traditional college student norms.[6] Their experiences also show how counterspaces enabled them to celebrate their differences as a positive contribution to campus diversity.

The Expected Ease versus Difficult Reality of Transcending Racial-Ethnic Boundaries

The first thing Lourdes mentioned when asked to describe herself was that she is a first-generation college student. "I'm the first person in my family to go away to college," she said. "My mom and my dad, they would both always tell me how they wanted me and my sister to go to college." Lourdes was aware she would be a minority in college but was motivated by the desire to serve as an example of upward mobility for her racial-ethnic group. "I wanted to [go] because I always hear how it's most just Caucasian people who go." She was also motivated by the desire to learn. "All my life I always got good grades," she said. "I usually liked [school], so it's not like I'm doing it just to have money. It's also because I like it."

Despite her convictions and love of learning, Lourdes was unprepared for the experience of being othered and the social isolation that came with being a minority in a historically White space. Lourdes was overwhelmed by feeling "like I was the only like Hispanic person there." These feelings of social isolation have academic consequences, because schooling is, in large part, a social experience.[7] Classroom learning is the result of many successful interpersonal interactions among teachers and students. Thus, when students feel disconnected or misunderstood, their learning is negatively affected.

The limited number of Latinx and Black students means that these young people are often in classes where they are the only member of their group in the class. As Lourdes noted, even after making a few friends on campus, classroom social interactions were still challenging. "In my classrooms I still feel [alone]. In classes I don't really have any friends. It was just friends outside of the classes. So I still felt kind of uncomfortable." As will be discussed later, this discomfort affected her willingness to contribute to discussions or ask questions in class.

Like many of his peers, Jerome, the valedictorian of his high school class and a Black man, was drawn in by his expectations of the quintessential college social experience.

> I wanted to go to college just so I can experience the college life. [In the brochures] it looked like all the students were happy, and then you can tell everybody was progressing. You want to be a part of something like that. I was kind of looking for a group of people that I can hang out with, . . . work together to get the assignment done. But it was kind of hard 'cause, I don't know, it's kind of hard relating to people at [Urban PrivateU-South], being a Black student . . . especially when you don't stay on campus.

As Jerome was learning to cope with the academic challenges of college, he had hoped to find solidarity with other students with whom he could share these struggles. His loneliness and isolation were undeniable the summer after his first year. He had not yet made any friends, which, he said, was disappointing. Jerome attributed much of his social isolation to his race-ethnicity, and was surprised at the sense of difference he felt, despite his efforts to bridge the gap.

> I think it is kinda harder being friends with people outside of your race. 'Cause you know that they have a different lifestyle. They gonna want to do different things outside of school, probably. And I tried, I tried to, I tell myself at the beginning of a course, like when it's new in a course, "Make a friend with somebody here." But then it's like, I don't, I don't know. I wouldn't. It was just, if I did want to be their friend it—I was just

> forcing the situation. And I didn't wanna do that. . . . It's hard right now to find friends. But I think I, I'll try to get, I'll try to get better at that.

While Jerome tried to sound confident, he didn't quite understand why he could not make friends, and he felt the palpable social distance that stands between him and the image he had of college life—a place where people make friendships irrespective of their different social backgrounds.

Students' experiences of social distance ranged from feelings of awkwardness or lack of understanding, to incidents of microaggression, to overt experiences of discrimination. As Sarah, a Black woman attending Suburban StateU, detailed, overt experiences of discrimination continue to occur, even if they are infrequent.

> I've always grown up with interracial relationships. When I went to [high] school there were Hispanics, African Americans, Caucasians, and so on and so forth. College, it is a bit more segregated. People are adults now, so they're fully brought up in their ways for the most part. I've seen a lot of people that have been blatantly disrespectful or racist to me. At work, in school and classes. Like, she'll say, "I don't want to work with her cause she's Black." And it doesn't really get under my skin or affect me. I don't care, I'm gonna meet the person. Screw her, take it or leave it. It is kind of unsettling to say that the majority of my [college] friends are African American, because they're not as cultured and diverse as I'd prefer it to be. 'Cause my best friend [from high school] is White, and a lot of people are surprised to see that. I can blend with any type of race or culture, I don't mind. I'm open-minded to anything and everything. A lot of people aren't like that on the campus.

This curious but understandable dismissal of the personal impact of prejudice and discrimination occurred often among the students we interviewed. When students described such an incident, they often followed it with statements that negated its psychological and emotional punch, like "bad things happen, but I've got to keep moving forward." Knowing the importance of obtaining their degree and believing that such incidents will occur wherever they go, students normalized discrimination as a nuisance aspect of their college experience.

The racial-ethnic aspects of the social transition were the most challenging for students like Sarah who attended diverse high schools. Sarah's selective high school in Chicago was nearly evenly split: 32 percent Latinx, 27 percent White, and 26 percent Black students. As a result, she and her peers thought their new college peers would be sophisticated about issues of race-ethnicity and would be like-minded regarding building friendships across racial-ethnic boundaries. They were disappointed and often hurt to discover this was not the case.

The Push and Pull into Segregated Peer Networks

Feelings of social awkwardness and distance push students toward segregated peer groups, and the need for social belonging further pulls them in. Students noticed the structural diversity of the student body and conceded that they were now living in close proximity with students of other racial-ethnic groups, but were also aware that they still lacked meaningful interactions with these peers. Rosa chose Urban StateU because it was diverse. However, her previous schooling contexts, like those of most students, were segregated, and she did not have the social skills or social comfort needed to build a diverse friendship network.

> Since I came from [a] school [that] was mostly Hispanics, like 99 percent, it was really hard to go up to someone and be, like, "Oh, hi, my name's this," and that's because you're not used to it, you feel kind of like you can't. You don't know how to do it. So that was tough. But I did make like one Caucasian friend and one Asian friend. And when I did talk to them, I'm like, oh my god, they're so cool and stuff. But like it really didn't last a long time. It wasn't as a great relationship as my friend Jenny who was Hispanic and who was like me.

People's understanding of who is "like me" is elusive and malleable. It is elusive because it is usually determined in an instant and is based on implicit biases rather than thoughtful considerations of commonalities. It is malleable because research consistently finds that interventions that create sustained opportunities for intergroup contact are "vital to reducing racial bias," according to Nida Denson, who focuses on understanding the effects of college diversity experiences on student development.[8]

Many institutions like Urban StateU have made considerable progress advancing structural diversity. However, these efforts generally stop once these students arrive on campus. Gary Pike and George Kuh, two higher education researchers, conclude that "attracting diverse students should be seen as a necessary, but not sufficient, condition for positive diversity outcomes. Learning to function effectively in a diverse society also depends on the types of diversity experiences a student has and the commitment of institutional leaders to creating the conditions needed for positive and productive interactions among diverse groups of students."[9]

Like Rosa, many minority students do not find the classroom to be a space to form diverse friendships. Most efforts seemed "forced," they reported. And yet opportunities outside the classroom were limited. Like Rosa, Raul, a Latinx man attending Urban StateU, thought the university was "a big bunch of racial cliques." But he added, "I think that's anywhere you go, though. People like to hang around people that look like them, near them, that have their same background and things like that."

Students do not necessarily understand the causes of campus segregation, but they certainly pick up on patterns of distance and othering. Raul and Rosa echo the voices of many students who were surprised at the difficulty of forming friendships that crossed racial-ethnic boundaries within the classroom. And, because there were few opportunities to build friendships outside the classroom, despite intentions to do otherwise, they often ended up re-creating the social segregation that is found in broader American society.

Raul was one of several students who chafed at feeling pushed into same race-ethnicity peer groups, like a "Latino help group," which he did not feel represented his primary interests and identities.

> They tried to put me in one at the beginning of the school year. I didn't subscribe to it 'cause . . . I'm both Filipino and Mexican, so I never really fit. I actually despise hanging around one singular race because I hate being labeled as one singular race. I'm not. And also the people that I'm with are like, Americans, like we're people. We're not one certain ethnic background, you know? I never really subscribed to any of the offices for Asians either. So basically, I just hung around multicultural kids. I actually I enjoy that, mostly.

Students for whom race-ethnicity was not central to their identities focused on forming activity- and interest-based friendships, and some were successful in creating their campus social network as a result. Raul was recruited through the swim team, which provided a built-in social network, and several of his high school peers also enrolled at Urban StateU.

Consequences of Othering and Vulnerability in the Classroom

Because many students from historically marginalized groups attended lower-resourced public high schools and are first-generation students, they harbor legitimate fears that they are less well prepared for college than many of their classmates. Many Americans continue to implicitly associate lower levels of preparation with an ability gap rather than a resource gap in K–12 institutions and a consequent lack of curricular offerings, academic rigor, discursive teaching styles, and instructional technology.[10] Students' self-doubt, coupled with their feeling scrutinized by White classmates and faculty, heightens anxiety and self-consciousness in the classroom. Lourdes expressed these sentiments.

> Sometimes, most of the time, I wouldn't even want to talk [in class] just because, I mean, I know I'm not dumb, but I just feel like, I don't know, I feel like they would probably judge the way I talk, especially 'cause most White people have a better, I don't know, like, words that they use is better than how I would talk. So it would just make me feel kind of like, oh, I would rather not talk. But, when I'm just walking around, I don't feel like that.

These initial fears were compounded by the othering they experienced in class. Many believed that peers and faculty assumed they were accepted to meet "diversity requirements" and doubted their academic abilities. Sharon Fries-Britt and Bridget Turner found these same experiences among Black students attending a predominantly White college, and that having to confront these stereotypes eroded students' academic identity.[11]

Students in our study also reported instances when faculty and teaching assistants made them feel "dumb" when they sought help, which discouraged future attempts to seek support. As Rosa said, "Like when you go get help, certain TAs, they're kinda like, I don't know, rude. Or where you go get help for math, it's so stressful. Some of them just look at you like, 'You don't know this? You're so dumb.'"

Despite awareness that this hesitance to speak up in class or go to teaching assistants for support may negatively affect their learning and grades, students can still be paralyzed by feelings of inadequacy. Many said they were reluctant to ask questions and contribute to the discussion out of fear of being judged ignorant. This reluctance has academic consequences. Classroom participation often matters for students' grades and for professors' perceptions of students' level of engagement.

We would do minority students a disservice if we left the impression that their anxieties about being negatively stereotyped are solely a matter of their perceptions. These students' inferences are correct; research does indeed show that members of low-status groups, such as Black Americans, have to do more than White Americans to prove their ability, and White Americans are allowed more latitude in making mistakes before people point to lack of ability.[12] Monica Biernat and Diane Kobrynowicz conclude that "the ultimate outcome for a low-status person is a longer, more difficult trek to document ability [because people ascribe to them] evaluations that are [subjectively] less positive than those awarded to similarly credentialed individuals from high-status groups."[13]

Furthermore, although all college students feel anxious about their abilities, minority students feel especially self-conscious, as they often bear the burden of being the only representative of their group in the class. Consequently, minority students fear that any failures will affect not just how they are perceived but also how their racial-ethnic group is perceived. Mary Fischer finds that this performance burden is associated with heightened anxiety and decreased academic effort and outcomes.[14]

In response to being asked what advice she would give to college administrators working with students like herself, Aliyah, a Black woman attending Rural StateU, explained this burden.

> I was a lot harder on myself. And I wish that there was more of, like, believing in people than underestimating people. I also wish that administrators or just all faculty should take more time to get to know their students, especially students who come from somewhere [other than the White suburbs]. Take the time to get to know the students, especially when they want to get to know you, because there is that gap there and we can't deny it. So it can be frustrating when a student walks into your class as a professor or as a TA, especially the TAs, and they feel like . . . because I'm a minority, I'm starting [low down] here and I have to work my way up to be respected or to be viewed as I'm just as smart as someone else. And then I also feel like I have to surpass them so that you can also see that I, too, am a good student.

The unstated aspect of this is that White students are advantaged by not having to struggle with the burden of marginalization.

As confirmed by numerous research studies, faculty members play a critical role in mitigating or exacerbating students' self-consciousness, self-confidence, and belonging.[15] As with most things, there are student and institutional factors that determine the types of faculty-student relationships that develop and how much support faculty can provide. Some of these institutional factors include the number of classes that are large lectures, the extent to which faculty are rewarded for mentoring students, and the level of diversity among the faculty. What is more important is that institutional and student factors interact to place subgroups of students at differing levels of risk for alienation.

Rosa noted how courses intended to "weed out" the unprepared only added to feelings of alienation and chipped away at her academic identity.

> Some TAs were kind of iffy. Like I had my calculus TA, he was so mean. . . . He just sent his emails, "I'm so disappointed in you guys. I don't want you to talk to me, if you're coming to my office hours and

> you guys aren't gonna be serious and you guys have dumb questions." And then . . . they failed about two hundred students or something like that for calculus because they decide to change the policy right before the final, and the final was really hard . . . [as were] all exams throughout the whole semester. And, with that class I felt so, you know, helpless because my TA, I did not feel comfortable going up to him or telling him this, or raising my hand in class 'cause he just made you feel stupid. . . . I was trying to stay on top of it, but it was horrible. . . . Coming to college and not knowing who to turn to or who to go to, that was really hard, and just tough to find someone that will help you.

College courses are intended to be challenging in order to motivate learning and advance students' understanding. However, without accounting for the varying levels of preparation and needs for support among a diverse student body, professors and teaching assistants risk reestablishing precollege inequalities.[16] For students whose academic identity is already brittle, criticism when seeking support renders simple "access" to academic supports meaningless.[17]

Intervening Role of Critical Consciousness

Critical consciousness—the critical understanding of oppression—emerged as a mitigating factor in the difference between students who responded to feeling othered by minimizing their presence and voice in the classroom and those who spoke up during classroom discussions. Students who demonstrate critical consciousness are able to critically analyze their personal experiences in relation to larger social inequalities and advocate for themselves and others who experience these inequalities.[18] For example, minority students demonstrated critical consciousness when they recognized that their professors' low expectations of them was due to broader stereotypes and inequalities rather than their own merit as a student. Critical consciousness can serve as an active coping mechanism, particularly when one's understanding of oppression creates a sense of agency.[19] Students who demonstrate critical consciousness are often politically active, and that community engagement is positively associated with individual well-being.[20]

The experiences of students in our study corroborate findings from previous studies that indicate that Black and Latinx college students are better able to cope with the challenges they face when they understand how these challenges are part of a larger struggle against racial-ethnic discrimination. With that understanding, they feel capable of advocating for themselves and taking action toward systemic change.[21]

Maria, a Latinx woman enrolled at Urban PrivateU-North, and Jerome, introduced earlier, at Urban PrivateU-South, often felt like outsiders on campus and experienced a gaping social distance with their new White peers. Jerome responded to his feelings of social distance by trying to figure out what was wrong with himself.

> I probably could have [friends] if I wanted to, being part of all that stuff like Rising Men of Color, but . . . I already got my head on straight. And I already try my best, so I ain't feel like I needed to be in a group like that. . . . I guess it's more about networking. I don't even have a Facebook, Twitter, or Instagram. I'm trying to ask myself, do I need it? . . . And then they say the friends you make at college are the friends you can grow with.

He also had to commute to school, which he thought impeded developing friendships, participating in clubs and organizations, and being part of study groups. This issue came up in his response to being asked what advice he would give college administrators trying to help a student like himself. Jerome blamed himself for not being able to stay on campus and felt ashamed by it. Consequently, he retreated from several opportunities to engage in activities that he believed were geared toward students who lived on campus.

In contrast, Maria's critical understanding of the roles of privilege and power in her feelings of being othered provided a critical frame for her active coping strategies.

> I obviously made friends, they were all nice to me. But at the same time they would talk about things that I knew nothing about. Like online shopping or that kind of thing, and I was like, "Ahhh, this is all privilege." . . . In my classes it's not always the majority White, but they're more strong spoken, and I feel like my role this past year has definitely increased in terms of participation, so I'm no longer holding back. I always wait for things to get to a certain level of like ignorant or problematic and I'll raise my hand. That's when I'll say some stuff that clears up whatever miscommunication or whatever misconceptions that person may have. I always address things directly, and I'm not afraid to hold back, considering the political climate we're in.

The political climate, she said, was forcing her to speak up. While she hated that the political issues "were a thing," at the same time they were "empowering because it's forcing me to speak up. Obviously, it's not the same for everyone, but for me in particular it's a fun challenge."

Her critical understanding of privilege enabled her to interpret experiences of othering within a frame of structural inequalities, and place the responsibility for feeling othered on her environment, rather than on herself.

> Every time I walk around, I'm very aware of privilege and oppression and how everything works. I'm always very conscious, and in the back of my mind I'm always secretly angry about it and I'm kind of resentful in that way. Don't assume your form of thinking is the correct way, and don't assume that everyone has the same priorities. I feel like a problem I had my first year was that a lot of administrators were very much like, "Oh you have these responsibilities and duties at school and like blah blah blah," and I'd be like, "Nah, screw that, [I have] my family. I have to go to them." Priorities are different in different cultures, and you need to understand that. That's part of cultural awareness, and you need to be able to accommodate that instead of always expecting others to accommodate to your ideologies.

Students like Maria, who were able to situate their experiences of difference within an understanding of cultural bias, were more confident in their own values and in their minority status and demonstrated higher levels of well-being overall. As research shows, this perspective is an important coping resource.[22] Students with critical understandings suffer less from feelings of inadequacy and self-doubt than those who, like Jerome, search for what is wrong with themselves when they feel othered.

While some students arrive at college experienced in adaptively coping with cultural marginalization, many others do not. Thus, it is important that students have access to campus counterspaces that enable them to collectively process experiences of marginalization.

Counterspaces Facilitate Critical Understanding

Minority students made friends in a variety of counterspaces, from social spaces to clubs, organizations, and offices oriented toward minority students.[23] Lourdes's feelings of isolation and homesickness that resulted from her struggles fitting in and making friends with the predominantly White student body diminished substantially once she began attending events sponsored by a Mexican coeducational fraternity. "I was like, oh, OK, this is where they're hiding. . . . And then I talked to [my new friends] there a little bit, and we just started talking like forever, and from there, we became really close." These connections improved Lourdes's outlook. "I actually really like [college] now," she said.

Contrary to what many assume, in racially-ethnically oriented counterspaces, race-ethnicity often recedes into the background, enabling minority students to relax and lower their cultural defenses.[24] In addition to social support, many minority-focused clubs offer academic support. Students who felt embarrassed or self-conscious asking for help in the classroom were emboldened by academic support provided in minority-focused counterspaces. Rosa described the difference she experienced when she started going to tutoring sessions offered at the Latino Center.

> [When you go to the tutoring center to] get help for math, it's so stressful, you go there and you need help, and some of them just look at you like, You don't know this? You're so dumb. I stopped going to that one actually, and I started going to [tutoring at the Latino Center]. 'Cause like I felt more with my race, you go, you gravitate towards them. They're more helpful, and they were kinder. They didn't look at you and stuff. I guess I like them 'cause they're like me. I understand them more.

Apart from the formal academic support that these organizations offer, students benefited from the informal networks of solidarity and mutual recognition provided by students facing similar challenges. In this case "like me" meant people who would not link one's race-ethnicity with intellectual stereotypes.

One of the primary functions of counterspaces is creating a critical mass of students of a particular marginalized social identity to help them form social bonds.[25] This enables marginalized students to move beyond relying solely on individual coping resources. Students revealed how counterspaces provided opportunities to share institutional knowledge that was critical in dealing with administrative difficulties. Maria had problems with her contract for student housing and some questions on available financial resources. A mentor in a Latino organization pointed her in the right direction. "I told [a friend I met through Colectiva Chicano] what happened, and I [had] just met her. And she told me, she was like, 'Oh, you should talk to Andrea,' which is the person who got my big help. And, so everything was like on, just from friends. Hearing from friends." For first-generation students whose families lack insider information, campus information networks are especially important.

Although all students face challenges as they adapt to college life, the transition can be particularly stressful for minority students transitioning to historically White institutions. These challenges are not only due to their lack of experience and comfort with being in a mostly White space; White students and staff are often equally, if not more, inexperienced and uncomfortable building bridges across racial-ethnic boundaries. Both microaggressions and overt discriminatory acts leave minority students feeling unwelcomed. As these experiences accumulate, minority students often begin to feel self-conscious, self-critical, and alienated from the college life they imagined.

Minority students long for their colleges to move beyond structural diversity and become brave enough to ensure that they have both counterspaces and spaces that actively foster interactional diversity. This is not an either/or proposition; as shown throughout this book, minority students arrive on campus expecting and wanting to build relationships with peers who are "not like me." All college students need institutionalized help to understand the dynamics of prejudice and how those dynamics play out in their daily interactions. They also need institutionalized help making connections that increase intergroup communication and reduce anxiety.[26] Institutional support is also critical in promoting frequent and sustained intergroup interactions. These sustained interactions can reduce prejudices, increase tolerance for diverse perspectives, and ultimately increase acceptance of racial-ethnic others.[27]

7

FINDING ONE'S PEOPLE AND ONE'S SELF ON CAMPUS

The Role of Extracurricular Organizations

With Gabriel Velez

Within the first few weeks of life as a college student, young adults must adjust to new living arrangements or commuting schedules, decide on a handful of classes to take from a course book that can span hundreds of pages, and meet hundreds of new peers, advisers, and professors. They must also adjust to much less contact with family and friends. This vacuum leaves college students searching for new sources of social support—the people who will anchor who students think they are and whom they want to become. Thankfully, a flurry of orientation activities offers opportunities for first-year students to become acquainted with the vast array of extracurricular activities that will help them "follow your passions, form friendships, learn new skills, network professionally and—of course—enjoy yourself."[1]

Activity fairs offer a dizzying array of clubs, organizations, sports, activities, and volunteer opportunities. The buffet of options alone may be overwhelming, and many college students see this as a high-stakes choice. Extracurricular activities are now a fundamental part of the college experience, with even more significance than classes for some students.[2] As one parent of a high school senior put it when asked about her daughter's likely major in college, "I have accepted that she is going to college for the social network, and will figure out the major and career stuff along the way."

This emphasis on networking and extracurricular activities begins long before students set foot on campus. During junior year of high school, students sit through presentations on finding their college fit and are repeatedly told that college is not just for higher learning. They are told that they are choosing the place that will be their whole world for at least four years, so they should figure out if it "feels" right, if it attracts the type of peers they can imagine as lifelong friends, if it has the social and extracurricular activities that will keep them entertained, and if they can build connections that will get them jobs when college is over. Continuing-generation students hear stories about joining that perfect club or Greek organization that connected them to the people who became their closest friends and who opened doors to that perfect job. From academic literature to popular psychology in teen magazines and movies, young adulthood is presented as the age of finding oneself.[3]

Racial-ethnic minority youth enter college with these same developmental needs, hold similar expectations of college life, and confront the same overwhelming menu of options. Within this context, extracurricular activities allow students to find their people and place on campus. This is evident in how Aliyah, a Black female student, talks about her involvement in a women's leadership organization, Women Engaging, Exploring, and Elevating (W3E).

> I think one of the highlights of my year was going on the new student retreat 'cause that was the first time that I felt like I was plugged in to something, or I had people I could call my own people. Living in that leadership community [of W3E] was fun because everyone's door was always open. So that was a nice way to transition into college, having that initial openness with everyone. . . . That's probably the reason why I'm going back to help the new W3E ladies move in. It was just something that I wouldn't trade for anything.

Regardless of race-ethnicity, all students are looking for a sense of belonging—integration, membership, participation, inclusion—on campus.[4]

The plethora of extracurricular activities today did not appear by chance. Their emergence as spaces for self-exploration is closely connected to what is expected of emerging adults. Arthur Chickering and Linda Reisser, two of the pioneers of research on college student development, suggest that during this time, young people are developing along at least seven vectors: developing competence, managing emotions, moving through autonomy toward interdependence, developing mature interpersonal relationships, establishing identity, developing purpose, and developing integrity.[5] College administrators have expended considerable effort structuring the extracurricular activities to support positive development on these vectors and ensure that students graduate with diverse skills and leadership abilities.[6]

Administrators also understand that during the transition to college, youth learn to inhabit a range of identities that are tied to the multiple spheres they traverse across campus. The notion that there is one core identity that does not change may still influence popular psychology, but it is based on outdated theories and understandings.[7] Each extracurricular group and organization offers youth opportunities to define various parts of who they are and meet different psychological needs. This includes finding a sense of belonging in a community, feeling capable and valued, demonstrating leadership, and developing a positive physical self-image, to name just a few.[8]

Racial-ethnic minority youth are no different in their expectations that participation in extracurricular organizations will define their collegiate experiences. At the same time, their decisions are inevitably connected to the experience of being a minority at a historically White college or university.[9] We again emphasize that there is no one minority experience; class, gender, sexuality, personality, talents, and interests are a few of the factors that differentiate minority students' choices and experiences. Nevertheless, the interviews with students in our study revealed interconnected themes in the ways that Black and Latinx youth navigate extracurricular spaces as they transition to college and how those spaces shape their understandings and presentations of themselves.

In this chapter, we take a critical look at extracurricular activities in relation to experiences of race-ethnicity at college and examine the role they serve in minority students' self-exploration. No one questions the existence of organizations like W3E, and most would applaud the benefits that Aliyah experienced from the group, yet many question why race- or ethnic-specific organizations such as the Latino Ethnic Awareness Association and the Afro-American Cultural Alliance exist, and believe that minority students do themselves a disservice when they anchor their college belonging in such organizations. This is, in part, based on the misconception that organizations that appear to be agnostic to race-ethnicity develop the whole person, while racial-ethnic-focused organizations develop only students' understandings of their racial-ethnic identity, possibly to the detriment of other aspects of themselves.[10] In opposition to this belief, we detail the role of minority-focused extracurricular spaces in how minority students cope with campus microaggressions and actively counteract stereotypes. We also detail how organizations that do not have a racial-ethnic focus can be leveraged as counterspaces by Black and Latinx youth.

Marked and Unmarked Spaces

Critics of racially-ethnically-focused activities and organizations argue that these groups are detrimental to the creation and maintenance of a common student identity and exacerbate racial-ethnic tensions by isolating students into "mutually suspicious and hostile ethnic enclaves."[11] This perspective assumes that this mythical common student identity is free of cultural bias and can be equally accessed by all. However, at historically White colleges and universities, minority students consistently report feeling excluded from this common student identity.[12] Similarly, on diverse campuses, White students struggle to identify with the mythical common student identity.[13] Silvia Santos and colleagues found that on diverse campuses White students perceive "that their ethnicity, personal needs, values, and interests as White individuals were not being adequately addressed or were simply ignored by the university. Furthermore, these students felt out of synchrony with their ethnic minority peers and with the campus culture."[14]

Returning our focus to historically White colleges and universities, what if minority-focused student organizations—most of which are only two to three decades old—formed in response to White racial-ethnic organizations and hostile campus climates? This brings us to the concept of marked and unmarked spaces.[15] Critics see minority organizations, such as the Asian Pacific Islander Club, as segregated spaces because they are racially-ethnically marked, and miss the fact that the overwhelming majority of Greek organizations are also segregated spaces because these activities are *formally* presented as racially-ethnically unmarked. However, minority students not only see Greek organizations as racially-ethnically marked spaces, but also experience them as spaces from which they are actively excluded, as shown in chapter 4. Numerous news media have detailed this active exclusion revealed through racist fraternity chants, social media posts, and other internal organizational documents.[16] Beyond exclusion from this one type of organization, Black and Latinx students often experience isolation more generally across the broader campus because of explicit and implicit messages about race-ethnicity in their daily lives as students.[17]

Jim Sidanius and colleagues underscored the similarities between explicitly minority-focused organizations and Greek organizations. They found that identifying strongly with one's racial-ethnic group is an important factor in minority students' decisions to join minority organizations, and in White students' decisions to join Greek organizations.[18] For White students, in-group bias, as measured by factors such as opposition to affirmative action, was an additional factor in joining Greek organizations. Sidanius and colleagues conclude that "while there has been a tendency to associate ethnically oriented student organizations with ethnic minorities, our results suggest that some of the most powerful ethnic environments among White students come in the form of sororities and fraternities."[19]

Defenders of minority student organizations argue that because a defining feature of being a minority in any given context is having to find opportunities to interact with others of the same social identity, minority-focused activities play a critical role in creating sites of concentrated interaction with members of one's group.[20] Consequently, minority youth choose minority-focused groups because they provide counterspaces in which these students can develop and express their racial-ethnic identity. This is especially important because counterspaces facilitate these coping responses within a broader campus context where minority students may be marginalized or poorly understood.[21]

Defenders also argue that minority-focused organizations contribute to campus integration by providing counterspaces where minority students can establish a sense of local belonging, from which they can branch out and connect to the broader campus. The empirical evidence is mixed. Some studies find that participating in minority-focused organizations enables minority students to experience greater comfort with their racial-ethnic identity. This comfort can then lead to more exploration of the broader campus social environment. Other studies find that this participation increases minority students' perception that groups are in competition and increases their feelings of victimization by virtue of race-ethnicity.[22]

These mixed findings may be because, as Kathleen Ethier and Kay Deaux conclude, there is considerable variation in students' actions once a social identity is made salient.[23] During the transition to historically White colleges and universities, minority students with robust precollege cultural identities were more likely to become involved with their racial-ethnic group at college and increase their level of racial-ethnic group identification. In contrast, minority students who did not express a strong precollege association with their race-ethnicity were more likely to perceive threats to their racial-ethnic identity in college, decrease their racial-ethnic group identification, and experience a drop in self-esteem associated with their racial-ethnic identity. This illustrates "the protective nature of group identity in situations in which the group is a numerical minority and is possibly faced with discrimination from the majority group."[24]

In this chapter, the experiences of four students show the variation in Black and Latinx students' need for and benefit from minority-focused extracurricular organizations. Jason, a Black man, and Maria, a Latinx woman, show that racial-ethnic-focused extracurricular activities can be spaces to actively push back on the marginalization they encounter on campus. These spaces also offer opportunities beyond race-ethnicity by allowing these young people to explore the many possible selves they can become. Aliyah, introduced above, shows that a racially-ethnically agnostic student organization can become a counterspace for examining racial-ethnic issues because it is a micro-community of peers who care. Lastly, Lucas, a Latinx man, expressly rejects the need for a racial-ethnic focus and instead builds his identity through activity- and mission-focused extracurricular organizations.

These four students cover a range of precollege backgrounds, college contexts, and first-year experiences. Jason was a captain of his high school football team, though sports did not earn him a scholarship to college. He wanted to go out of state, but tuition was too high, so he stayed in state and enrolled at Suburban StateU. The second of six siblings, he has an older brother who completed two years of college before leaving. Jason knew his experience would be different; he would obtain a degree in business and succeed in his goal of becoming a human resources manager, as well as be the first in his immediate family to obtain a college degree. He was inspired by his grandfather, an army veteran who often talked about not having had the kinds of educational opportunities available to Jason and his siblings. Jason attributed the success of his first year of college to the varied academic, social, and personal supports he found on campus.

Maria was a first-generation college student whose parents instilled the value of schooling from a young age. Her parents worked in manual labor jobs and wanted a different future for her. She also asserted that she "wanted a different lifestyle, like what you see on TV or whatever," and believed that college and a degree in business were the way to achieve this. Her elementary and high schools were almost entirely Latinx, and she was in an ESL (English as a second language) classroom until fourth grade. The cultural gap between high school and Urban PrivateU-North was a bit of a shock, but she successfully managed the transition, partly because of the Latinx organization that, a few years earlier, had first introduced her to the idea of going to college, as well as similar organizations she found on campus.

Aliyah also went to college for business. Her Ghanaian parents conveyed to her from a young age the importance of college. On top of this, she felt pressure from the success of her two older sisters, who both went to a prestigious private university. Aliyah chose Rural StateU because of its business program, which she believed would help her get a good job and set her on the path to one day becoming a business owner. She described the transition to college as a bit difficult, especially because of issues with her roommate. The rough patches, however, were balanced by a great community she found in her extracurricular activities, which included W3E, a faith group, and a society of women in business.

While Lucas was also a first-generation college student, he had one older brother currently in college and one who had already obtained his degree. His siblings' descriptions of collegiate life and advice shaped his expectations of college as a place to experience new things and become involved in as much as possible. His brothers filled the gaps in the support that his Mexican parents, who had only a grade school education, could not provide. A self-labeled competitive person, he wanted to do even more and have even more success than his brothers had. He jumped right into being involved in a number of extracurricular activities at Suburban StateU with the goal of meeting a diverse range of people.

In managing the transition to college and the accompanying questions about themselves, all four students described how their extracurricular involvement provided them with peer support and exposure to new challenges and possibilities. Jason and Maria joined minority-focused organizations to cope with racial-ethnic tensions and stereotypes on campus. Jason joined in reaction to feeling marginalized, and Maria joined immediately upon arrival on campus to preempt potential feelings of racial-ethnic isolation. Aliyah joined non-minority organizations and unexpectedly found herself leveraging the peer relationships she built in those organizations to assert her own racial-ethnic identity as distinct from stereotypes or expectations that others placed upon her. Lucas rejected being involved in minority-focused activities and became involved in activities that allowed him to establish a group of friends, associates, and contacts outside the Latinx campus community. These varied coping strategies demonstrate that individual young people find their own personal ways to respond to and counteract the expectations and stereotypes attached to their race-ethnicity.

Minority-Focused Counterspaces Are Maturational Spaces

Minority-focused extracurricular organizations may be understood as developmental counterspaces that provide structured activities and opportunities for minority students to cope with racial-ethnic tension and pressures on campus. When Jason arrived on campus, he found academic support from tutoring initiatives and monetary help from the financial aid office, but also an environment permeated by racial-ethnic stereotypes and tensions. When asked how he would describe the racial-ethnic interactions on campus, he mentioned a particular verbal assault.

> They rode past. They was like speeding. And a White guy hung out the window. He was like, what's up, bitch. And we were like, what? And they just kept going. So I don't know if he had some alcohol in his system or what. But I mean, it's like a little racial tension. I have a bunch of White friends, and I'm not, you know, racist or anything. But it's one little incident, and like, wow, you know, things are still, you know, kind of like happening.

The event prompted Jason to think more broadly about racial-ethnic tensions on campus and what it meant to be Black on his campus.

Research has demonstrated the powerful impact of small, frequent, and often overlooked experiences of discrimination in the classroom, in living spaces, and in social spaces across college campuses.[25] These racial-ethnic microaggressions include feelings of being invisible in classrooms, facing lowered or negative expectations or double standards, and other implicitly conveyed stereotypes. Many minority students respond to these subtle experiences of discrimination and racism by withdrawing, attempting to minimize their racial-ethnic identity, or disengaging from campus. Others, like Jason, develop active coping responses to combat stereotypes and structural inequities. For example, some Black and Latinx students responded by vocalizing their experiences, confronting aggressors, and bonding with other students with similar racial-ethnic identities.[26]

Jason demonstrated exactly these coping responses in the "image busting" activities that his minority-focused student organization, Collegiate Black Men, offered.

> Image busting is we dress up, we have on nice suits. We go shopping together, like, for dress code. We have on a nice suit and tie, certain ties. We do that every Monday for whole day. We also have meetings, every Monday from five to six-thirty. We image busting. What we do to image bust is normally when some other people see a Black man in a suit, they think of them as going to a funeral or going to an interview or something. That's the thing, so we image bust. We don't cut that stereotypical thing. We dress up just to look nice, it's like that.

Collegiate Black Men exists to mitigate any barrier that stands between Black male students and graduation. By including tutoring, mentorship, and social support, the organization helps Jason and others thrive. This organization provides a space to more thoroughly counteract the challenges Black men face.

Collegiate Black Men became Jason's campus home because it was all-inclusive and pushed his overall growth and development.

> The CBM really helped me get off right. Getting my college career off right. Other organizations, AASU [African American Students United], it's all right, but AASU that's more leaning towards throwing more parties. It's a good organization, but they wanna like throw more parties and get people more involved on campus by just getting them out of their dorm rooms. . . . I could do it, but I want something that has events but at the same time will help me school-wise, too. . . . So I just ended up kind of leaning towards CBM. It gave me an opportunity to do some events as well as get scholarships and a bunch of more stuff. Make me better. . . . They really told me, just give everything a try.

Like Jason, students often described their involvement with minority-focused organizations as not solely about developing their racial-ethnic identity, but also their overall growth and development. Actively developing one's whole self and the diverse aspects of one's identities is critical for minority students who often have to code-switch—develop and deploy different aspects of themselves to cope with the distinctive situational demands of their social status. Counterspaces can help students develop a core sense of self, which can alleviate the pressures of code-switching. Minority students may draw on these counterspaces and the experiences they offer to assert control over how much they adapt their self-presentation to meet the often stereotypical assumptions of others.

Minority-Focused Counterspaces Are Bridging Spaces

Minority-focused extracurricular organizations also helped bridge the cultural divide associated with transitioning from a minority segregated high school to a historically White college or university. For some youth, the pathway to college is distinctly shaped by the intervention of organizations focused on increasing the numbers of minority students in college. Consequently, their college experiences are framed from the beginning as finding academic success and belonging through the support of minority group members.

Maria fits this profile. She became interested in Urban PrivateU-North when participating in a college-bound, career-focused organization for Hispanic high school students. This early exposure to Urban PrivateU-North made her college choice easy and also put her on a path to college and through college by focusing on becoming a Latinx businesswoman.

> I guess I first stumbled upon [Urban PrivateU-North] because I was in the summer program, it was through the National Society of Hispanic MBAs. . . . The program was actually held at [Urban PrivateU-North]. So I had experience with the campus. . . . So I was like, oh, so this is a nice place. I applied there, and I got in. Being in that program, I met a lot of professionals. And they were all Latino. So I saw that people [like me] did it obviously, so like, OK, why not? They all had MBAs and that kind of stuff. And I was able to socialize with them. And I felt like that was cool. So, I'm like, OK, I fit in! I'm not like a black sheep or anything.

Once on campus, she immediately connected with the Latinx groups, knowing that in these spaces she could find the cultural understanding, belonging, and support that would help her succeed in college. As Beverly Tatum argues, it is developmentally supportive for minority youth to seek out racially-ethnically defined spaces to establish and affirm this aspect of their identities.[27] This sense of belonging may be particularly important for minority students because a strong sense of belonging within micro-communities can extend to feeling greater loyalty to their institution, which in turn may lead to greater persistence.[28]

When Racially-Ethnically Agnostic Spaces Become Counterspaces

Not all minority students join minority-focused organizations, and some explicitly decided on spending their extracurricular time with organizations that were racially-ethnically agnostic, choosing instead to focus on career pathways, spiritual and religious interests, athletic pursuits, and so on. These racially-ethnically agnostic organizations and activities, however, became counterspaces when the close peer relationships that develop create meaningful opportunities for minority students to actively combat racial-ethnic expectations, stereotypes, and microaggressions.

Unlike Jason and Maria, Aliyah became involved in extracurricular activities not directly tied to race-ethnicity, but, like Jason, she found a space that still allowed her to push back, vocalize her thoughts, and actively define what her race-ethnicity meant to her. Aliyah built tight relationships and a sense of belonging through her faith-based and women's leadership organizations, which then gave her the courage to embrace the role of being the "spokesperson for Black people."[29] While no one specific moment raised her awareness of the continuing significance of race-ethnicity on campus, she became increasingly aware of a divide.

> At first, I thought that everyone was like kumbaya, doesn't matter, and then it was about December or January when I realized that there actually is a lot of tension on [Rural StateU], because even—there's the Black people and there's the Indian people who hang out together, and then all the Asian people—it's very segregated almost. And then even within, especially the Black community . . . there's like Africans and then there's the African Americans. I didn't understand why that was important, but my roommate would only hang out with Africans. So that was a shock to my system. And then also, just there was a weeklong [protest] where Black people would stand on the quad with their mouths taped because they felt like they couldn't say anything because of their race. And then outside of that, there were a lot of, I don't know if you saw in the news, racial tension.

Aliyah was challenged by this new experience. She had attended a high school that was 70 percent White, 15 percent Latinx, and 6 percent Black, where she learned to build close relationships with students from different racial-ethnic groups. At college, in contrast, "even though no one knows each other, they're just forming these [racial-ethnic] cliques already. So it was kind of hard for me who's used to being friends with people from a bunch of different backgrounds."

Students like Aliyah who had a diverse peer group in high school are more likely to have a diverse college peer group and experience less dissonance in relation to the "chilly" racial-ethnic climate on historically White campuses.[30] It is not that minority students coming from diverse high schools do not experience racial-ethnic alienation on campus, but the intensity of their high school peer interactions offered opportunities to develop skills that make it more likely for them to engage diverse peers in college.

Amid a "nerve-racking" transition to college, Aliyah described taking solace in her faith-based group and the women's business club. She was drawn to these spaces because they were sympathetic with the social identities that she brought with her to college and with the aspirational identity of herself as a future businesswoman. In talking about these organizations, she often switched back and forth between them in her descriptions, which suggests that she was also integrating these two aspects of who she was on campus.

Because she was only one of few Black students in these organizations, she often felt backed into the position of representing and speaking out on racial-ethnic issues, for example after a police shooting of a young Black man made the national news.

> It came to one point where I was talking to this one [White] girl at Interfaith Leadership Council, and we just had like a three-hour lunch. She just asked me how I was doing with the whole [police shooting] thing, and then at first, I was like guarded because I wondered, Are you only asking me this because I'm Black, or is this something that you actually care talking about? But then as the conversation progressed I realized that it's something that if you . . . don't say something, it looks like you're condoning it, whereas I'm not condoning it, but it just like, it aggravates me to think about it.

The pressure to represent her race-ethnicity weighed on Aliyah. However, because she had built close relationships with these peers, she felt empowered to respond. Thus, Interfaith Leadership Council served as a counterspace because it provided a supportive micro-community to whom she could vocalize her perspective and what her race-ethnicity means to her. "I for some reason am like a spokesperson for Black people," she said, "and that became very stressful very quickly because

I'm lucky enough to not have to know anyone that's been personally victimized like that, and you can't put the weight of that on me. That was kinda stressful, but I also thought it was great because it was a way for me to talk about it while people listened. So I don't know, it kinda went back and forth." Because Aliyah experienced Interfaith Leadership Council as an ideational counterspace—a micro-community of peers who cared about her as an individual Black student—it became a counterspace that allowed her to have a voice about broader societal marginalization of Black people. As Andrew Case and Carla Hunter note in their detailing of how counterspaces can promote adaptive responding, "the enhancement of one's sense of self in the face of oppression can and often is facilitated through the presence of strategic others."[31]

Lucas's two older college-educated brothers prepared him with a mind-set oriented toward thinking ahead to connections, job referrals, and personal development that could be gained from extracurricular activities. Prepared by the stories his older brothers told, Lucas arrived with a plan for engaging in campus-wide extracurricular activities: "They said look for more opportunities that were offered and not to just slack around and just goof off. . . . You've got to start looking for bigger opportunities. And luckily for me, I actually got an opportunity [to take on a leadership role] my freshman year. . . . So that was something that was very influential. I was constantly looking for more and more opportunities."

Amid the tumult of unexpected challenges tied to independence and responsibility, Lucas found a sense of stability and ways to define and develop who he was becoming through his involvement with extracurricular organizations.

> Once I got more involved [with a fraternity], it helped me grow in confidence. That's when a more leadership role actually started appearing in my mind. . . . I want to become a better leader, but the only way for me to become a better leader is to be a better leader. So that's something that I just kept on looking forward to, and I thought the best thing I can do is just try my hardest at everything that I do. So that's what I've been doing is I've been trying at Frisbee, I've been trying at my Greek organization, and so it's made a big success for me, and it's helped me grow in the sense that I'm meeting new people every single day because I sort of have to. . . . It's sort of that I need it. My organizations need me to do this, and they expect me to do it, so I have to do it. So getting a push in the right direction, being forced to do something, even though you don't want to, it's actually beneficial for you.

His experiences led him to believe that engaging widely created the sense of connection that is at the core of the collegiate experience.

> There's so many kids out there that say that the school is boring and there's nothing to do, even though there's plenty of things to do out there; but they're just not willing to explore. And that's something that I feel like many students fail to do, [and] which makes them believe that the college experience isn't for them. And that's an unfortunate thing because there's so much things that every different school has to offer, and [Suburban StateU] is unique in the sense that it's a great, great community—really tight-knit. Also, tight-knit within Greek organizations.

Students like Lucas may choose extracurricular activities because they provide a space to meet "others not like me." Similarly, research shows that for Black youth, participating in predominantly White student organizations provides them with the opportunity to build cross-cultural communication skills, learn from others, and create feelings of connection with other populations.[32] For Lucas, this strategy worked, and he did not just join but created his campus micro-community.

> I became a founding father for my Greek organization . . . to give me a leadership role. And that's something that was very important to me. I wanted it to be something that I could control. Something that I could mold into my own and something that I could call mine, for example. So, I mean, it was basically like an entrepreneur to building a business. It's just [that] I want to build something, and I want to mold it, and I want to see it grow.

Lucas explicitly noted participating in activities not related to race-ethnicity, but the underlying purpose can still be understood as seeking a micro-community to actively push against feelings of marginalization and isolation on campus. For Lucas and students like him seeking "others not like me," extracurricular activities offer opportunities to reject others' determination of boundaries or definition by race-ethnicity.

Scaffolding the Transition

The college transition brings with it an array of new opportunities and new possibilities for defining who one is in new social contexts. These prospects of defining and redefining oneself come at a critical stage of identity development, a time in the life course when questions of "who am I?" and "what is my role in my various communities?" are in flux. Minority students at historically White colleges and universities are additionally confronted with how to define their selves in relation to stereotypes, while also learning how to balance institutional versus personal identity and group belonging, and ideally integrating the two. Minority students must navigate these identity challenges all the while attending to academic success.

As the four students detailed in this chapter illustrate, minority students have varied preferences and needs for minority-focused extracurricular organizations and adopt different strategies to deal with racial-ethnic marginalization. Yet the end goal is the same. Whether these students are interacting with others "like me" or "not like me," extracurricular activities may serve as counterspaces in which they can define, develop, and assert their racial-ethnic identity. For some youth, having a cultural home on campus is critical for their sense of belonging, while also offering academic, leadership, and career supports that foster the development of many aspects of themselves.[33] For others, participating in activities with students of different racial-ethnic backgrounds may provide opportunities to demonstrate that they do not conform to expectations and stereotypes, while also building cross-cultural, leadership, and career skills, and developing a sense of belonging within a micro-community.[34]

The interviews revealed that, at times, being in counterspaces where one's social identity blends into the crowd enables individuals to focus on other aspects of themselves, while simultaneously contesting and counteracting stereotypes and expectations. It will be particularly important for college administrators to pay attention to a problematic narrative that emerged from the interviews: the perceived need to choose between being a member of social identity-based groups and being a member of the institution.

Lucas appreciated all the different resource centers—the Latino, African American, and Asian American Resources Centers. "There's different resource centers for everyone," he said. He found that the Latino Resource Center helped him grow in his racial-ethnic identity and cultural knowledge, but lamented that because there was no programming that brought the centers together, students had to choose. "You're getting a better sense of [your] community and what your culture is. But then you begin to realize that you're sort of missing out on other opportunities and other cultures that are out there."

However, once we recognize that this need to choose is socially constructed, it can be deconstructed. Lucas had an inkling of this.

> But no one is going to tell you [that] you cannot do something. So I could easily just go to an Asian American parade or an event, and they won't judge me for it. They'll actually be happy that I actually went to an event and [can spread the word]. So then that brings more people in, because that's what all these organizations want. But unfortunately, with the titles that they already give themselves, it sort of just tells people not to come in. That's the unfortunate thing.

Counterspaces are not defined primarily by the social status characteristics of the participants, but by the common ideals and goals that form the basis for coming together. The goal of the Asian American Resource Center can be shared by students who are not Asian American. However, in the current polarized environment in America, organizations must clearly state the welcome. A recent flyer for a Latin American Dance Association at another university explicitly noted that one does not have to be Latin American to participate.

The task for university administrators is to foster a campus culture that does not marginalize minority-focused organizations as being solely for the development of one's racial-ethnic identity. This means that while the counterspaces provided by minority-focused organizations and cultural or racial-ethnic centers are important in and of themselves, they also need to provide students with experiences, opportunities, and supports beyond those directly related to counteracting stereotypes and feelings of isolation. Positive development of all students would also be facilitated by a campus culture that promotes involvement in both minority-focused and minority agnostic interest-based organizations, while promoting opportunities for multiple organizations to work on collaborative university-wide events. Essentially, universities might serve student identity development best by promoting a diversity of spaces and allowing belonging, integration, and development to occur in micro-communities, rather than pushing for universal affiliation with the mythical common student identity that is supposedly free of cultural bias.

8

SPLIT BETWEEN SCHOOL, HOME, WORK, AND MORE

Commuting as a Status and a Way of Being

With Hilary Tackie and Elan Hope

The challenge of commuting is often much more than the physical distance between home and school. Many commuting students are moving between divergent social worlds. Their focus and energy are split between environments that abide by different norms and priorities, forcing them to shift their self-presentation throughout each day. This lack of coherence can make college more challenging than it is for students who reside on campus. Each day, commuting students leave their college environment, which can restrict their access to academic resources and support. In addition, students often decide to commute for financial reasons, necessitating paid employment to manage the financial burdens created by their college enrollment. Consequently, as several studies show, commuting students are at greater risk of dropping out or disconnecting from college.[1]

Nestor, a Mexican American commuting student who attended Urban PrivateU-South, described a divide between commuting and residential students. The students who lived in dorms knew one another, and the commuters knew the commuters. On his campus, there was not much intermingling. Asked whether commuting made him feel like an outsider, he said, "kinda, because you'll see [people] hanging out, but it's because they all dorm together. They all know each other from their dorm. But it's like, oh, I'm a nobody. It's not like I'm invisible, but there is that separation between commuters and people that dorm."

This separation presents, at least for Nestor, an "us-versus-them" dichotomy in experiences, identification, and identity. Given that racial-ethnic minority students have the highest likelihood of commuting to campus, we would be remiss not to examine the experiences of students at the intersection of these two identifications.[2] Commuting matters. Several of the students labeled themselves and qualified their experiences by stating, "I am a commuter." Because this status affected their connections to campus and their approach to college life, understanding the first-year transition experiences of students who classify themselves as commuters is integral to illuminating the ways such young people make sense of who they are as college students.

As highlighted throughout this book, there is no single best way to be a successful student. Similarly, there are many different ways to be a successful commuting student. Among our larger sample of 533 students surveyed, slightly more than 60 percent of those who stated that they lived with their parents were Latinx. In addition, among the seventy students interviewed, those who highlighted their commuting experiences were almost exclusively Latinx. The experiences of Latinx students attempting to bridge the gulf between home and school that are detailed in chapters 9 and 10 illustrate the difficulties of bridging the many cultural disjunctures associated with living in an environment where family members do not understand the time and energy required for being a successful college student, particularly the cocurricular commitments, and especially when those commitments conflict with family obligations.

This chapter explores the first-year experiences of three Latinx students—Sammy, Kara, and Lucia. Besides being commuters, all three are first-generation students in immigrant families, and these identities add additional complexities in how they experience the transition to college. We show commuting as both an identification and identity through the experiences of students who range in their ability to successfully transition as commuting students—from experiencing their residential status as simply a factor of their reality to experiencing it as the central obstacle to fully becoming a college student.

Commuting Students Possess Many Overlapping Minority Statuses

The most recent examination, which was of a 2003 cohort of students enrolled in four-year colleges, found that 21 percent lived off campus, 67 percent lived on campus, and 12 percent lived at home—the group that we call commuting students in this chapter.[3] Commuting students are more than simply students who cannot walk from their dorm or apartment to their classes. Often, these students are also likely to work more than twenty-five hours per week, are first-generation students, and are financially independent.

Sammy, who attended Urban StateU, was an excellent student in high school. Although he claims to have slept through several classes, he managed to maintain a 3.8 GPA and scored a 29 on the ACT. His high school served mostly other Latinx youth like him. Sammy's parents immigrated to Chicago before his birth. His sister was the only other person in his immediate family to go to college. Despite working and living at home, Sammy was highly connected to his campus; he joined profession clubs and the rugby team, made many friends, and started dating a girl from his chemistry class. He believed that having to balance many competing responsibilities during his first year of college taught him "how to start living like a real adult instead of like a kid still stuck in high school." After college, Sammy hoped to become both a neurologist and a teacher.

In contrast to the average college student, while growing up Sammy had to manage family and community insecurities stemming from undocumented immigration status, family and neighborhood poverty, and neighborhood violence. This meant that his college search was not only about his academic ability, but also his ability to pay for college.

> Especially me being from the South Side, you know, we have a lot of Hispanics who are middle class, low class. Many are barely making it by, maybe they're making it by but they're struggling a bit, and they have to watch where they're stepping. And especially immigration, like deportations, ICE. There's so much more fear within us about college. Especially with our parents, they were like "Oh, he doesn't have his papers, we don't have the money for this, can he even go, should he even try?"

From the start of his application process, Sammy was fairly certain he would commute. He knew that it was highly unlikely that his family would be able to pay for dorm living, but cultural factors and his parents' wishes also figured prominently in that decision. "I told my parents I want to experience how it is to live outside my house," he said, "and they started putting me on a guilt trip like, 'Oh you don't like living with us? You don't like it here?' I'm just like 'No, I want to experience it.' You know, houses on campus, I could do what I wanted, I could basically just do what I want, but I wasn't completely independent, as they [say]."

Research shows that Latinx students have one of the highest likelihoods of commuting to campus and experience substantial internal conflict, as well as conflict with family regarding the decision to live on campus.[4] Despite the challenges associated with commuting, living at home enables first-generation, racial-ethnic minority and immigrant students to maintain family cultural connections, and it lessens the psychological and emotional distress of feeling that succeeding in college comes at the cost of weakening one's family ties.[5]

Kara attended Urban PrivateU-South as a business major. Because she could not afford to live in a dorm, she had a ninety-minute train and bus ride to campus. Like Sammy, Kara had parents who expected her to live at home and viewed providing housing as part of their support for college. "My family," she said, "was just like, 'Oh, we're not charging you for rent or anything.' Cause that's like in our culture."

In addition to being a full-time college student, she worked full-time at a retail outlet less than ten minutes from home. Working full-time was the only way she could afford college. Because of these many demands on her time, she went to campus solely for the academics. She did not join any clubs or organizations. Because of this disconnection from campus, she entered her sophomore year feeling like she had yet to make a true transition to college.

Kara, for the most part, worked through the application and enrollment processes alone, as her parents had neither the experience to help her apply nor the finances to help her pay. She debated between a university that gave her a full-ride scholarship and Urban PrivateU-South, where she would have to pay a high cost for the opportunity to attend. Her parents told her it was up to her—go for free or pay. "But it was my dream, since I was little, to come to [Urban PrivateU-South] downtown," she said. "And since it was like a really good business school," she opted for the downtown campus. She also got "a better feel" from Urban PrivateU-South, she said.

Kara was the first woman but not the first person in her extended family to attend college. However, because her enrollment challenged the gendered cultural expectations of her Latinx immigrant family, she was not privileged to the valuable information held among the college-educated men in her extended family. "They saw it as a man thing to go to college . . . but not like completely like, 'Oh don't go to school,' or like, 'Get married 'cause you're twenty already.'" (This gendered aspect of her college transition is detailed in chapter 9.) Advice from the college-educated men in her family might have been pivotal in helping her to understand the value of accepting that full ride from Urban StateU rather than the partial scholarship from a much more expensive private institution. To cover the out-of-pocket costs, Kara was forced to increase her shifts at work such that, by the start of the academic year, she was working full-time as well as attending school as a full-time student.

Lucia enrolled at Urban PrivateU-North with interests in medicine and the sciences. Lucia's parents were both from Mexico and worked hard to support their children's educational aspirations while struggling with poverty throughout Lucia's childhood. Her parents' hard work inspired Lucia to do well in school and instilled in her a hope that she would eventually go to college. She finished high school with a 4.0 GPA and scored a 27 on her ACT. Lucia's older siblings had attended a local community college, so she grew up believing that community college or work were the only options available to her. "I didn't think that I would be able to afford something like [four-year college]. And it's just the topic, my parents would always talk about school, school, school, and that's why they worked so hard, but they would never bring up any university or anything like that, so it just didn't cross my mind."

During high school, her counselor and her sister encouraged her to apply to college, which changed her aspirations. Despite this encouragement, Lucia, like Kara, received little informational or instrumental assistance from her family.

> If I had questions I would maybe ask my sister, but she didn't live with me because she's already married. But it was just mostly me, 'cause my parents don't speak—they're divorced—and they don't speak English, and they don't know anything about it. It wasn't difficult as much as it was a tedious process. I applied to a lot of colleges, so I just had to rewrite the same information, and sometimes I had to get a lot of my essays revised by teachers. I didn't think it was difficult at all. It was just time-consuming process.

What Lucia did get from her parents was encouragement and motivation to make them proud.

> We have always been struggling with money issues, mostly when I was younger. And I saw how hard they worked to give us [anything], . . . 'cause the only reason we came over here was that so me and my siblings would be able to get an education. . . . And I saw how hard they worked to allow us to get an education, and that was really my main priority. I really, really like school. I've always really, really liked learning. I love learning new things, and I really want to be able to use my education to be able to help other people and to be successful, so I really wanted to end up going to college.

Getting accepted into Urban PrivateU-North was a long shot, she knew. She also assumed that college, especially a four-year institution, was not a financially viable option. To avoid any unnecessary expenses, she started out living at home in the suburbs, enduring an arduous commute to campus involving trains and buses.

Work, Finances, and Campus Engagement

Working to afford college was a central theme in commuting students' narratives. Although nearly half of full-time students work more than twenty-five hours a week to afford school, this percentage is substantially higher for commuting students, who are also more likely to work off-campus and work longer hours, making it challenging to engage in campus life.[6] Although commuting may have reduced their financial stress, the distance and travel time often served as additional stressors.

When Kara started college, she commuted to campus four days a week. By the spring quarter of her first year she had figured out ways to reduce the commute to two days a week by packing her courses into fewer days and taking classes online. Kara never spent time on campus that she did not absolutely have to. This meant she was rarely able to take advantage of campus-based academic supports. Referencing impromptu study sessions hosted by professors or teaching assistants, Kara complained,

> I just don't feel comfortable when they're like, oh, they have specific times and they don't want to make [other] time. Well, there's only so much, I can't go in at the specific time you ask. Especially 'cause of that distance barrier. So, it's like, "Oh, we have a study session on Friday, you can come later." It's like, "Oh, well, I have to make that hour drive to come over here, that hour commute." So it's really not to my advantage to come.

Kara's professors had little sympathy for her need to work full-time and did not understand that enrollment was contingent on working full-time to pay for it. A professor told Kara that she should not be working more than twenty hours while in school. "I'm like, 'Well, there's really not much I can do if I can't pay for school,'" she said. Her situation also meant she had no time for extracurricular activities. "Soccer was the one thing I was really hoping to do, because I loved playing soccer," she said. The need to work also kept her from applying for scholarship opportunities that would have helped her pay for college. "I know there's a lot of scholarships available to Hispanics, and low-income and stuff. But it's like, that whole work, yeah, is preventing me from that."

Kara was stuck. Working enabled her to enroll in college while simultaneously impeding her ability to engage in college. Recognizing the importance of campus engagement, she considered taking an on-campus work-study position. But she quickly discarded that idea when she learned of the lower salary. "I really can't make less, because I've already figured out how much it takes me to pay for [school]. If I do work a work-study job, I would have probably have to keep another part-time job."

It's important to note that lower campus engagement does not mean that commuting students are any less engaged during class or display less academic effort. Education researcher George Kuh and colleagues show that although residential students may display slightly higher scores on measures of engagement, commuting students, despite balancing multiple responsibilities, exert equal effort in the classroom.[7]

Lucia's parents paid as much of her college costs as they could. Her mother, she said, paid more than half the year's tuition, and her father gave her his unemployment checks; "that ended up being a lot of money, so I used it for that. It was always my plan that my parents were really gonna help me pay for it." Lucia also worked a full-time job the summer before college and then part-time once school started, but she still did not have enough to live on campus.

Lucia relied heavily on a loan and a number of scholarships to afford an eventual move to campus. Several of those scholarships demanded her time to attend sponsored events, tutor students, and participate in mentoring meetings. A women's leadership scholarship, for example, asked that she read the next cohort's essays. "It's about fourteen girls that get a $16,000 scholarship. . . . so I had to read through about four hundred applications with four differential essays, with recommendation letters and like a résumé. I had to read through about two hundred of them during the school year." Another scholarship required her to mentor a student from a lower-income neighborhood. "They're part of this afterschool program, and I went to go and tutor them. I had a specific student that I mentored. He was in middle school. And it was once a week . . . and then we also had separate meetings with all their tutors." In addition, she was part of a mentoring program for "students of color and first-generation college students. They had events every month that I went to."

Essentially, Lucia's scholarships came with a tax on her time that was especially difficult to manage when working part-time and commuting to campus. This left her feeling very restricted, because she could only become minimally involved in clubs of her choosing. Again, doing the work necessary to obtain the financial resources to enroll in college limited her ability to engage in campus life.

Despite minimizing student debt, or simply making college possible for those with no access to student loans, commuting can quickly become untenable. It took Lucia nearly two hours to commute to campus on public transportation. It was "terrible," she said. Before the end of her first term, it was clear that she was not going to be able to sustain it for the remainder of the year. "I was really close to transferring to a college closer to home. But then, I remember my sisters, they told me not to. They told me just to stick through."

Following the receipt of some additional scholarship money, Lucia was able to move to campus at the start of her second semester. With more time, she joined several clubs and began to have the college experience she desired. "The transition from commuting to dorming was a great, great one. That was one of the best decisions I could've made. I don't think I'll ever commute again."

As in Lucia's case, the challenges of commuting and learning to balance many competing responsibilities can also be a growth experience, as long as the stress does not exceed one's coping abilities.[8] "I learned a lot about myself during this whole year of college, I learned, 'cause my first semester was hard 'cause I was working a part-time job and I was commuting and I was taking seventeen credit hours. It was hard, but I learned, like, life is always gonna be hard no matter what."

Commuting, Working, Studying, and Playing

Despite a substantial financial aid package, Sammy struggled financially. He wanted to be able to buy what he wanted but was also committed to managing his financial aid wisely. To have more spending money and to be able to build up a savings account, he took a part-time job in a grocery store. "I'm gonna try to split [my paycheck] off into separate expenses. My first paycheck probably gonna be for books. Each paycheck after that is gonna be my living expense. . . . I don't want to go into debt, since I don't have to worry about my tuition; more for me it's just paying to live. That's basically why I work," he said.

Sammy was also planning ahead for the possibility of taking more than four years and needing to pay the full amount of tuition. "That's why I'm hoping to put a lot of money that I'm earning into savings accounts. . . . I have to be able to support myself. If I have to go the extra that I won't be struggling, and I won't be miserable, and I'll be able to finish. And I said that I want to go to med school—that means I'm going to have to save even more money now, put ten dollars away from every check and start saving up."

Although this is an admirable goal, putting ten dollars each week into a savings account will do little to reduce the student loan debt he will incur should he go to medical school. As So-Hyun Joo and colleagues note, students must establish a critical balance between not taking on an overwhelming amount of student debt and not working so many hours that they cannot meet their academic responsibilities.[9] Failing to find this balance puts students at risk of dropping out.

Despite a full schedule, Sammy was able to become engaged in organizations for students interested in medicine and joined the rugby team. He felt confident about managing his time.

> To be honest I didn't really have a lot of trouble with managing my time. As I grew up I sort of tended to become more detail orientated, or I liked to believe so. So, you know, I would always carry a watch around, and I would time things. I would time how long it would take me to get to my train station. How long it would take the train to get there. Intervals between each train. Intervals between late trains, 'cause that happens way too often, and then how long it takes me to get to one location and then wait for a bus, how long that usually takes, then go to [Urban StateU]. So in that sense, I was sort of able to start mapping out my schedule in my head.

He would arrive on campus at 9 a.m. and leave at 5 p.m. During a three-hour gap, he scheduled time for friends and fun. "Within those three hours, I separated—maybe two hours were for friends and maybe an hour for myself to do whatever else I wanted to."

Despite being involved and social, Sammy still felt somewhat set apart from residential students. Because he lived in a high-crime and high-violence neighborhood, he often had to cut short his social time on campus to avoid walking from the bus stop to his home late in the evening. On several occasions he relied on friends to let him stay in their dorm rooms. It was when facing these time constraints that Sammy, like Nestor earlier, felt like an outsider.

> The one thing I sort of don't really enjoy is how much—what's the word—how selective do I have to be about the things I want to do? I come from the South Side—not the safest part of Chicago, not the most dangerous, but not the nicest place to be around ten or eleven at night. So I had to be sort of selective about the things I want to do. People who dorm or have apartments around [Urban StateU] are sort of more capable of going out, doing more of the events that [Urban StateU] might provide. Maybe they start at 8 [p.m.] and don't end till like 10. I would promptly be there for an hour, and then I would leave, and that's before like anything really starts. So I feel sort of left out at times, because you know people are doing all these things, and I sort of had to be at home and to sort of learn how to deal with it.

Despite these challenges, Sammy spent a great deal of time on campus and optimized his time there. He prioritized connecting to campus life and taking part in a variety of on-campus opportunities. As we discuss next, institutional supports helped Sammy have a successful college transition as a commuting student. Urban StateU has received the highest national award of excellence "for transforming higher education through outstanding programs, innovative services, and effective administration" for off-campus, commuter, and other nontraditional students.

A Space of Their Own on Campus

Commuting students have bounded opportunities to establish connections and build a sense of belonging on campus. Their time on campus is bounded by work hours, public transportation schedules, and other nonacademic obligations that create roadblocks to socializing and campus-based activities.[10] Their lack of a place on campus puts them at a disadvantage in establishing the type of campus-based peer support networks that are important for smoothing the transition to college.[11] Kara, Sammy, and Lucia found that they could no longer rely on their high school friends to get them through this life transition, as many of those friends either went away to different schools or did not attend college.

Lucia noted the importance of her new college friends in supporting her through the transition.

> I learned a lot from my three really good [college] friends, and every time I hang out with them I learn something new, and it's like they have kind of like the same goals . . . and expectations that I have for my future, so that really helps 'cause my friends back home they're not, they don't enjoy doing a lot of the same things that I, that we enjoy doing. . . . They like doing different things, and then not a lot of things are educational activities. [My friend] that lives on campus, she's been a really, really good friend; she's really supportive and everything, she always tells me to apply to different things, she tells me what's going on, like scholarships or events that she knows I'm interested in, and that's really helpful.

Lucia had initially bonded with other commuters on campus since "we were going through the same [orientation] process." But she discounted those connections as not being as deep as the ones she made after being able to move into the dorm during the second term. This suggests the need to rethink orientation strategies that separate commuting and residential students into distinct orientation groups. Lucia's shift from commuting to living in the dorms "was awesome" and helped her redefine what it meant to be a college student. "I had a lot of fun, I was able to join a lot more clubs, and I really like college, I really, really like learning, and I'm definitely going to keep going for it even after I'm done with my undergraduate education. I want to do an MD-PhD program."

In contrast, Kara, who despite having an academically successful first year, never felt like she was fully becoming a college student. "I really haven't had much of a college experience. My transition has been basically transitioning from working two days when I went to high school to now working a whole week. If I go to campus it's just to go to class. I rarely stay on campus." This resentment was exacerbated by the fact that her experience differed from that of most of her high school friends who moved away for college, and from her best friend who was living in a dorm at another college that was close to Kara's. The majority of her friends were now living a college life that she could not relate to. "Most of them they don't even work, from what I've heard. Because, oh, like they don't want to work or stuff, or they think it's too stressful, or their parents are paying for school. So they don't feel that need to work."

Kara described her first year of college as overwhelming and never once mentioned receiving any support in balancing her schedule, reviewing her finances, or socially integrating into campus. These were all responsibilities that required her initiative. When asked who helped her through stressful experiences, Kara replied, "Well, I don't think I did receive much of help."

Kara saw moving into a dorm as the only way to improve her college experience. "I really wish I could dorm [when I get to senior] year, because obviously then I'll have, since I'll have all my credits, then I'll be able to get an internship downtown, maybe. But I don't know, because of I'd have to get a good job and make sure I could afford to dorm, and to pay for school. I feel like that the whole paying for it is a huge barrier in whether I can actually have a college experience." By the end of her first year, Kara still hadn't "made, like, legit friends like I had in high school." Not having any "legit friends" on campus, as well as having to justify her college goals to her family, made for a difficult college transition.

Sammy also recognized the role that living on campus played in connecting to a supportive peer group. He used his friendliness and outgoing personality to make those connections with classmates. "It was sort of something I had to figure out on my own," he said. "Everyone had their own ideas of what to do, oh, 'cause you know some people are like, 'Oh yeah, I got my cluster mates, I have my roommates, people on the same floor as me.' I can't have that kind of experience. But I can experience going to a class, I'll sit next to someone, and I'll be like, hey, you don't understand it. They'll be like, [and] there we go [a conversation started]." Sammy had friends in the dorms, and he leveraged his relationships with them to build a stronger connection to campus. "You know, I have some friends who lived on campus, I would go over here and sleep here. You know, maybe there's a concert going on. . . . So I'd come over here, maybe I'd sleep here."

While there were definitely social advantages to having access to the dorms, Sammy found ways to participate in campus activities without being a residential student: “It was sort of something I had to figure out on my own.” When asked about the most stressful part of first year, Sammy, who is admittedly precocious, said,

> I guess sort of finding out where I belong. There’s all kinds of organizations, all kinds of choices, all kinds of people. Do I start hanging out like smokers, or with the people, like a small group of Mexicans, do I branch out, and if I branch out, will people accept me? There’s a lot more of a world for me whether or not I can find people who understand, who I can actually be happy with. But for me I like to talk a lot, obviously, I like to talk. So that was a little bit weird for me, ’cause I didn’t want my college life to be similar to my high school life, where I was just outside and alone. I just sort of wanted to try and be out.

Without the benefit of situational bonds formed through simply spending hour upon hour together via residential living, commuting students are limited to interest-based bonds.

Sammy’s institutional identity was helped significantly by Urban StateU’s focus on commuter student belonging. By giving commuting students a place of their own on campus, where they could store things, relax, and commune with each other, the school at least afforded commuters the luxury of passively building campus connections. Sammy made many of his friends at the campus’s commuter center.

> It’s basically a place you can study and just relax. It’s hard being a commuter sometimes. You dorm here, you could leave half your shit in your room and then come back out and then come back in and grab whatever you want. For us we have to carry everything. I go to work now, and I have to carry my uniform on me for [work]. So it’s either carry around my uniform with me everywhere I go, or have it on me the entire day. Button-down shirt, a tie, black pants, black shoes—you know I’m not going to feel all too comfortable in it. What the commuter center does [is] they give you lockers, they give you access to a kitchen, they give you access to computers, and if you just like an area to sit and chill and you meet other people that you’ll get to know and someone has your charger, same kind of phone, and then you ask them for a charger. They’ll have game days and snacks, movie days. Most people only go in there for like the lemonade and cookies, though. But, yeah, it’s a nice thing going on there.

As Sammy's experiences illustrate, such spaces and the targeted services they provide, such as lockers, not only connect but validate commuters as valued members of the campus community.

All students need a campus home, and Urban PrivateU-South also recognized the need to create focused services for commuting students. However, the programs and services offered there were much less a priority and much less robust than at Urban StateU. Lucia thought the services were understaffed and largely unhelpful, and instead found her campus home in offices directed to racial-ethnic minority students.

Students' level of integration into the academic and social life of college is measured by the strength of the connections they have with other members of the campus community, including fellow students and professors.[12] These connections help them develop a sense of institutional belonging and are informal sources of cultural, informational, and instrumental capital about how to navigate college. Consequently, students like Kara, who are only loosely connected to their campuses, have a higher risk of attrition. The most recent examination of students attending four-year colleges found that students who lived with parents were about 23 percent more likely than on-campus students to drop out during their first year. This increased risk was largely due to lower levels of academic integration, such as participating in study groups, meeting with academic advisers, and talking with faculty outside of class.[13]

Students who are only loosely connected to their colleges are forced to rely almost exclusively on their own motivation and formal sources of information, rather than being buoyed by peers who are on the same journey. Lucia longed to be more socially integrated into campus life and did not hesitate to move to campus when the opportunity presented itself. This move transformed her college experience, strengthened her academic identity, and increased her educational aspirations. Even though Sammy would have enjoyed dorm life, his personality and targeted institutional supports ensured that commuting was a manageable challenge to developing a sense of campus belonging.

Some students, like Sammy, are able to make commuting work for them and remain engaged and connected despite their distance from campus. Meanwhile, other commuting students, like Lucia, experience both a physical and social distance from campus that can only be rectified by the campus integration that living in dorms provides. Although Kara would benefit from dorming, she is not doing college wrong. By working full-time and adjusting her course schedule to maximize her limited time on campus, she is doing college in the only way that her financial resources allow. She is determined to reach graduation day and hopes to live in a dorm for her senior year, when it would be financially viable.

Much of the existing research on commuting students takes a deficit framework—that is, commuting is viewed as a deficit imposed on the student rather than a disconnection between the student's status as a commuter and the institutionally expected residential student status. This deficit framework denies the skills, such as time management, initiative, experience in the job market, and cultural code-switching, that commuting students, especially historically marginalized commuting students, learn to master. Understanding and adequately supporting commuting students requires attending to structural inequalities that position them as deviant from and marginal to the ways that residential students are integrated into campus life and supported in finding a campus home.

9

OUT OF THIN AIR

When One's Academic Identity Is Not Simply an Extension of One's Family Identity

With Emily Lyons

Academic identity—students' beliefs about themselves as learners, beliefs about themselves as belonging to particular educational institutions, and beliefs about the importance of schooling for their futures—plays an important role in shaping students' educational trajectories.[1] Transitioning to college comes with many challenges and shifts in roles and responsibilities; having a strong academic identity can help students persevere when challenges and failures arise.[2] Several factors influence the ease with which students maintain strong academic identities during the transition to college. One of these is the coherence among students' multiple identities.

As discussed in chapter 2, we all have multiple identities that become more or less salient, depending on the context.[3] When our multiple identities cohere, growth in one identity domain can strengthen and facilitate growth in other domains. For instance, a student who enters college with a strong activist identity could strengthen this aspect of her identity as she furthers her academic identity as a political scientist. Conversely, when there is conflict or tension between identities, growth in one domain can weaken other domains. For example, a student who enters college with a strong religious identity could feel tension between this identity and his emerging academic identity as a physicist. Maintaining conflicting identities is most challenging when the conflict occurs between two or more highly salient aspects of one's sense of self.

Along with introducing new tensions between different aspects of one's identities, the transition to college and associated changes in social context for racial-ethnic minority students often increases their exposure to social identity threats—experiences that challenge the value, meanings, or enactment of some aspect of one's social group identifications.[4] Exposure to social identity threats can lead students to adapt in ways that result in changes in the meaning of the threatened identity, how openly they express the threatened identity, and even restructuring how they perceive the salience of the threatened identity to their sense of self.[5] As illustrated in the comments of one Latinx female student attending Urban PrivateU-North, these social-identity-threatening experiences are often subtle, but they have meaningful consequences.

> I feel like sometimes some people have, like, expectations. . . . They expect me to have a lot of scholarship money, and that's why I can afford to go to [Urban PrivateU-North]. I feel like sometimes, it's kind of weird being, 'cause most of the time I'm . . . the only Hispanic person in my small classes . . . but this is just me being self-conscious or something. I feel like the professors, they didn't expect me to do as well as other students.

Research on racial-ethnic microaggressions shows that although these experiences are relatively infrequent, they have lingering effects, causing marginalized students to question themselves, question the motivations of others, and question their belonging.[6]

The identities that students take on as college students and as members of their family are two aspects of the self that students described as being central to who they are. For many students, tensions between their academic and family identities are moderate to none. For first-generation students, however, the very decision to enroll in college may mark a divergence from their parents' trajectories and the trajectories expected of them. This is because schooling plays a large role in socialization, and college plays a particularly large role in shaping people's beliefs, habits, preferences, and behaviors.[7]

First-generation students often have a difficult time explaining their academic obligations and responsibilities to their families, particularly when these conflict with family responsibilities.[8] Likewise, professors, who hold idealized assumptions about what an undergraduate's life is like, often demonstrate insensitivity to students' responsibilities and obligations outside the classroom. Consequently, first-generation students often find themselves having to "live simultaneously in two vastly different worlds" in order to succeed academically.[9]

Living in two worlds requires constant code-switching—being one person on campus and another with family. Elizabeth Aries and Maynard Seider describe how lower-income students compartmentalized the aspects of themselves that showed up at home and those they presented on campus. Only by keeping these aspects separated could their conflicting identities coexist.[10] This separation of home and school can result in an extremely disjointed lived experience.[11] Students often work to assimilate on campus by censoring the aspects of their off-campus life that would highlight differences, or they overcompensate by attempting to get perfect grades. At home, these same students may minimize school and censor any aspects of their identities that relate to their lives on campus.

Some first-generation students, however, are able to express more adaptive behaviors at home by modeling positive academic behaviors for younger siblings. Bringing aspects of their academic and family identities together in this way helps bring coherence to students' lived experiences and also plays an important role in supporting younger siblings' emerging academic identities. As will be highlighted in the next chapter, having an older sibling to guide them through the college process can substantially improve outcomes for first-generation college students.

First-Generation, Latinx, Female Students in Immigrant Families

The Latinx female first-generation students in our study reported particularly sharp tensions between their academic and family identities. *Familismo*, "a [Latinx cultural] pattern that privileges family interests above those of the individual," leads to one's place and role within the family being an especially salient aspect of the self.[12] Accordingly, research shows that family connections and responsibilities can support the educational success of Latinx women, but many Latinx women also report feeling conflicted about who they are expected to be within their families and the identities they are expected to take on to be successful students.[13]

In this chapter, these identity and role conflicts will be described through the first-year transition experiences of Kara and Cindy, two first-generation, Latinx, female college students with immigrant parents. The similarities in their experiences illustrate how "trying to live simultaneously in two vastly different worlds" can lead to feeling marginalized in both contexts. The differences in their experiences illustrate how ideological counterspaces can facilitate more adaptive coping.

Most have heard about *machismo* in Latinx culture—strong or even aggressive masculinity, which in the context of *familismo* corresponds to men's feelings of strong responsibility toward family, such as being the breadwinner and decision maker. There are corresponding cultural expectations for women called *marianismo*. Modeled on the Catholic Virgin Madonna, the cultural expectations of marianismo call for women's humility, spiritual purity, and prioritization of family. Familismo, coupled with marianismo, "creates an expectation that the 'good Latina woman' will always prioritize family needs above her own individual needs."[14] As Roberta Espinoza notes, education can be seen as helping Latinx men fulfill the expectations of familismo because it can improve their ability to provide for their future families. For Latinx women, however, familismo often dictates prioritizing a caregiver role over educational advancement.

This cultural expectation is in sharp contrast to the expectations of college faculty, who often assume that students can set aside all responsibilities and commitments beyond classes to focus on college.[15] This assumption is unrealistic for many individuals of any gender or cultural group, but for women like Kara and Cindy, these assumptions are so far removed from their reality as to be damaging for their sense of self. For Latinx women whose identities and sense of belonging are tied to close family connections and whose academic identities are tied to their sense of personal accomplishment, tensions between family and school can create what Roberta Espinoza terms the "good daughter dilemma." This dilemma places Latinx women pursuing higher education "in a cultural bind between meeting the demands of their individualistic-oriented school culture and their collectivist-oriented family culture."[16]

As Kara's experiences illustrate, tension between being a good daughter and being a good student can be especially pronounced when family members express ambivalence about going to college. Yet, as Cindy's experiences show, even if one's family unambiguously supports going to college, there can still be a substantial gap between family and academic expectations. The juxtaposition of Cindy's and Kara's stories also shows that there are actions faculty and administrators can take to make it easier or, conversely, more difficult for students to integrate their family identities within their growing academic identities.

Kara's Story: Gendered Familial Ambivalence

Kara lived at home with her parents and two younger brothers her first year of college and commuted about an hour to Urban PrivateU-South, where she was pursuing a degree in marketing. As noted in chapter 8, attending Urban PrivateU-South had been Kara's dream since she was a little girl, partially inspired by an alum who was a close female family friend. Although Kara received a full scholarship from a different school, she chose to enroll at Urban PrivateU-South despite receiving limited financial aid. This meant that in addition to commuting, she worked more than thirty-five hours a week to pay for school.

Kara had found high school easy to navigate. She got good grades, took several AP classes, played soccer, and still had time to spend with friends and family. Likewise, she found the academic aspects of college easy to navigate. She describes herself as always having been "school smart." By objective measures she was academically prepared for college, entering her first year with several AP classes already under her belt, a high school GPA of 3.35, and an ACT score of 25.

For Kara, as for many first-generation students, the decision to pursue a college degree means, to some extent, defining herself in opposition to others in her family. "I'm gonna be my first girl in my family to go to college. I've always been kind of school smart. I know some people in my family, they just really hate school. So I'm like, well I should go to college, and I really want a better living standard when I grow up." As is too often the case for first-generation college students, Kara cannot turn to her family for college advice or support.

> My parents didn't even get the chance to finish high school; they went to school in Mexico . . . so they really don't understand what it's like to go to college. . . . I don't have anyone that's graduated school to tell me, "Oh, this is what you can do." So [I] just kind of play it by ear. If it's something relating to school, I try to go to a counselor, ask my friends for advice, friends that I have that are a year older than me or have kind of already done with school.

Research shows that parents without college degrees hold high educational aspirations for their children.[17] But tensions still exist. These tensions are exacerbated when parents are ambivalent about their children's college enrollment.

For Kara, her parents' ambivalence is tied directly to expected gendered roles and responsibilities at home. Although she would be the first female in the family to attend college, she had college-educated uncles. "It was mostly they saw it as a man thing to go to college." But, she added, "I can go to college. Just because I'm a girl doesn't mean I can't go. That I shouldn't go. I want to have the same education like they did." Kara's father was particularly ambivalent. He didn't exactly object, Kara said, but yet, "It's a similar mind-set but not completely like, oh, don't go to school. . . . It's not that strong, but there's still a little bit of 'Oh, you shouldn't be doing this. You shouldn't be out going to the city every day on public transportation because you're a girl.' Stuff like that."

Despite Kara's perception that her family would have been more supportive of her college aspirations were she male, today Latinx women are more likely to enroll in and graduate from college than their male counterparts.[18] Sarah Ovink, who studies the sociology of higher education, found that whereas college-age Latinx men expressed "a sense of automatic autonomy" regardless of whether they earned college degrees, Latinx women sought college degrees "as a means of earning independence."[19] The women Ovink interviewed saw obtaining a college degree as essential for "achieving independence and avoiding traditional patriarchal power structures." Given this, Latinx parents may experience ambivalence about their daughters' college aspirations and may see their daughters' gains as their losses.

For Kara, her parents' lack of college experience, coupled with their ambivalence, translated into receiving limited instrumental or emotional familial support and involvement in her college experiences, beginning with her applications. "My parents weren't really involved in that," she said. "They didn't actually go to [Urban PrivateU-South] until I had decided, and they [the school] invited us to go for the Homecoming event or something like that. So that's the first time my mom went to campus. My dad actually hasn't been to campus yet." Although her parents may not have been able to offer large amounts of financial support—her father works as a manager at a factory, and her mother works in a restaurant kitchen—Kara believes they could have done more to help and probably would have been more willing to extend themselves financially were she male. In Kara's view, her parents are making a choice to focus on other financial goals, leaving her to take full responsibility for paying for college. "I have to take out another loan," she said, "but it has to be under my name, because my parents won't take out a loan." This unwillingness to contribute to college costs created challenges for her interactions with the financial aid office, because based on her parents' incomes they were not meeting the federally determined expected family contribution. As Kara noted, "Even though my parents' incomes count, they're not helping me pay because they're paying for other things. All they look at is, just what your family makes."

Family financial support is not just about reducing students' stress about bills; it also functions as a signal to students that their families value their ambition and efforts to obtain a college degree. As Douglas Guiffrida notes, this could be as small as "money for laundry . . . which [symbolizes] the family's support and willingness to make sacrifices for them."[20]

During her first year, Kara struggled mightily to fulfill both familial and academic expectations. Although her parents did not charge rent, she was expected to work and contribute to family expenses in addition to covering her college expenses. As Roberta Espinoza states, it is not uncommon for Latinx parents to expect their daughters to continue to contribute to the family while pursuing higher education. Indeed, the cultural value of marianismo "creates an expectation that the 'good Latina woman' will always prioritize family needs above her own individual needs."[21] For Kara, this balancing act created a lot of stress and was a barrier to becoming involved in campus life.

> It's been overwhelming. . . . There's really not much in my experience besides just going to school, work, and then balancing time to sleep in between of everything. Well, at the beginning I was sleeping at most six

> hours, the first couple of weeks, because I was just overwhelmed with work and then school. My college experience was just that I go to class, I have a break, I do some homework, and then I head straight over to work. So I really haven't had much of a college experience.

Her parents' limited understanding of the academic demands made her feel alienated from her family. During the most stressful time in her first year—finals week—she had no one to turn to who understood. Her father, in fact, was "on me" for being away from home too much.

> He was mostly on top of me for being out all day. . . . And then it's like, "Oh, you should be sleeping now because you have to wake up early." I'm like, "I have to get my work done before I go to sleep or else I can't sleep." Or I would be thinking, oh, I didn't do this, so I have to wake up early tomorrow to do it, and I can't wake up early. I really didn't have anyone. I just had to work it out for myself.

On top of it all, Kara's employer required a minimum of twenty-five hours a week to maintain her employee benefits. And she commuted an hour to campus.

Alienation from Both Home and School

Kara's parents offered little support, but neither did her academic advisers and professors, who were either unaware of or insensitive to her off-campus responsibilities. Research shows that this feeling of alienation from both home and school is common among first-generation students.[22] During her first two years, the only time Kara met with a professor outside of class was when it was required for her English literature class. This one meeting left her feeling criticized for working at her job too much when she asked the professor to be more flexible about potential meeting times to accommodate her work schedule. "So, she just told me, 'Oh, you shouldn't be working a full-time job while you're in college. And you have to make time for your studies, and to meet with your professors if you want to do well in college.' I was like, 'OK, well I'm trying to pay for college in the first place.'"

As a result, she seldom sought out assistance from professors, or she hid details about her off-campus life. "After that I was just like [I] kinda don't wanna speak about working another job . . . cause I know . . . you're gonna tell me the same thing or you're just gonna be like, 'Well, you should really take care of school more.'"

Kara also felt that her academic advisers were not being sensitive to how her needs differed from those of traditional college students. She had seen an academic adviser only twice. "I don't wanna say they're not helpful, 'cause they do answer my questions," she said, " but I feel like sometimes they could be more helpful as far as trying to relate to like, oh, what I'm doing, instead of just making it seem like, OK, you're just like all the other college students here living on campus. You have the same situation. So I feel like it's not as understanding as they could be." What Kara needed was answers to questions that she did not know to ask, as was implied in her response to being asked what her academic advisers could do to be more helpful: "I don't know, I feel like there's some things that I kind of figured out by talking to people where I wished they [the advisers] could have assisted me more with that, 'cause I know the advisers know a lot more about what I can get in school to help me out. And the school obviously has a lot of connections that could probably get me to, I don't know, assist me as far as like progressing in my career."

As we will see in Cindy's story, institutional agents can and should help students bring their whole selves to campus. This is made possible when academic advisers use their insight and foresight about what it takes to be a successful college student to fill in missing information, recognize and validate students' off-campus lives, and help them navigate competing demands.

Cindy's Story: Family Emotional Support Coupled with Institutional Ideational Support

The challenges of balancing family and academic identities arose even for Latinx women whose parents, like Cindy's father, were extremely enthusiastic and supportive of their daughters' college aspirations. This was in part because, unlike students whose parents attended college, first-generation students must expend considerable energy trying to communicate and explain their academic responsibilities to family members, particularly when those responsibilities conflict with family responsibilities.

Cindy attended high school in a suburb that was nearly all White and located about an hour outside Chicago. She believes that being such a racial-ethnic minority in that community was a reason for the lack of support she received from her guidance counselor.

> I was one of two Hispanic people [in the school]. So my guidance counselor just pushed me to go to community college, and that's something I didn't want to do, and so I kinda just tackled it on my own. . . . I was extremely happy to get out of [that school]. . . . I feel like they didn't think that [college] was something that I would be successful in or I would be able to pursue. Without them having to say that, I could see

> it in the tone and the way that they dismissed me. So from there I just didn't expect anything from them.

This is guidance that she desperately needed, because, like Kara, Cindy had a father who was unable to offer instrumental support. "My dad, we're really, really close, but he just doesn't know. Even now, I'll call him and tell him things, and he just doesn't understand, either how big they are or how little they are. He just knows I'm going to school, and that's pretty much it."

Cindy arrived on campus prepared for both the academic work and the independence after years of being a "motherly figure" to her little sister and becoming "an extremely independent-do-everything-by-myself person." She enrolled at Urban PrivateU-North, moved into the dorm, majored in accounting, and was "loving" her new life in the city.

Like Kara, Cindy frames her decision to pursue higher education as, to some extent, defining herself in contrast to her experience growing up. Continuing-generation students often talk about going to college to provide the same type of lifestyle for their own future children that they had growing up. Conversely, similar to many of the first-generation students in our study, Cindy talked about going to college as a way to provide a lifestyle that would be different from the one she had growing up.

> I know how my dad struggles, and I know how he lives paycheck to paycheck and can barely stay above water sometimes. And I know how much of a struggle it was for me to just have basic things, and I don't want that for my children, and I don't want that for myself either. I'm not saying that I want to be showering in money or anything like that, but I just wanna be comfortable, and I don't want a worry in my life to be something financially based. I just think that that's an awful way to waste away your life, to be worried about money.

Although many argue that this transactional and utilitarian approach to college is problematic because college is supposed to be about self-development, others highlight that a career-oriented perspective enables first-generation students to undertake the considerable leap of faith and economic risk that college entails.[23]

Familial Emotional Support Is Not Enough

Cindy and Kara are also similar in their doubts about whether college will indeed pay off in the end. "I've done more than both my parents have done in their entire life, on an academic basis and on a career basis, and you sit there and think, should I, can I keep going, is it going to work," Cindy said. The first-generation students we interviewed expressed notable ambivalence. They believed that they had to obtain a college degree to have a chance at a financially stable adulthood but doubted that obtaining their degrees would guarantee them a good-paying job. Some mentioned fears of becoming that iconic college-educated barista at Starbucks.

Unlike Kara, Cindy had the benefit of an older sister in college and an incredibly supportive father. His unambivalent emotional support contributed to her academic success. Her father reminded her of the harder road ahead because she was Hispanic. He told her she would have to put in "three times the effort just to be looked at as an equal" and that she would have to give it her all, "because they're gonna scrutinize you and look at you critically because of who you are." As a result, she said, "I always keep that advice in the back of my head. I always give everything my all."

Cindy also knew that if she ever had financial difficulties, her father, despite meager financial resources, would do whatever he could to help. Nevertheless, her father's enthusiasm about having daughters in college did not protect her from experiencing tension and strife when family and academic obligations conflicted. Indeed, Cindy says that the conflicting identities were the most challenging part of her first year. "You get so involved in school and in classes and in things that you're this whole different human on campus, and then you forget that there's a life back home and you still have family."

When she would forget to call her father, he would FaceTime her, and "he would be like, 'Why aren't you calling me anymore? Do I not exist to you anymore? I'm still alive.'" She didn't intentionally blow him off, she said, but "trying to juggle between giving a lot of time and effort into school and also remembering that my family is still a thing and calling them, I guess is probably one of the most stressful things. And my dad likes to call me. I'm the child he goes to, to talk about all of his, just his feelings and emotions and whatever is going on in his life. I'm his confidant."

Balancing a new life at school while maintaining connections to one's old life at home is a challenge that all college students face. Much of the early research on this issue suggested that to succeed at college, students must separate from their families and fully engage themselves in campus life. However, more critical research that allows for racial-ethnic and other group differences has found that students differ in their need to stay closely connected to family, as well as their family's need for them to stay close.[24]

The tensions between family and academic responsibilities are intensified for Cindy because of the maternal role she assumed toward her younger sister after her parents divorced. She continues to feel responsible for her younger sister's well-being.

> I'm kind of the mother input. But sometimes, because I'm working on an eight-page paper, and it's two in the morning, and I get a phone call and my little sister hasn't called back or isn't home, now I have to worry about that. I'm trying to look on the Yellow Pages to look where her friend lives and finding the address and all these things. I think certain situations, dealing with stuff back home, really, really put me in a stressful position, because I'm here and I don't really have the option to shoot back home overnight. . . . So sometimes, explaining that to my family puts me under a lot of stress.

Unlike Kara, Cindy did not have to negotiate the balance between home and school each and every day. Because Cindy lived on campus, she had more control in responding to her family's expectations and was able to immerse herself in campus life. However, she did have to help her father with expenses at home when he had "no idea how [he was] going to pay rent." She was quick to say that he did not expect her to pay the rent, but she nevertheless felt an obligation. She gave him money for rent because "I didn't need the money at the time." However, she added, "I could've saved that money for the following year for school or whatever or other expenses that would've eventually come up." But in the end, she said, "that's my dad, that's my family, and I want him to have a roof over his head obviously."

Cindy also gave generously to her younger sister. "She's like my baby, my child really. So if I know there's something that she wants like school related, . . . or, you know, something to help her progress academically, or just for her development in general, and I don't mind helping her out with stuff like that. She doesn't ask a lot, but when she does I do."

This experience of giving rather than receiving financial and other material supports to family is not uncommon among first-generation college students. Research shows that first-generation students feel guilt and selfishness when they are unable to contribute to their family's financial needs.[25] This violates the traditional expectation of a one-directional support relationship between students and their families.

Cindy did not compartmentalize her family and academic identities entirely. Instead, she sought ways to bridge these two important parts of herself, bringing aspects of her family and culture to her college campus and sharing details of her college experience with her family. Unlike Kara, who did not talk to her family about what was going on at school, Cindy did not see her father's lack of knowledge of college as a reason to keep silent about what was going on in her life on campus. Instead, she found that, at times, her father's limited experience with college was a plus when it came to dealing with academic stressors.

> Sometimes it's good that he doesn't know how serious some things are. Because when I'm like, "Oh, it's finals week" and he doesn't know what that means, I'm like, "Oh, I have tests in class." Other parents who have had experience with college put a lot of pressure on their kids and are calling them all the time, like, "Are you studying? Are you doing this? Are you doing that?" And for me, my dad's like, "OK, well, call me when you have a chance. Good luck. I know you'll do fine." Cause he doesn't understand how big finals week is, so he's kinda very chill and calm, so it doesn't put a lot of pressure on me, which is a good thing.

Perhaps because Cindy lived on campus and did not feel the stress of negotiating daily the conflicting demands of family and academic identities, she was able to share more about her experiences as a college student.

Institutions' Role in Helping Students Bring Coherence to Conflicting Identities

Cindy's experiences also illustrate how what universities do can aid students in integrating seemingly disparate aspects of themselves. Cindy spoke of the importance of campus cultural organizations and the programming that targeted the needs of first-generation students in navigating the challenges of adjusting to college and bridging home and school.

> I got involved in the Association of Latin American Students, which is really cool because I really like how [Urban PrivateU-North] embraces diversity and accepts everybody no matter what religious, ethnic, sexual orientation, whatever. It's just everybody there really embraces everybody. Not just coexisting, but recognizing those people and embracing them.
>
> So we would go out to [a Hispanic neighborhood] and get Mexican food or go to the museum for Mexican culture, and stuff like that. So just doing things to really stay in touch with your roots, and even though you're away from home or away from that culture, still being able to connect to that. Then I was also part of Exceptional College Students. It's for first-generation, low-income students, and they put on a lot of workshops. And we had a banquet, which was really fun, but the workshops were based on things you could possibly do in the future . . . just general stuff that you think for some people would be just common sense, [but for us] may be information you may not know.

Equally as important in allowing Cindy to bring aspects of her family and cultural identity into her life as a college student was having professors and academic advisers who cared about her off-campus life and were able to recognize the unique challenges that she might be facing. "I love all the professors," she said, "[but] my physics professor . . . he goes out of his way to help you out in the classroom. . . . I go in there and not only talk about physics, but my life in general, and he sits there and listens to me talk, and he's just a listening ear." She described a time when she had been sick and missed class and felt lost before a test. "He sat there with me and did every single question on that study guide and didn't go home until I finished," she marveled. Professors on campus, she believed, went out of their way to keep her on track and even more, so "that you're happy in the classroom and you're happy in the environment that you're in, which is really cool." They also made personal connections and made the time for students, which was important to her. This contrasts sharply with Kara's experiences with inflexible and somewhat oblivious professors.

The physics professor's mentorship and support is an illustration of an ideational counterspace, in which "two or more people come together for a specific purpose over time."[26] Counterspaces are *defined* by the ideas, supports, and resources shared through interpersonal interactions. It is simply that these identity-validating and supportive interactions are more likely to occur when marginalized individuals of a particular social identity are brought together in a physical space. The support and mentorship Cindy received from her professor provided a counterspace within her classroom experiences—a sliver of space for Cindy to experience localized belonging that she then extended to how she perceived all other faculty on campus.

Furthermore, in contrast to Kara's experiences with academic advisers who did not go beyond the formal requirements of their role, Cindy's academic adviser went out of his way to recognize and validate her experience and obligations beyond academics. "Oh my God! I absolutely love, love, love, love my academic adviser. I cannot express how vital he has been to my success here. He is just so supportive." After her father lost his job, Cindy feared she might not be able to return to school the next year. Depressed at the prospect, she didn't want to tell anyone, but she broke down in her adviser's office. "I just started crying and sobbing . . . and he sat there and cried with me." Together, they devised a plan, him running interference with the financial aid office or finding out the correct information for her. "I don't know what that experience would have been like for me if I didn't have [him] as my academic adviser. . . . I just am so grateful to have been blessed to meet an individual like that and even more so to have him available to me as a resource for four years."

Enabled by supportive ideational counterspaces, Cindy enhanced and further integrated her family and academic identities, which allowed aspects of one identity to inform aspects of the other. Lacking supportive counterspaces, Kara minimized both her family and academic identities and relegated each to separate spheres of her life.[27]

It is important to highlight that despite the unique challenges that first-generation, Latinx, female students in immigrant families faced in negotiating academic and family identities, they did not need formal counterspaces exclusive to students with those exact social status characteristics. The women we interviewed found support in a variety of counterspaces that broke with the hegemony of the idealized unfettered college student, free of all concerns other than fully immersing one's self in the college experience. They found this support in physical counterspaces dedicated to Latinx students, first-generation students, and Black students. They also found support in ideological counterspaces with non-Latinx and non-female institutional agents who first listened and then responded with advice that validated how their off- and on-campus lives differed from those of the idealized college student.

10

A GUIDING HAND

Advising That Connects with Students' Culturally Situated Motivational Orientations toward College

With Tasneem Mandviwala

While White young adults are significantly more likely to graduate from college than Black and Latinx young adults, within these two minority populations there is a further disparity: women are significantly more likely to graduate than men.[1] Both Black and Latinx women academically outperform their male counterparts even when socioeconomic and other factors are taken into account. Although research and the media have paid significant attention to the "endangered Black male college student," less attention has been paid to the Latinx male student.[2] Notably, there are numerous universities with programs called either the "Black Male Initiative" or the "African American Male Initiative" that are focused on increasing the numbers and success of Black college men.[3] Few such programs exist for Latinx men.

Only recently have we begun to hear of the "vanishing" presence of Latinx men in college—"vanishing" because of their erasure from college campuses.[4] In 2015, 43 percent of all Latinx college students were men, compared to 54 percent in 1976.[5] The attention and programming directed to Black men is warranted; Black men make up only 5 percent of undergraduates at degree-granting colleges.[6] However, Latinx men are not doing any better. They currently make up less than 8 percent of undergraduates at degree-granting colleges. As Victor Sáenz and Luis Ponjuan note, "despite these trends, research attention to [Latinx men] has been minimal, and public outcry has been almost nonexistent."[7]

Given the previous chapter, a puzzle presents itself: Why is it that Latinx women, despite facing more cultural challenges to college, surpass Latinx men in attaining higher education? Unless we believe that there are gendered cognitive differences among Latinx youth, we must turn to sociocultural factors to help elucidate the disparity between men and women's persistence rates. Julio Cammarota suggests that though *marianismo*—prioritizing caring for others and attending to responsibilities inside the home—presents challenges for women's college success, it is also a motivator, because obtaining a degree is a meaningful route through which Latinx women can gain greater autonomy.[8]

As in the previous chapter, we again take a racially gendered approach to understanding students' experiences. A simplistic application of what has been learned from research on Latinx women because of shared Latinx heritage, or learned from Black men because of shared maleness, would fall short and ignore the complexity and nuances of the Latinx male experience.[9] Although there are many similarities, our interviews revealed that Latinx men differ from Black men and from Latinx women in critical ways. We found that compared to Latinx women, Latinx men were less likely to incorporate a love of schooling in their academic identities and also less likely to state that they were going to college for self-development. These factors may place many Latinx men at odds with their institutions' cultural orientations and at risk for early departure.[10]

In comparison to Black men, Latinx men were more likely to come from very low-educated and immigrant families. This means that their home life did not include access to a knowledgeable adult who could guide them through the college process, from its very beginning in dealing with applications, school choice, and financial aid, to advice for managing the stress of finals week or support in persistence decisions. We found that Latinx men were woefully reliant on institutional guidance for a successful college experience; 37 percent had parents with no education beyond high school (17 percent had parents who did not complete high school), compared to 20 percent of the Black men whose parents had no education beyond high school (only 4 percent did not complete high school).

As with Latinx women, it is necessary to consider the combined effects of sociocultural factors such as first-generation student status in conjunction with cultural factors such as definitions of masculinity and success. Accordingly, with a focus on college persistence, the current chapter details the various sociocultural factors Latinx male students face. Many administrators at historically White colleges and universities are not only unfamiliar with these factors but are often entirely ignorant of them.

To avoid the trap of invoking surface-level social and cultural stereotypes for the observed outcomes of racial-ethnic minority groups, we examine how attending to students' social and cultural norms and needs adds nuance to traditional theories of college persistence. Traditional theories of persistence state that in addition to academic challenges, many students leave college because of their inability to adjust to the college context.[11] Students who do not succeed are believed to have difficulty managing their emotions about being away from home, do not find belonging on campus, and struggle with their new autonomy.

The commonly accepted solution to these challenges is greater campus engagement.[12] The belief is that by separating their sense of self from family and precollege friends and immersing themselves in their academic identity and campus activities—essentially making campus their new home—students will see themselves as integrated into the institution and as valued members of it. However, as noted throughout this book, many have criticized these traditional theories for not fully considering how this model of persistence ignores the lack of belonging and cultural exclusion that many racial-ethnic minority students experience.[13] White students, higher-income students, and students with college-educated parents may be able to transfer their sense of home to campus by immersing themselves in campus activities, but historically marginalized students may not find that sense of home on campus, argue David Pérez and Victor Sáenz, regardless of how much they "abandon family traditions, customs, and values to gain membership in predominantly White institutions." Instead, the authors continue, abandoning one's culture for the sake of campus belonging "can have a detrimental effect on the psychological well-being of Latino male undergraduates."[14]

By comparing and contrasting Latinx men who had difficult transitions with those who had successful transitions into college, we are able to identify culturally situated insights that may help such students gain solid footing in educational settings, and what educational institutions can do to provide effective supports.[15] This search for variation within is, as higher education scholar Terrell Strayhorn argues, in direct contrast to much of the existing research on social and cultural capital, which "treats minority students as a homogenous group whose experiences and capital reservoirs are uniformly deficient and decidedly different from that of majority students."[16]

Even though we begin at entry into college, the full story begins with these students' K–12 educational experiences. As with all other American youth, minority boys receive the message that "college is not only an expected part of the life plan, it is the ultimate symbol of independence."[17] However, these youths receive the fewest K–12 educational supports that would enable them to prepare for college. They also must contend with negative educational stereotypes. Black and Latinx boys have the highest rates of suspensions, expulsions, and special education assignment, and the lowest rates of placement in advanced courses and gifted programs.[18]

The Latinx men in our study gave four general reasons—"motivational orientations"—for why they enrolled in college. These motivational orientations include, from most to least frequently cited, (1) future financial stability, (2) receptivity to school-based mentorship, (3) earning family pride and honor within the community, and (4) joy of learning and self-development. Although we differentiate between these motivational orientations, they were not exclusive, and students often offered multiple motivational orientations. That said, one particular orientation tended to dominate and frame the thoughts of the men in our study.

The three students we detail in this chapter—Marco, José, and Lucas—were all first-generation Latinx students who combined financial aid with work to pay for school. However, they varied in their access to mentors who could guide them through the college process.

Marco attended Urban StateU, a decision he made on his own because he felt that particular school was the best balance between his interests, financial resources, and family obligations. His dominant motivational orientation toward college was joy and interest in academic learning. This was, out of necessity, a self-motivated goal, as Marco had received minimal support with the college process. For him, the aimlessness of some of his peers was the spur to focus on education as an avenue to a successful and fulfilling life. His four sisters were significantly older than he was, and the only one of them who had attended university had left home years ago, so he had little mentorship in the application process. Marco commuted to campus, and during his waking hours when he was not in class he was either doing homework or working to cover his own financial needs and contribute to the family's finances. Despite his high level of self-discipline and self-reliance—or perhaps because of it—his transition into college became increasingly difficult. He entered his sophomore year feeling exhausted and on the verge of burnout.

Like Marco, José commuted to college during his first year at Suburban StateU and worked full-time. José's high school had a high dropout rate, and he was not sure he would attend college until the final months of his senior year. It was then that the direct encouragement and guidance of his counselor and teachers helped him decide, and his motivational orientation for attending college solidified. He wanted to earn pride and dignity for himself and his family in the community. With no sibling or parental support, José quickly learned that turning to the right school-based mentors was the difference between failure and success. This receptivity toward school-based mentorship would help him later. As he made his way through sophomore year at college, it was clear that his success was the result of not being afraid to ask for institutional help as he pursued his goals.

Lucas—who was chronicled in chapter 7 as well—was also enrolled at Suburban StateU. Sharing many of the same background characteristics with Marco and José, Lucas grew up in an immigrant family with parents with no schooling beyond high school. However, by getting him into private Catholic schools, his parents were able to give him access to a college preparatory curriculum. His two older brothers had graduated from college when Lucas was a high school senior, and they reinforced the expectation that he would get a college degree. They were also able to help him through the college application, enrollment, and transition process. Lucas had high aspirations for college and was motivated by future financial stability. He combined this motivational orientation with support from home and receptivity to school-based mentorship.

The Role of the Self

Traditional college culture encourages—actually expects—students to attend college for the sheer love of learning, intellectual exploration, and overall self-enhancement.[19] Although Latinx women were much more likely to cite these reasons as motivations for attending college, Latinx men like Marco were also motivated by this aim.

> I always knew I was gonna go to college since I was five. . . . But when I seriously knew I was gonna go to college must have been in high school, when I was passing my classes.
>
> Well, I was always into science, so that, I feel, solely drove me towards my education. . . . I've always been very, an academically oriented person that way. I always want to teach myself, like watch educational shows and stuff, so I always wanted to go to college to get that scholarly experience.

Marco was majoring in biology with his eye on neuroscience. "For a long time, I've been telling myself I'm gonna do medicine, but like I said, the science, there's so much you can do in that field. I wouldn't even know; sometimes it's like, just the idea of being a scientist is enough."

It was clear later in the conversation that Marco had a hard time justifying his love of learning as the main reason for attending college. His hesitancy stems from the distance that claim interjects between him and his community. As Richard Rodriguez wrote in his autobiographical essay, "as [my parents] watched me advance through my education . . . they seemed to know that my education was separating us from one another, making it difficult for us to resume familiar intimacies."[20]

As a first-generation student in an immigrant family, Marco found himself in a complex liminal cultural space. Without navigational resources, including the right sociocultural language to speak openly and comfortably about their experiences, students like Marco struggle to make it through to the other side.

Performed masculinities and cultural scripts for manhood shape men's perceptions of themselves and their life trajectories. These factors are critical to understanding the minority male view of college.[21] Latinx men add another important orientation: going to college for respectability, *machismo*, *caballerismo*, and *dignidad*. These are important gendered cultural values that emphasize men's roles in providing for their family, be it materially by providing financial support or more abstractly by increasing the clout and social standing of the family within the community.

The term *caballerismo* was developed in large part in response to the negative deficit approach of the dialogue around machismo. However, instead of focusing on the destructive aspects of masculine control, caballerismo focuses on "chivalrousness, family centeredness, nurturing stances, and approaching of problems from a more emotionally connected perspective," according to critical higher education scholars Victor Sáenz and Beth Bukoski.[22] Interwoven into both machismo and caballerismo is the idea that men must value and prioritize their families; to not do so would be considered unmanly or weak. Having a successfully masculine reputation would include maintaining dignity, or *dignidad*, for one's self by maintaining it for one's family by graduating from college.[23]

Machismo and caballerismo are reflected in Latinx men's focus on going to college to "give back" to their families and communities. These values, though, are misaligned with the traditional expectation that students should go to college to learn, explore, and improve themselves. This may account for Marco's feelings of "weirdness" surrounding his desire to go to college primarily to learn rather than to contribute to the social and financial capital of his family and community. "It's just that I feel people think it's weird," he said, "when you say this. Like, 'Why do you wanna go to college?' 'I wanna go to college to learn.'"

These Latinx cultural scripts of masculinity are often listed as obstacles when they are forced into an uncritical comparison with traditional college norms. However, they can be transformed into assets if students and universities recognize and engage them, as they did with José.[24]

José describes himself as "a typical Mexican" and is well aware of the underlying structural and sociocultural factors that Latinx men grapple with. "My parents didn't finish high school. I'm the first one to finish high school and enroll to a four-year institution. My [first-year] college experience wasn't the best, 'cause I was commuting. I had to come back to work because I had expenses I had to pay, as well as help my family out. So college the first year wasn't the best, but I really enjoyed it, even though I didn't do as many activities as I wished to." He has the prototypical interdependent, community-oriented understanding of why he is going to college.

> My main reason is the same as it was since day one: I want to make myself known to people, to be respected, to be dignified, have dignity. I want to get my parents out of working. That's my main goal. Help out people that I really wish to help out. Like help my community for more. Start programs for kids, like it's not just high school. You could have more education, start funds and everything-wise. And for my family, future-wise. To give them what my parents couldn't give me.

His parents were surprised at his decision to go to college and told him they had no money for it. He reassured them of scholarships and financial aid options. He also knew he would be commuting, which "will help me by saving thousands of dollars," as well as working. But still his parents "weren't 100 percent. So I finished my first semester. It was a tough semester, since I didn't have that much encouragement from my family. But afterwards they found out I was doing better. And they were encouraging me even more to further my education, to finish up in four years."

In sharp contrast to the experiences of the Latinx women discussed in the previous chapter, José was able to quickly overcome his parents' doubts; and his gender—an integral aspect of who he is—was never implicated in their reservations about his college aspirations. Although these Latinx men also commuted to campus and had to manage the bulk of their college expenses, their parents made space for them to focus on school without the added burden of family caretaking obligations.[25]

The Many Roles for Others

Most of the research on family support for college focuses on parents, but we found that having a college-going or college-educated older sibling substantially improved the outcomes of younger siblings in first-generation families. That was certainly the case for Lucas.

> My two brothers were actually the biggest help. My parents, they're from Mexico, they barely speak English, so it's very hard for them to understand the whole process of applying to a school. . . . My brothers, they gave me a more detailed perspective of what each college was because they . . . lived through it. They've gone through every little thing. They told me my freshman year, it's an important year, but it's something that people understand that it's a rough transition. People understand if you get little bumps on the road. They'll understand that. But, they said, your second year, third year are extremely important for not only your education, but also for jobs.

Later in the interview, Lucas clarified that it was his parents who created the expectation that college was something he "had" to do, but it was his brothers, along with teachers and a guidance counselor, who were "constantly pushing it," who helped him realize his goal. His guidance counselor's push, in fact, was what "got me to where I am today."

> It was my last three months of my senior year. It was a quick process. She kept telling me that if I wasn't enjoying life, if I wasn't enjoying my future life earning $8.50 or $10, if I was OK how I was living or if I wanted to do better. And I wanted to do better, I wanted to earn more money. I really wished to make my parents don't work anymore. And she told me if I go further in education, then I could earn more money and have better benefits for my future kids as well.

In essence, Lucas's parents, his brothers, and his school mentors—each offering contributions from their different funds of knowledge—worked together with him to ensure a successful transition into college.[26]

In our interviews, José touched on all four motivational orientation patterns: desire to contribute to his family, future financial stability, influence of a school-based mentor, and the desire to improve one's self and expand one's sphere of being. Without mentors within the educational system, he would have struggled to translate his motivations into the language that resonates with college administrators.

> [My teacher and guidance counselors] assisted mostly by just encouraging me, giving me support, inspiring me to pursue my education. They were helping me at my application, the basic things that I didn't do very well. I'm not sure at the moment how to explain it, but they helped me on my personal statement. They told me how to become a better person, become a leader. Make like, an advance and everything, get my name out there [through extracurricular activities]. We redid [my college essay] like over ten times. And it came out really good.

José's experiences with school-based mentors in high school and then in college led to his awareness that asking for help has been one of the most effective approaches to his college success, and is the primary advice he would give to others.

> Second semester [of the first year] was easier. It was way easier. 'Cause this time I wasn't like, mostly afraid. I was more on top of things and asking for more help. I would always get to class like fifteen minutes before. I would ask my professor or I would go to their office hours, and

> I knew some [other students in my classes], so I would text them or call them, like "Hey, are you busy right now?" to let them know, "Oh I had problems with this, I don't understand. Can you help me out with this?" So it was more flexible.

First-generation students need many sources of support to lower the barriers created by their lack of insider knowledge.

However, even when first-generation students like José recognize the need for and benefits of asking for help, their outside responsibilities, like commuting or working, may pose barriers to receiving help. José would do his homework after work, at night, when his professors were unavailable to help with questions. His schedule never aligned with their office hours, which was frustrating for him. "And that's why my grades were lower," he said. "So my job was bringing me down 'cause it was full-time." As will be seen, a set of informal networks would later help him manage his work-school conflicts.

By his sophomore year, José had stopped commuting and became more involved in campus activities, like joining a fraternity and other extracurriculars. It was in his second year that he also recognized the need for another type of support: emotional. This is significant in two ways. First, asking for or accepting emotional help would seem counter to stereotypical masculine norms of Latinx culture, as well as American culture.[27] Second, belonging and emotional well-being are central aspects of theories of college persistence.[28]

In contrast to José's path, Marco's college transition was arguably less successful. Of course, such a comparison requires the disclaimer of differences in individual histories, personalities, and talents. As evident earlier, Marco's dominant motivation to attend college was a desire to learn and develop himself. It is interesting then that Marco would struggle more in college than José, whose primary motivational orientation—to support his parents and future family—would be considered less than ideal.

One substantial difference between José's and Marco's approaches to college was their emphasis on the self. Marco wanted to go to college "to learn," but he also wanted to "teach myself," and "always told myself I was gonna go to college." Whereas dominant American norms laud individualism and a focus on the self, Latinx norms tend to prioritize communal actions and goals. This is a potential disconnect for Latinx students, particularly those whose families recently immigrated. Because of these students' need to lean on others to fill their knowledge gaps, an interdependent approach to college may lead to greater success.[29]

The challenges associated with Marco's independent mind-set can be seen in how he approached the college application process, ultimately leading to a less successful outcome than José's. Despite his statements describing the many ways that his high school helped, Marco believes that he got into college with little help from anyone.

> I just did it myself. My dad . . . I wouldn't ask him to help with college applications and stuff. I just did it myself. It wasn't too bad. And I had teachers give me advice here and there. During the time of the applications I was also getting prepared for my testing. And so we're getting bombarded by work there, we have to make sure we do all these applications, essays, meet deadlines. And I mean, it's tough, but it's a good thing I'd say because it makes you take it seriously and really make a decision on that.

When asked who helped him from his high school, he said teachers inspired him to push harder, but no one "helped me too much with my applications." Instead, he said, "a few teachers pushed us to meet those deadlines. They got on our backs." His homeroom teacher "was doing that to everyone," he said. His science teacher was also willing to write recommendations, though she told students to write the letter and she would sign off, "so you could express what you wanted it to express. So, yeah, it wasn't all me."

Marco's experience reveals subtle but important differences from José's. Like José, Marco describes his high school teachers as helping and pushing him along, but unlike José, he did not personalize their support; it was simply something they did for everyone. Research shows that personalized support from faculty and academic advisers is pivotal for first-generation students' success in college.[30] Because Marco never personalized his high school support, he had limited skills for how to obtain it in the future, making his first-year transition harder than necessary.

> I went to [my academic adviser] whenever I needed to . . . it's kind of similar to any counselor. I never really talked to my high school counselor that much, either. They don't really baby you or anything like that. They're just there for you when you need to ask them a question and stuff, and to talk to. And when I need to talk to them, I tell them my questions or my thoughts on what I'm trying to do. Talk to her about the classes I need and make sure I'm on track. But I don't need to talk to my counselor about personal stuff. I guess some people do do that. I never have.

Marco focused on accessing formal supports, but his commute and full-time work schedule were barriers. His interactions with professors, he said, were "too few," especially in large classes. "You know, they have a line of students going up to meet them at the end of every class. It's discouraging, because three hundred people aren't gonna ask questions at the end of class." Office hours did not align with his work schedules. He did, however, take advantage of tutoring sessions before tests. Though there, too, he sometimes struggled to find a good fit. "It's kinda hard when you don't know who's a good tutor, though, when you're new. Man, I just asked a girl a question, and she's like, 'I don't know. Hold on, let me Google it.' And I was like, what're you gonna do for me?! I can Google it."

While the tutoring services he mentioned helped, they certainly were not as helpful as the professor would have been. Seeking academic help and being given a peer tutor who "can Google it" would be understandably disheartening to a student who must be maximally productive to balance competing responsibilities.

The Latinx men in our study often already had vague guidance from their parents. What they need from advisers was clarity and direction from someone who had traveled the road before, someone who could help them ask and answer questions they did not know to ask. We found that this kind of support occurred when students and their advisers were able to build a rapport that allowed them to talk about more than just school. Marco believed he did not need that kind of personal interaction. José, on the other hand, saw his advising relationship as a friendship. José viewed all the relationships he made with advisers and peers as a potential source of help. "I made friends with my counselor, and she helped me, offering me like math tutoring. She introduced me to this guy named Roger [a junior], and he's been my mentor, tutoring me and mentoring me at the same time. Helping me, so it became easier." In fact, most of the friends José has made on campus are, he believes, for tutoring and asking advice.

Marco, in contrast, assigned his college advisers and friends a much more circumscribed role in his life—more as "a backdrop like, oh, I need to wind down, rather than, oh, I'm gonna seek out help. But I did have the friends who I studied with. That's definitely necessary. You gotta have study groups."

Succeeding in college is about much more than academics, and Marco was left to navigate all these other aspects of college based on what he could figure out for himself.

> I feel like I didn't really get financial advising, really. I didn't get told what would be the best options for me. They kinda just pushed me towards like, oh, you can apply to try and get a job here or something. I didn't have someone talking to me about where to go, walk me through my options, tell me if I can do work study and what not. I guess I can't. I called them up, and they said I'm not eligible for whatever reason. I didn't know that at the time, how it worked. Some people would tell me, "Oh, I'm getting paid money on the side for coming here." And I'm like, what are they doing?

This independent approach would become more of a hindrance than an asset, which was evident in his sentiment that things got progressively harder from the first to the second semester of his first year. In contrast, for José and many other Latinx men we spoke with, the college experience was something they settled into, something that felt much more comfortable after the initial adjustment challenges. However, for Marco, despite becoming more accustomed to the campus and general expectations of college, he seems to have found the challenges growing as time wore on. By the spring of his first year, he was still burned out from the first semester, he said.

> I definitely feel like the fall was tougher, but at the same time I feel like I did better in the fall, just because in the spring I was already so tired out from the fall. I had already gotten used to it, but at that point, I was so burnt out from the first semester. I was making sure I was getting things done, but I wasn't doing necessarily my best because I was kinda taking it easy. Unfortunately, I didn't pass my calculus class. I'm retaking it now.

In the end, seeking help seemed to make the difference between success and burnout. Neither Marco nor José lived on campus for the first year. Both faced immense financial challenges and work responsibilities. Both have immigrant parents who are not college educated. Marco has a college-educated older sibling. So why, then, is José's experience noticeably more successful, with less burnout—a transition that will potentially encourage him to persevere and complete his degree? The answer may be because while Marco shied away from having more than formal and academic discussions with institutional agents and college peers, José's "talk to everybody" approach maximized potential avenues of support and guidance. It appears that through engaged help-seeking—hearing more advice, sharing more emotions, and consciously pursuing help—José gained the edge needed to help overcome his knowledge gaps about how to navigate college and prevent burnout.

Help for students should not be one-directional, only sought but not offered. Academic advisers and faculty should be actively offering help. If engaged help-seeking is taking advantage of potential resources by "talking to everybody," engaged help-providing is first listening to understand "where students are coming from" and then offering advice that fills the gaps. Marco himself says that it is this lack of engaged help that is missing from the institutional side of the interaction.

> I feel like advisers look at the paper a lot, too much. They're more looking down at the paper than at you. Which of course is important—they don't really know you, so they're trying to get to know you from

> the sheet of paper, which has its advantages, though, I mean, you don't really know a person. . . . I mean, I don't blame them at all. They have so many students they have to talk to. And they have to make friendship with everyone. They're not gonna be able to get to know everyone super-well to help them their best, but definitely try to like make the most eye contact as they can. And try to reach out and encourage them to talk to you or email you or stuff like that.

The experiences of the Latinx men detailed in this chapter confirm the critical role of social support in college success. Social support can be instrumental assistance, such as study partners, class notes, homework assistance, or it can be informational assistance, such as advice on norms and expectations. It can also be cultural advice about formal and informal resources and opportunities.[31] Social support also has academic benefits by helping to improve emotional well-being, such as reduction of depression and anxiety that can impair cognitive functioning and attention. All the preceding chapters also illustrate the pivotal role of social support in the development and maintenance of academic motivation and the likelihood of responding to stressors with active problem solving versus withdrawal and disengagement.[32]

Not all students are aware of their need for a strong campus-based social support network, and not all students have the social skills to make friends with their academic adviser. Therefore, administrators and faculty should be more proactive in building friendships with students and practicing a more engaged and socioculturally sensitive understanding of historically marginalized students. This latter component is perhaps the most challenging, because of the demands for change it makes. Because of that, it is also potentially the most beneficial.[33] A socioculturally engaged institution would become proactively aware of and responsive to variations in the challenges, strengths, and opportunities within subgroups of the student body. This requires understanding not only the obvious socioeconomic stressors that subgroups of historically marginalized students face—such as working full-time and commuting to campus—but also the more intangible cultural stressors, such as the difficulty conceptualizing college as being about self-development versus preserving the honor and dignity of one's family. Actively recognizing a broader range of culturally situated motivational orientations toward college would enrich the broader campus culture by better incorporating historically marginalized students.

11

(DIS)INTEGRATION

Facilitating Integration by Carefully Attending to Difference

Colleges and universities can take a range of positions toward the broad category of identity-conscious supports, and identity-affirming counterspaces in particular. Any given institution's position would likely be associated with its active commitment to advancing interactional diversity. Institutions that take a matter-of-fact position regarding lack of structural and interactional diversity would more likely attempt to neutralize students' attempts to create counterspaces. Institutions that believe that the job has been accomplished once they have enrolled a statically diverse cohort would more likely place the burden of creating and sustaining counterspaces on historically marginalized students. Institutions that recognize that historical marginalization is often sustained by present-day disenfranchisement, discrimination, and stereotyping would more likely provide resources and opportunities to create and normalize formal and informal counterspaces.

Advocating for identity-conscious supports and campus counterspaces as one specific category of such supports does not negate the importance of academic preparation and the role of K–12 schools in ensuring that historically marginalized students arrive on campus ready to engage in college-level work. Differing academic preparation is a significant factor in racial-ethnic gaps in college persistence.[1] Schools vary widely in their educational resources and course offerings, and these variations are strongly associated with the racial-ethnic composition of the student body.[2] Among the 533 students in our study, those who attended predominantly White high schools were much more likely to report that their high schools prepared them for college compared to those who attended predominantly non-White high schools.

The question is whether academic preparation is enough. The research-based consensus says no.[3] Black and Latinx students have lower college grade point averages (GPAs) and are less likely to graduate than White students, even after accounting for SAT and ACT scores and high school GPA.[4] This is because even when ability and academic preparation are equal, Black and Latinx students have unequal access to the cultural and social resources that historically White colleges and universities require.[5] However, when colleges and universities take proactive steps to provide identity-conscious supports, racial-ethnic differences in outcomes narrow considerably.[6] As highlighted throughout this book, these cultural and social resources go beyond racial-ethnic identity to include how race-ethnicity is associated with the increased likelihood of having other marginalized social identities, such as being a first-generation student, a lower-income student, a commuting student, a working student, and a student from an immigrant household.

Black and Latinx students have responded to the call to go to college, but colleges and universities have been slow to change in response because they believed they could assimilate these students and remain unchanged.[7] Higher education has shown itself to be a revolving door that puts too many Latinx and Black students right back outside their walls, with student debt and without a degree that would lead to the wages needed to service that debt. Although I foreground the persistence problem, the broader goal of campus counterspaces is fostering persistence coupled with psychological, emotional, and cultural well-being. Too many studies show that for historically marginalized students, educational success comes at a high personal cost.[8]

Diversity as a Process Rather Than an End Goal

For too many institutions, enrolling students from a diverse range of social categories has largely been the first and only step toward campus diversity. Because such universities perceive the goal as achieved once students enroll, they pay much less attention to the post-recruitment process. The result is universities with structural but not interactional diversity, an outcome that is evidenced by a reliance on enacting diversity through institutional statements rather than through institutional actions. As Claire said in chapter 4, it felt suspicious and insincere when Urban PrivateU-South administrators regularly touted their high level of campus diversity, given the difference between those statements and her experiences.

> The administration also definitely plays up their diverse aspects. When you go to presentations for the first week or whatever, when they were doing introductions, they would be like, "We have this and we have this, and we're so tolerant of everyone" and blah. It's just so strange. You shouldn't have to do that, you should just [say] we have this, like it's really cool, this culture's pretty cool, you should check it out. Not advertising it. Or bragging about it. Which is definitely something that you find there a lot.

Research shows that, like Claire, students take note and interpret this overreliance on diversity statements as evidence of the institution's token commitment to diversity.[9] Students with both diverse and segregated friendship networks take note of when diversity is primarily enacted through institutional statements. The authors of *Making Diversity Work on Campus* call attention to this issue because students' perceptions of the institution's commitment to diversity affect their individual willingness to build relationships that cross racial-ethnic boundaries.[10]

As Julissa, profiled in chapter 2, said, the lack of interactional diversity is clearly visible to nearly anyone who paid an ounce of attention to the issue. The campus itself, bars and restaurants, and events were all typically segregated, she said.

> You have Black people hanging out from the hours of 11:30 and 2:00, and they take over a certain part of the quad, and you see other races and groups that are afraid to walk through the Black group to get to the student union, so they take the long way around to get to the front. . . . If it was a Black event [at Friendship Park], you would see Black people there, but if it was a White event, there would be a larger turnout on campus in general. So there was a lot of segregation there. Even when Black people started taking over the common area of [the food court], you would see a lot of White people not really eat at the convenience store during those hours, but as soon as that Black rush left, that's when it would be when it was busiest. So a lot of apparent segregation that you would really just have to sit at a table and watch and pretend like you're doing work to notice and see what's being interpreted by different races about one another.

This ease with which the lack of interactional diversity becomes visible means that administrators cannot say they did not know; they can, however, say they did not care to know.

Without taking steps to foster interactional diversity, institutions invite the negative outcome of structural diversity: increased levels of racial-ethnic conflict.[11] As noted in *Making Diversity Work on Campus*, "while racially diverse campuses provide important opportunities for teaching and learning that racially homogeneous campuses do not provide, they also present significant challenges that must be addressed if the educational benefits of campus diversity are to be achieved."[12] The conflict itself is not the negative outcome. It is whether the institution uses that conflict to further productive understandings of others.[13]

Silvia Santos and colleagues found that one potential negative outcome of increased diversity is White students' feelings of "identity threat," that is, perceiving reverse discrimination, perceiving that their racial-ethnic identity is not valued, and that educational resources and supports are being diverted to members of racial-ethnic minority groups.[14] The conflict or discomfort that comes from feeling that one's assumed privileged position or perspective is not the standard can be used to spur self-reflection, perspective taking, and other aspects of interpersonal growth.

Instead of making productive use of these conflicts to further the institution's commitment to diversity, many colleges and universities suppress and minimize the conflict. For example, one way that colleges have responded to critiques of race-conscious policies is by symbolically shifting their language to appear more race-inclusive and less race-conscious. Afeni Cobham and Tara Parker argue that after a brief flirtation with moving toward a race-conscious orientation, universities have pivoted and moved toward what I call false racial-inclusivity—celebrating similarities across racial-ethnic diversity and downplaying historical and contemporary differences in how race-ethnicity is experienced.[15] As Cobham and Parker note, one manifestation of this is removing "minority" from the names of administrative offices designated to serve underrepresented students and replacing it with "diversity" or "multicultural." My own university changed its "Office of Minority Student Affairs" to "Office of Multicultural Student Affairs" in 2007, and then to the nondescript "Center for Identity + Inclusion" in 2016.

In crafting a plan for diversity that is central to their educational and intellectual mission, universities should take stock of their efforts to avoid the trap of making statements about diversity instead of taking action. The expectation that students will somehow figure out how to overcome a lifetime of explicit and implicit biases and engage with diversity with minimal institutional supports is negligent.[16]

For administrators who do want to know more, begin by surveying your students and other members of your campus community. Campus climate surveys can provide insight into how perceptions and experiences of the campus differ based on several social categories that identify subgroups with a history of marginalization. I led the development of my institution's 2016 campus climate survey, and the following examples are a good starting place. Students were asked to indicate their level of agreement with the following statements:

1. I feel that I belong at this university.
2. I feel welcomed at this university.
3. I feel valued by other students.
4. I feel valued by faculty.
5. Students of my race-ethnicity/gender identification/sexual orientation/ religious affiliation are respected at this university.
6. I feel comfortable expressing my views regarding race/ethnicity.
7. Attending a diverse university is important to me.
8. I have considered transferring to another school because of my experiences of discrimination/harassment at this university.
9. I have considered not recommending this university to a prospective student because of my experiences of discrimination/harassment at this university.
10. Racial-ethnic/gender identification/sexual orientation/religious affiliation discrimination may have been a problem at this university in the past, but it is not a problem today.

It is important to examine how responses to these questions differ by several social status categories. Some students may experience marginalization due to their race-ethnicity, for others it may be class-based, and yet others may feel that their gender identification or religious affiliation is the marginalizing aspect of who they are.

In the remainder of this chapter I offer a few critical actions for universities to engage racial-ethnic diversity that is simultaneously about repairing past injustices while creating a more equitable and inclusive future.

Structuring Diversity into Campus Orientation Programs

Those who argue for identity-blind campus integration believe that people's group identities can be submerged either by stripping away salient group markers so that students think of themselves only as individuals or by creating a new single group institutional identity so that students think only of being part of the institution.[17] However, as we have highlighted throughout this book, color-blind integration defies students' lived experiences.[18] Color-blind integration ignores power, privilege, and inequality, factors that are intimately tied to students' experiences of race-ethnicity on campus. Color-blind integration is complicit with the idea that the historically privileged group's culture is the superordinate identity into which all others should be subsumed.[19] Consequently, color-blind integration can only occur in theory and never in practice.

Recognizing the futility of asking historically marginalized students to submerge their cultural or group identities under some larger humanist or institutional identity, Patricia Gurin and her colleagues argue instead for supporting students to maintain intragroup solidarity while developing intergroup alliances; neither is done at the expense of the other.[20] Social psychologists who believe that historically marginalized students need identity-conscious supports to succeed in college argue for difference-education interventions.[21] These interventions provide students with insight into how their different backgrounds matter for the challenges they will likely experience and the resources they will need to succeed. In addition, they explicitly and implicitly communicate that it is OK to self-acknowledge the aspects of one's social identities that may make one's college experience different from that of the idealized traditional college student. Difference interventions can be programs that focus on a single identity group, where students focus solely on the experiences of others like themselves and learn success strategies that take their identity into consideration. However, they can also be done as intergroup programs that simultaneously engage students' belonging to a range of identity groups to explore how each identity characteristic can shape the college experience.

Nicole Stephens and colleagues detail a one-hour difference-education intervention held early in the first year that reduced the achievement gap between first- and continuing-generation students by 63 percent. It also reduced first-generation students' stress and anxiety and increased their academic and social engagement. In the intervention, incoming students heard from first- and continuing-generation seniors about how they adjusted to and found success in college. Seniors discussed their social class backgrounds and how it affected their precollege and college-going experiences, and, in turn, how those experiences determined the resources they lacked and supports they needed to succeed. Stephens concludes that "the intervention provided students with the critical insight that people's different backgrounds matter, and that people with backgrounds like theirs can succeed when they use the right kinds of tools and strategies. . . . Specifically, difference-education can help students to make sense of the source of their particular experiences in college and, at the same time, equip them with the tools they need to manage and overcome the challenges their different backgrounds might present."[22]

Because there is no one profile of *the* Latinx student or *the* Black student, there is no one answer for how colleges should respond to the needs of their increasingly diverse student bodies. The educational benefits of diversity can only be achieved by living in the dynamic space of recognizing both the individual and the group, and not placing the needs of one group as subordinate to another.

Curricular Diversity

Universities are sorely lacking in diverse curricular offerings. To many, it is surprising to hear that the overwhelming majority of colleges and universities are lacking in curricular diversity. Yes, there are literally thousands of courses offered each year at each institution. However, almost all of those courses use a colonial framework—course syllabi dominated by the intellectual and scientific contributions of White scholars, particularly White men. To spur change, several student petitions have called for "decolonizing the college curriculum."[23]

In response, most administrators point to their racial-ethnic studies offerings, but this relegates curricular diversity to the limited number of electives that students have space for or to the limited number of students who major in a racial-ethnic studies discipline. Racial-ethnic studies courses have been and are the lifeblood of academic counterspaces, where, while engaging in core intellectual activities, racial-ethnic minority students reduce their feelings of cultural isolation on campus, develop critical cultural identity, and build supportive student-faculty relationships.[24] However, curricular diversity must be envisioned in more expansive ways and include seemingly identity-neutral fields such as mathematics, ostensibly universalist fields such as psychology, and traditionally colonial fields such as history and political science.

Only a limited number of research articles and books can be covered in any one course, and this limited set of readings is often composed of the seminal articles that have always been used and more recent articles by the professor's known network of contemporaries. Given this, to achieve curricular diversity, universities should diversify their faculty. Faculty who come from historically marginalized groups would be more likely to broaden the range of articles considered seminal to any given field and have a more diverse network of contemporary colleagues from which to draw.

Minority students have long reported that their perspectives and experiences are not represented in college curricula.[25] Imagine the increased sense of membership that historically marginalized students would experience if the intellectual contributions of members of their groups were explicitly integrated into the syllabus. Priyamvada Gopal, a faculty member at the University of Cambridge, writes in the *Guardian* in October 2017 of the impact of such a curriculum. "A decolonized curriculum would bring questions of class, caste, race, gender, ability and sexuality into dialogue with each other, instead of pretending that there is some kind of generic identity we all share." She argues that education should enable self-understanding for all students and enable understanding of others, and this can only be done if the intellectual contributions of members from all social groups are deliberatively integrated into the curriculum.

Interactional Diversity

There is now a clear consensus that structural diversity does not lead to interactional diversity without intentional institutional action.[26] Structural diversity should be seen as a prerequisite to creating campus environments that deliberately teach students how to identify and move beyond their biases, understand broad group differences as well as the diversity of individuals within groups, and develop meaningful interpersonal relationships across group boundaries. These are skills, not natural inclinations nor character traits, and because of the segregated nature of American K–12 schools, most college students lack these skills on arrival.[27]

Fostering interactional diversity is a critical aspect of preventing the negative aspects of structural diversity. For White students, increased social interactions with students of other racial-ethnic groups increase their likelihood of holding positive views about multiculturalism on campus and valuing the goals of promoting diversity.[28] The nature of majority and minority experiences in any given society is such that interactions with diverse groups may be particularly beneficial for students who belong to the majority group. This is because they are less likely to have encountered views that contradict their worldviews than people who belong to minority groups. For racial-ethnic minority students, fostering interactional diversity reduces their feelings of isolation on campus and results in a more successful first-year transition.[29]

Fostering interactional diversity has both campus-wide and individual student benefits.[30] On campus, interactional diversity has broad normative effects, such that campuses with higher levels of interactional diversity also have greater student appreciation and awareness of persons from other racial-ethnic groups. That said, the benefits of interacting with others of another race-ethnicity is greater on campuses with more segregation. In other words, students benefit most from opportunities to interact across racial-ethnic boundaries on campuses where students primarily interact with their own racial-ethnic group.[31]

Nicholas Bowman examined more than fifty studies and concluded that the effect of diversity on students is determined by the level of peer interaction with diverse individuals, particularly interactions outside the classroom.[32] Frequent interactions with diverse peers is positively related to a range of student outcomes, from civic attitudes and behaviors to cognitive outcomes, such complex thinking and problem-solving skills. Josipa Roksa and colleagues believe that this cognitive growth is spurred by interpersonal encounters that provide experiences and information that are different or discrepant from one's previous experiences.[33] Nida Denson and Mitchell Chang conclude that "although interactions with diverse others may initially seem more difficult and effortful than interactions with similar others, they are associated with several benefits."[34]

Given the importance of interactional diversity, I highlight several promising actions that universities can take to enhance the quantity and quality of intergroup social interactions.[35]

1. Semi-informal, facilitated events to help students gain the tools for cross race-ethnicity dialogue while also building friendships.
2. Peer education that uses older students with diverse peer networks to educate incoming students of their same race-ethnicity about diversity issues. This approach increases student comfort with discussing sensitive topics.
3. Intentional community-building efforts using repeated interactions that sustain the level of interaction necessary to build genuine friendships.

Meaningful and sustained interaction, and not simple proximity, are crucial. Theories regarding the psychological processes that lead to changes in attitudes or biases toward members of other groups, particularly stigmatized groups, emphasize how knowledge about a group, emotional or affective ties with group members, and experiences alter one's perceptions of group members.[36] Essentially, there is little utility to recruiting a statistically diverse student body without taking the next steps of fostering interactional diversity.

Counterspaces

So why, after arguing for the importance of interactional diversity, do I close this book by re-emphasizing the need for institutionally supported counterspaces for students with minoritized, marginalized, and stigmatized identities? Counterspaces, particularly physical counterspaces, do promote the separation and segregation of subgroups of students from the broader institution. However, it is for brief periods of time and for the strategic purpose of helping students develop the adaptive coping resources and skills that enable them to re-emerge and engage more fully with the broader institution.

As Tabitha Grier-Reed notes, racial-ethnic supports are needed to counter racial-ethnic stress.[37] Charles R. Lawrence, one of the founding critical race theorists, notes that in the absence of deep and meaningful campus diversity historically marginalized students—and faculty—turn to counterspaces for a community of "trusted friends, [where one can] seek refuge and dress wounds of battle and places for hard conversations, where differences can be aired and strategy mapped, where we can struggle with and affirm one another."[38] Later, Lori Patton used this quote to capture her belief that campus culture centers, such as the Black or Latin American Student Unions, provide spaces of resistance against identity disaffirming campus experiences.[39] I use this quote to signify that counterspaces are critical spaces where marginalized students challenge each other to push beyond stereotypical narratives, develop counterstories, and learn adaptive strategies from others who are navigating similar struggles. Essentially, counterspaces take many forms—ideational, physical, curricular, cocurricular, formal, and informal—and do many things. They counter discrimination, build critical group identity, become culturally affirming while fostering institutional belonging, provide psychological and physical safety, support academic achievement, and provide a social community.[40]

What I have gathered from media coverage and conversations with colleagues who oppose racial-ethnic counterspaces, as well as from a few scholarly articles on this topic, is that opposers tend to equate being admitted to college with being welcomed and integrated into campus life. As discussed in chapter 1, when one's understanding of discrimination and oppression is personal (only personal engagement in blatant and overt acts of discrimination are considered) and ahistoric (there are no current laws or formal policies that directly disadvantage historically marginalized groups) and when structural factors are ignored, one can easily claim that discrimination and oppression are nonissues. Under this thinking, institutionally supported counterspaces are perceived as unfairly "catering" to students from historically marginalized groups.[41]

Based on this belief that enrollment equates to full inclusion, opposers imagine that students who choose to participate in counterspaces are choosing to separate and segregate themselves from this imagined inclusive campus community. Consequently, when students of color "are observed associating with each other, their same-race affiliations are lamented in the public and private discourse as the cause for the racial balkanization of college campuses. . . . In other words . . . affiliating with your own racial-ethnic group in college is presumed to have a negative influence"[42] However, there is no truth to the myth that campus segregation is due to the actions of minority student self-segregation. The empirical evidence is clear: minority students are much more likely than White students to have both casual social interactions and close friendships that cross racial-ethnic boundaries.[43] Each and every time counterspaces are threatened, unwavering acknowledgment of the fact that racial-ethnic minority students have the highest levels of diverse campus interactions would go a long way to demonstrating institutional recognition of the true nature of campus segregation.

This discrepancy in perception is also found among students; counterspaces appear to be perceived differently based on whether students feel that members of their identity group are threatened versus welcomed on campus.[44] White students are more likely to view explicitly racially-ethnically marked organizations in negative, segregationist terms and experience their existence on campus as obstacles to meaningful intergroup relationships. In contrast, minority students view these organizations as a means of self-affirmation and growth, both of which increase their likelihood of social engagement with majority spaces on campus. And, as discussed in chapters 4 and 7, racial-ethnic minority students experience many of the university's long-standing organizations as implicitly marked White spaces from which they are actively excluded.

White student segregation is fostered in these long-standing unmarked White spaces that are seen as simply part of the history of the institution. As the authors of *Making Diversity Work on Campus* concluded, "It is important to note that historically White colleges and universities have a much longer history of exclusion than they do of inclusion and that this history continues to shape racial-ethnic dynamics on our campuses. One product of this history of exclusion is that, on many campuses, benefits sustained for particular groups go unrecognized and often work to the detriment of groups that have been historically excluded by the institution."[45] Again, the point is understanding that racial-ethnic counterspaces, and counterspaces for other subgroups of students, developed in response to feelings of exclusion, marginalization, and alienation.

Racial-ethnic minority students also need counterspaces because in those spaces their race-ethnicity fades into the background. The students interviewed noted the relief they felt while in such spaces and on realizing that their adjustment and integration challenges were normal. Counterspaces ensure that minority students do not have to struggle alone. They allow students to share empathy as well as information. As a result, students were better able to cope with the challenge of being othered. For historically marginalized students to take full advantage of the learning opportunities that abound on college campuses, they need to feel comfortable exposing their vulnerabilities, asking questions, and making mistakes. As discussed in chapter 6, for Black and Latinx students this requires a context where they feel that they will not be judged more harshly than their White peers who make similar mistakes, and their accomplishments will not be dismissed as exceptions.

When one is the only member, or one of only a few, of a marginalized social group in a given context, experiencing identity-threatening microaggressions can lead to withdrawal and avoidance coping.[46] This is because being in the extreme numerical minority places students in the untenable position of having to choose between ignoring the microaggression or responding and risk being singled out as too sensitive, someone who sees racism and discrimination in innocuous comments, or as someone who manipulatively plays the race card. Several researchers have noted this Catch-22 dilemma.[47] Being tagged with any of these labels has potential negative ramifications for students' educational and professional careers. Counterspaces enable healthy shared processing of microaggressions. Marginalized students can share and deconstruct their experiences, obtain emotional validation through the recognition of shared experiences, obtain critical insight, and develop adaptive coping.

Counterspaces also provided the Black and Latinx students in our study with compensatory supports they needed to counterbalance the low-quality guidance that many reported receiving from White academic advisers and professors. The majority of the students we interviewed first went to their assigned advisers, teaching assistants, and campus-wide academic support centers. They received advice and academic supports that were somewhat helpful but did little to consider the aspects of their precollege experiences, current circumstances, and aspirations that differed from those of the idealized college student. At times, those institutional agents only increased the students' feelings of academic inferiority. Students pointed to the gap between their and the institutional agent's racial-ethnic and class backgrounds as the reason for the limited guidance and support received. As Aliyah noted of the teaching assistant's favorites in chapter 6,

> Administrators should take more time to get to know their students, especially students who come from, this is going to sound really mean, but if you're not like White and suburban.... Especially the TAs, because TAs always have their favorites, and then they, it's like sometimes they're investing more time in their certain students, which I personally don't think is fair. Invest the same amount in every student, and then if a student comes to you for help, that's what should set them apart. Not whether they come from, not, and some TAs talking about like what they did on the weekend with the students. And I'm like, that's fine, develop a relationship with your TA. But if that means that you're going to help them more than you're going to help me, I don't know if I'm OK with that.

The higher quality of guidance and support that happens between White institutional agents and White students goes unacknowledged, because White institutional agents are presented as racially-ethnically neutral. However, minority students do not experience them as racially-ethnically neutral.

As Derick Brooms found, Black male students credited a counterspace for Black males with providing access to critical campus resources. "Although [the black men] asserted that many of the resources were in place already for all students, they felt disconnected from many of these opportunities or shared that they held little to no knowledge on how to access them."[48] The counterspace created Black male peer networks that shared strategies and resources for overcoming challenges, while simultaneously building members' sense of self and collective identity in ways that inspired and motivated their academic efforts.

I cannot close this book without directly addressing the claim that racial-ethnic minority counterspaces are divisive spaces. Counterspaces are only divisive spaces to the extent that the culture of the institution presents racial-ethnic minority students with the false choice of identifying with and belonging to the larger institution versus finding their micro-community of local campus belonging. Campus belonging, at least for racial-ethnic minority students, is a fluid process that involves student agency in making dynamic decisions about when they do and do not identify with the larger institution versus their micro-community on campus.[49] When students feel that they do not belong to the larger institution, they take active steps to locate or create localized belonging on campus. For minority students, this may mean going between majority and minority spaces based on needs that are satisfied, neglected, and marginalized in each space.

Counterspaces are not a panacea for increasing Black and Latinx students' college persistence. Institutional, family, and individual differences all played a role in the extent to which students used physical, social, and ideological counterspaces to successfully counter social identity threats and maintain belonging to their communities of origin while also developing a strong sense of belonging on campus. It is also important to moderate expectations that all racial-ethnic minority students will welcome counterspaces as an adaptive coping support, as shown in the preceding chapters. In addition, for too many of the students interviewed, it was clear that although counterspaces were supportive, in the absence of substantial alleviation of financial distress, these students yet risked joining the ranks of those who leave college with debt and no degree. However, even with these caveats, without counterspaces, historically marginalized students are left to their own individual coping resources to navigate a system that is dominated by implicit unwritten cultural and political rules.

As Benjamin Bowser and his colleagues state,

> Universities and colleges as formal organizations and in outward appearances look like fair and equitable organizations. . . . But if we look at universities and colleges as informal organizations with unwritten

> institutional cultures and practices, then [we see that] is where actions are taken or not taken to produce inequities in the use of resources, participation, and influence by race. Through the informal life of an institution, one can maintain historic racial and cultural privileges while professing and giving the appearance of fairness.[50]

By providing historically marginalized students with identity-affirming supports, administrators are institutionalizing mechanisms that simultaneously acknowledge and challenge "sedimented or past-in-present racial formations where unquestioned racial ideologies create understandings that appear to be the natural and inevitable."[51] Counterspaces facilitate radical growth—coming together to first affirm one's marginalized identities so one can then critique deficit and deviant representations of those identities, for the strategic purpose of developing new counternarratives.

Methodological Appendix

Students, their families, and others who have a hand in their college success are prioritized as the audience for this book; therefore, the research methods have largely been rendered invisible to the reader. For those interested in how the data was collected and analyzed, and the validity of the claims made, I offer this brief methodological appendix. In it I discuss the sample, data collection, and methods used to study not just the factors affecting the persistence of Black and Latinx college students, but also their making of meaning along the journey. In addition to the objective aspects of the study, I outline the primary analytic decisions and the collaborative process that led to the findings reported in this book.

The findings presented here emerged from the sequential narrowing of issues discussed in the research literature, news media, and among the cohort of Latinx and Black students interviewed. First, as discussed in the introduction, we zeroed in on college persistence because of the current centrality of obtaining a college degree for the future financial stability of American youth, particularly Black and Latinx Americans. Second, the focus is on Black and Latinx students because the majority of them who enroll in college, taking on substantial loans to do so, won't obtain their degree, making college a high-risk, high-reward venture. Third, issues of academic preparation are backgrounded for three reasons: (1) based on their SAT and ACT scores, the ability of these students to do college-level work is not an issue for the sample recruited, (2) being academically prepared for college is necessary but not sufficient, and (3) we have limited understanding of the nonacademic barriers to graduation. Lastly, how Black and Latinx students' many social identities are marginalized and minoritized on college campuses is foregrounded because it is an often-discussed but under-researched barrier to persistence.

The following process was used to ensure that this collectively authored book was written with one voice. First, all coauthors interviewed participants and/or transcribed interviews and coded transcripts, so all were very familiar with the content of the conversations. Second, two research articles, one on identity and one on counterspaces,[1] and two op-eds, one against and one for campus counterspaces,[2] were read by all coauthors before they began analyzing the data. Third, all coauthors contributed to a collective online mind-mapping of how the framing issues, listed above, related to what participants discussed in their end-of-first-year interview. Fourth, I collaborated with each coauthor to identify the central focus of each chapter. Fifth, each coauthor identified one transcript that illustrated the focal issue to be examined in their chapter, then all coauthors reviewed the full list of focal transcripts to prepare for a two-day retreat. Sixth, during the two-day retreat all coauthors spent one hour collectively discussing each chapter. This was followed by me writing the introductory chapter that outlined the student persistence problem, and the second chapter that framed the centrality of identity for Latinx and Black students attending historically White colleges and universities. Lastly, all coauthors engaged in a collective review of these two chapters before beginning the process of coauthoring each subsequent chapter.

Sample

The Minority College Cohort study included seven waves of survey data collection between September 2013 and October 2017, and four waves of interviews between July 2014 and August 2018. This study tracked a sample of Latinx and Black young adults who graduated from high school and enrolled at historically White universities in the fall of 2013, with high expectations of obtaining at least a bachelor's degree. Of the full sample of 533 participants, on a scale from zero to 100 percent, they averaged a 92 percent confidence that they would obtain their bachelor's degree, and a 78 percent confidence that they would obtain a graduate degree. Based on the final survey, approximately 50 percent had obtained a bachelor's degree within four years of graduating from high school, and an additional 32 percent were still enrolled as full-time students.

Participants were recruited in the fall of their first year of college, approximately two months after the academic year began at their respective schools. Administrators associated with the registrar's office at each university sent two recruitment emails, approximately two weeks apart, containing a description of the research study and a link to the online survey. Across the five universities, the proportion of Black undergraduates ranged from 3 percent to 18 percent, with a mean of 8 percent; the proportion of Latinx undergraduates ranged from 9 percent to 25 percent, with a mean of 16 percent.

The recruitment email was sent to students who met the inclusion criteria: full-time, first-time, first-year students who self-identified on their college application as either African American / Black or Hispanic / Latina / Latino. Approximately 35 percent of participants who responded and consented to participate in the study were enrolled at Urban PublicU, 28 percent at Rural StateU, 24 percent at one of the two Urban PrivateUs, and 13 percent at Suburban StateU. The mean age at recruitment was eighteen years old, and 48 percent of Black and 69 percent of Latinx participants were first-generation college students. Only 25 percent of Black and 43 percent of Latinx participants are men. This is despite extending the enrollment period for men beyond the dates listed in the recruitment emails. As noted in the introduction, this gender gap is reflective of the current gender imbalance in college enrollment in the US.[3]

The recruited sample was 41 percent Black and 59 percent Latinx. Participants were asked to identify their ancestral and/or country of ethnic origin and could select "American," specify something not on the list, or select "none" as their ethnic origin. The ethnic composition of Black participants was 84 percent African American, 6 percent African, 2 percent Caribbean, and 9 percent multiracial. The ethnic composition of Latinx participants was 68 percent Mexican, 8 percent Puerto Rican, 5 percent South American, 2 percent Central American, 2 percent Dominican, 1 percent Cuban, 4 percent Other Latinx, and 9 percent multiracial. Only 8 percent of participants were foreign-born; 25 percent of Black and 81 percent of Latinx participants had at least one foreign-born parent.

Participants graduated from 255 different high schools; over 85 percent were public high schools located in the Chicago metropolitan region. Participants' high schools spanned the full range of student racial-ethnic diversity compositions. Specifically, 24 percent of Latinx and 32 percent of Black participants attended predominantly same-race ethnicity schools (their racial-ethnic group was 70 percent or more of the student body), and 20 percent of Latinx and 10 percent of Black participants attended predominantly White schools (White students were 70 percent or more of the student body).

The Survey

Before we began participant recruitment, we had a collective meeting with at least one administrator from each of the five participating universities. Each administrator had a role in "minority" or "diversity" student support services. This was an important part of establishing the institutional relationships needed to ensure that our recruitment emails would be sent out by each institution's registrar's office. This meeting was also used to review and revise the planned survey and identify additional survey topics. The additional topics that resulted from this meeting focused on financial, academic, emotional help-seeking expectations, actions, and experiences, particularly in relation to seeking support from institutional agents in high school and college. These topics emerged from administrators' discussions about one of their biggest frustrations: students who wait until it is too late to seek support, particularly students who left college because of problems that could have been resolved or minimized had they been more open to seeking and expecting institutional responsiveness to their needs. The survey took about forty-five minutes to complete and also included the following topics:

1. Postsecondary aspirations and expectations
2. Career aspirations and expectations
3. College preparation and planning experiences and supports during high school
4. Social network and social support from family, peers, and other adult mentors
5. Risk-taking behaviors and health and well-being during high school
6. High school curricular and cocurricular experiences and achievements
7. Mental health: anxiety, depression, and stress scales
8. School-based racial and ethnic microaggressions and discrimination scales
9. Racial-ethnic identity scales
10. Civic engagement and political activism scales
11. Romantic relationship experiences
12. Student debt and financial distress

This formed the base survey, with question wording updated at each wave of data collection.

A total of seven waves of survey data were collected: Wave 1 (September to October), Wave 2 (January to February), and Wave 3 (June to July) of participants' first year post-high-school graduation; Wave 4 (September to October) and Wave 5 (June to July) of participants' second year post-high-school graduation; Wave 6 (June to July) of participants' fourth year post-high-school graduation; and Wave 7 (July to September) of participants' fifth year post-high-school graduation. Wave 7 had an extended data collection window to ensure the highest possible final response rate. The response rates for Waves 2 through 6 were above 90 percent, and the final response rate for Wave 7 was 87 percent. This is a high response rate for a five-year longitudinal study that provided only a twenty-five-dollar Amazon.com gift card for each completed survey, increased to thirty-five dollars for the final survey. Though small, the incentive was meaningful for participants, and many emailed a thank you at each wave. When the study was over, one participant emailed that he would remember this study as buying the backpacks that he had through college. During the year in which data collection was paused, participants' third year post-high-school graduation, we sent e-cards for Thanksgiving, Christmas, and Valentine's Day.

After data collection was concluded, many participants emailed that they would miss being asked about their experiences and opinions. At initial recruitment and at each wave of data collection, we framed the need for their participation in ways that centered the importance of including their experiences and voices in the decision making about policies that would affect the students coming behind them. I believe that this contributed to the high response rate. The high response rate was also because a substantial number of the survey questions asked identity-relevant questions and asked not just about their experiences, but also how they felt about those experiences.

After the final wave of data collection, all participants received one final emailed question: "Please tell us about how participating in this study affected your thoughts, feelings, and any other way that participating may have affected you." The primary response was that completing the surveys gave them an opportunity to reflect on their experiences and "brought out good memories and bad memories." The second-most-frequent response was that the surveys were also opportunities to process their emotions about their life experiences: "I distinctly remember exactly how I was feeling each time I filled out the survey. Observing my emotions in retrospect have allowed me to firmly grasp my personal triumphs and tribulations."

The Interviews

A phenomenological framework undergirded the qualitative aspects of this study.[4] Under this framework the researcher identifies the phenomenon to be understood and then seeks to unpack the diversity of experiences associated with that phenomenon. To gain a phenomenological understanding, researchers must first familiarize themselves with each interviewee's experiences of the phenomenon and then their meaning-making about those experiences. We focused on participants' understandings of themselves during the transition to adulthood, and for most this centered on how their college campus experiences mediated their understandings of themselves, their future, and American society as they transitioned to independent adulthood.

Stratified random sampling was used to select the interview subsample. The sample was stratified by race-ethnicity, gender, and financial distress. Because financial factors figure prominently in determining college persistence and it was a substantial issue for most of our participants, the subsample was stratified by low, medium, and high financial distress at the start of college. Financial distress was the average of three survey items: (1) how much difficulty, if any, are you having paying your bills? (2) how upset or worried are you because you do not have enough money to pay for things? and (3) how concerned do your current financial conditions make you about the chances you can afford to complete your college degree?

The stratification by race-ethnicity, gender, and financial distress resulted in twelve mutually exclusive categories (see table 1 below). Random sampling with replacement was used until we reached the quota of six participants for each category. For the initial establishment of the interview subgroup we waited one week after sending the final interview request reminder email before categorizing prospective participants as unresponsive and replacing them with another randomly selected participant. We had substantial difficulty recruiting Black men with moderate and high financial distress into the interview subsample, so we oversampled Black men with low financial distress.

The first interview was completed during July and August of 2014, the first summer after participants enrolled in college. Interviewees were then invited to complete follow-up interviews during July and August of 2015, 2016, and 2018. Each interview lasted one to two hours, and participants received thirty-five dollars for each interview. The first interview was done in person with all but sixteen participants who were not residing within driving distance of Chicago.

The primary goals of the first interview were to (1) obtain retrospective information about their process of deciding to enroll in college, (2) learn about many aspects of their transition and adjustment experiences, (3) explore issues associated with the financial costs of college and understand its role in persistence, and (4) build a trusting connection that would facilitate future interviews, which would be conducted by phone. Given these goals, semi-structured interviews were used. Semi-structured interviews combine the systematization of an ordered set of questions with the flexibility for the interviewer to deviate from the question order and add questions.[5] This is the best method for ensuring that a base set of questions are asked of all interviewees while creating a conversation-like experience and enabling the interviewer to explore unanticipated topics.

TABLE 1 Number of participants interviewed in each stratification category

STRATIFICATION CATEGORY	PARTICIPANTS INTERVIEWED
Black, female, low financial distress	6
Black, female, moderate financial distress	7
Black, female, high financial distress	6
Black, male, low financial distress	9
Black, male, moderate financial distress	5
Black, male, high financial distress	1
Latinx, female, low financial distress	6
Latinx, female, moderate financial distress	6
Latinx, female, high financial distress	6
Latinx, male, low financial distress	6
Latinx, male, moderate financial distress	6
Latinx, male, high financial distress	6

The interview protocol (questions, probes, and transition statements) for the first interview was developed using the following process. First, I drafted the initial protocol based on a very preliminary analysis of the first three waves of survey data. Second, the two postdoctoral co-investigators edited the protocol and added questions based on their research foci (within-racial-ethnic group cultural insults such as being accused of acting White, and engagement in extracurricular, civic, and political activities). Third, the interview protocol was tested with a few undergraduates at my university and then revised. Fourth, once trained, interviewers conducted one to two interviews with study participants and then met to discuss and review the interview protocol.

The interview protocol began with chronological questions about high school experiences, including preparing for and applying to college. We then asked about the transition to college, including managing independence and academic demands; interpersonal interactions with peers, professors, and administrators; and participation in extracurricular activities. The interviews then moved to discussing adjustment issues that would be particularly salient for Black and Latinx students attending historically White colleges and universities, such as racial-ethnic interactions and microaggressions. We also asked broad questions to determine what interviewees perceived to be the most positive and negative aspects of their transition to college. The last major block of questions asked about financial factors, college persistence, and career aspirations. We then closed by asking about advice they would give to college administrators and to other students like themselves.

This interview protocol served as the base protocol for all follow-up interview protocols, with the removal of retrospective questions about high school. The second follow-up interview included questions about racial-ethnic injustice and immigration in America, with a focus on Black Lives Matter and DACA activism. The third follow-up interview included questions that asked participants to detail one personal incident of racial-ethnic stereotyping. The final follow-up interview included questions that asked them to broadly reflect on their life experiences during the five years since graduating from high school. All follow-up interview protocols included branching questions for participants who were not enrolled in school during the preceding six months. The following topics were included for participants not enrolled in school: process of leaving college, current employment and career aspirations, student debt, and aspirations and plans for re-enrolling in college.

A team of Black male and female and Latinx female graduate students and postdoctoral scholars conducted the interviews. Interviewees and interviewers were matched on race-ethnicity and gender, except Latinx male interviewees, who were interviewed by Black male interviewers. As interviewing proceeded, the two co-investigators periodically reviewed interview tapes and provided interviewers with helpful feedback.

The interviews proved to be an invaluable tool in four major ways. First, they provided detailed data on participants' varied experiences and perceptions of those experiences, particularly regarding their campus social interactions and meaning-making about those interactions. Second, the interviews enabled us to examine ambiguous concepts that we asked participants to define for themselves in their answers to the questions. For example, participants were asked to describe how their first year was different from what they expected. Third, interviews provided opportunities for participants to indicate not just whether they had a particular type of experience but also detail a specific story illustrating the experience and their perception of it. For example, participants were asked to tell us about any personally stressful racial-ethnic experiences they had in a given year, and elaborate on what the other person(s) did, what the participant did, and how it made them feel. Lastly, the interviews allowed us to examine the experiential, attitudinal, and perceptual factors underlying quantitative findings from the surveys.

Analysis of Interview Data

Transcribed interviews were coded by a team of trained coders using Dedoose qualitative analysis software. Initial coding focused on identifying broad thematic codes that emerged inductively from the transcripts and deductively based on primary themes used to develop the interview protocol. The thematic codes that would be applied to all transcripts were determined through an iterative process in which all coders individually coded the same set of randomly selected transcripts and then collectively discussed their findings with the aim of identifying a limited set of broad codes.[6] Once an agreed-upon set of codes was established, all interviews were double coded using consensus coding. Once the first randomly assigned coder completed coding the transcript, the second randomly assigned coder reviewed the transcript and flagged coding disagreements. Both coders then met to resolve coding disputes, which could be resolved by agreeing on a single code or agreeing on adding multiples codes to a segment of text. The following thematic codes were applied to all transcripts:

1. College-going support
    a. Support from family
    b. Support from friends
    c. Support from high school teachers and administrators

   d. Support from university professors and administrators
   e. Other support
2. Reasons for going to college
3. First-year transition and adjustment
   a. College adjustment experiences
   b. Campus racial-ethnic interactions
4. Stress
   a. Family stress
   b. Roommate, peer, friend stress
   c. Coping
   d. Other stress
5. Finances
   a. College financial planning and understanding
   b. Financial stress
   c. Work and employment
   d. Other finances
6. Romantic relationships
7. Racial-ethnic and immigration societal and political issues
8. Most positive experience this past year
9. Advice offered to university administrators
10. Advice offered to other students

Each coauthored chapter used the following sequential data analysis process. First, a limited number of the most relevant thematic codes were identified based on the focus on the chapter. Second, all excerpts of each code were examined to determine the associations and patterns that best explain the phenomenon being studied.[7] Third, demographic characteristics of the cases were examined to determine whether the phenomenological associations and patterns were particular to various subgroups.[8]

Rigor, Reliability, and Trustworthiness

I believe that the steps and processes detailed in this methodological appendix resulted in the collection, analysis, interpretation, and presentation of trustworthy findings.[9] Beginning the process with trained interviewers who had completed their own undergraduate experiences only a few years earlier and also matched participants in race-ethnicity and gender (matched by gender for Latinx Men) resulted in conversational interviews and data that was highly contextualized with information about how participants made meaning of their experiences. The process of having the transcripts double coded by eleven coders with varied gender, racial-ethnic and socioeconomic status, and immigrant histories resulted in reliable and valid first-stage thematic coding of the data. The collective process of analyzing and interpreting the coded data for each chapter resulted in a nuanced understanding of the many ways that identity structures Back and Latinx students' transition and adjustment to historically White universities. Lastly, the coauthoring of chapters allowed for thick and rich descriptions that are accurate representations of participants' experiences and their meaning-making of those experiences.

Notes

INTRODUCTION

1. John L. Hoffman and Katie E. Lowitzki, "Predicting College Success with High School Grades and Test Scores: Limitations for Minority Students," *Review of Higher Education* 28, no. 4 (2005): 455–74; Stephen B. Robbins et al., "Do Psychosocial and Study Skill Factors Predict College Outcomes? A Meta-Analysis," *Psychological Bulletin*, 130, no. 2 (2004): 261; Michelle Richardson, Charles Abraham, and Rod Bond, "Psychological Correlates of University Students' Academic Performance: A Systematic Review and Meta-Analysis," *Psychological Bulletin*, 138, no. 2 (2012): 353.

2. Sara Goldrick-Rab, *Paying the Price: College Costs, Financial Aid, and the Betrayal of the American Dream* (Chicago: University of Chicago Press, 2016).

3. John F. Dovidio and Samuel L. Gaertner, "Aversive Racism," *Advances in Experimental Social Psychology* 36 (2004): 1–52.

4. Eduardo Bonilla-Silva, "Rethinking Racism: Toward a Structural Interpretation," *American Sociological Review* 62, no. 3 (1997): 465–80.

5. Robert D. Reason and Nancy J. Evans, "The Complicated Realities of Whiteness: From Color Blind to Racially Cognizant," *New Directions for Student Services*, 120 (2007): 70.

6. Linda M. Alcoff, *Visible Identities: Race, Gender, and the Self* (New York: Oxford University Press, 2005).

7. William A. Smith, Walter R. Allen, and Lynette L. Danley, "'Assume the Position . . . You Fit the Description': Psychosocial Experiences and Racial Battle Fatigue among African American Male College Students," *American Behavioral Scientist* 51, no. 4 (2007): 551–78.

8. Patricia Hill Collins, *Black Sexual Politics: African Americans, Gender, and the New Racism* (New York: Routledge, 2004), 55.

9. Digest of Educational Statistics, "Table 306.40, Fall Enrollment of Males and Females and Specific Racial/Ethnic Groups in Degree-Granting Postsecondary Institutions, by Control and Level of Institution and Percentage of U.S. Resident Enrollment in the Same Racial/Ethnic Group, 2014" (Washington, DC: National Center for Education Statistics, n.d.), https://nces.ed.gov/programs/digest/d15/tables/dt15_306.40.asp.

1. OUTLINING THE PROBLEM

1. Tanya Golash-Boza, "A Critical and Comprehensive Sociological Theory of Race and Racism," *Sociology of Race and Ethnicitynicity* 2, no. 2 (2016): 11.

2. Anthony P. Carnevale and Jeff Strohl, "How Increasing College Access Is Increasing Inequality, and What to Do about It," in *Rewarding Strivers: Helping Low-Income Students Succeed in College*, ed. R. D. Kahlenberg (New York: Century Foundation, 2010), 71–190.

3. US Bureau of Labor Statistics, "Employment Projections: Unemployment Rates and Earnings by Educational Attainment, 2017" (Washington, DC: BLS, March 27, 2018), https://www.bls.gov/emp/ep_chart_001.htm.

4. Digest of Educational Statistics, "Table 104.10: Rates of High School Completion and Bachelor's Degree Attainment among Persons Age 25 and Over, by Race/Ethnicity and

Sex: Selected Years, 1910 through 2015" (Washington, DC: National Center for Education Statistics, n.d.), https://nces.ed.gov/programs/digest/d15/tables/dt15_104.10.asp.

5. Jens Manuel Krogstad and Richard Fry, "More Hispanics, Blacks Enrolling in College but Lag in Bachelor's Degrees (Washington, DC: Pew Research Center, 2014).

6. Digest of Educational Statistics, "Table 326.10: Graduation Rate from First Institution Attended for First-Time, Full-Time Bachelor's Degree-Seeking Students at 4-Year Postsecondary Institutions, by Race/Ethnicity, Time to Completion, Sex, Control of Institution, and Acceptance Rate: Selected Cohort Entry Years, 1996 through 2008" (Washington, DC: National Center for Education Statistics, n.d.).

7. John Wirt et al., "Financing for Postsecondary Education: Debt Burden of College Graduates," in *The Condition of Education 2004* (Washington, DC: National Center for Education Statistics, 2004), section 6, 98.

8. Tracey King and Ellynne Bannon, *The Burden of Borrowing: A Report on the Rising Rates of Student Loan Debt* (Boston: Public Interest Research Group, 2002); College Board, *Trends in Student Aid 2017* (Washington, DC: College Board, 2017).

9. Eric Bettinger, "How Financial Aid Affects Persistence," in *College Choices: The Economics of Where to Go, When to Go, and How to Pay for It*, ed. C. Hoxby (Chicago: University of Chicago Press, 2004), 207–238; Rachel Dwyer, Laura McCloud, and Randy Hodson, "Debt and Graduation from American Universities," *Social Forces* 90, no. 4 (2012): 1133–55; Glenn Waddell and Larry Singell Jr., "Do No-Loan Policies Change the Matriculation Patterns of Low-Income Students?," *Economics of Education Review* 30, no. 2 (2011): 203–14.

10. John E. Grable and So-Hyun Joo, "Student Racial Differences in Credit Card Debt and Financial Behaviors and Stress," *College Student Journal* 40, no. 2 (2006): 400–408.

11. Lawrence Gladieux and Laura Perna, *Borrowers Who Drop Out: A Neglected Aspect of the College Student Loan Trend* (San Jose, CA: National Center for Public Policy and Higher Education, 2005); Sara Goldrick-Rab, Robert Kelchen, and Jason Houle, *The Color of Student Debt: Implications of Federal Loan Program Reforms for Black Students and Historically Black Colleges and Universities* (Madison: Hope Lab, University of Wisconsin–Madison, 2014); Jacob P. K. Gross et al., "What Matters in Student Loan Default: A Review of the Research Literature," *Journal of Student Financial Aid* 39, no. 1 (2009): 19–29; Caroline Ratcliffe and Signe Mary McKernan, *Forever in Your Debt: Who Has Student Loan Debt, and Who's Worried?* (Washington, DC: Urban Institute, 2013).

12. James E. Rosenbaum, Shazia Rafiullah Miller, and Melinda Scott Krei, "Gatekeeping in an Era of More Open Gates: High School Counselors' Views of Their Influence on Students' College Plans," *American Journal of Education* 104, no. 4 (1996): 257–79.

13. Margaret Cahalan and Laura Perna, *Indicators of Higher Education Equity in the United States: 45-Year Trend Report* (Washington, DC: Pell Institute for the Study of Opportunity in Education, 2015).

14. Deborah Hirsch, "Access to a College Degree or Just College Debt? Moving beyond Admission to Graduation," *New England Journal of Higher Education* 23, no. 2 (2008): 17–18; James E. Rosenbaum, "The Complexities of College for All: Beyond Fairy-Tale Dreams," *Sociology of Education* 84, no. 2 (2011): 113–17.

15. Mark Huelsman, *The Debt Divide: The Racial and Class Bias behind the "New Normal" of Student Borrowing* (New York: Demos, 2015).

16. Karen K. Inkelas et al., "Living-Learning Programs and First-Generation College Students' Academic and Social Transition to College," *Research in Higher Education* 48, no. 4 (2007): 403–34; Laura I. Rendon, "Validating Culturally Diverse Students: Toward a New Model of Learning and Student Development," *Innovative Higher Education* 19, no. 1 (1994): 33–51.

17. William G. Bowen and Derek Bok, *The Shape of the River: Long-Term Consequences of Considering Race in College and University Admissions* (Princeton, NJ: Princeton University Press, 2016); Douglas Massey et al., *The Source of the River: The Social Origins of Freshmen at America's Selective Colleges and Universities* (Princeton, NJ: Princeton University Press, 2011).

18. Maria Ong, Janet M. Smith, and Lily T. Ko, "Counterspaces for Women of Color in STEM Higher Education: Marginal and Central Spaces for Persistence and Success," *Journal of Research in Science Teaching* 55, no. 2 (2018): 206–45.

19. Valerie Purdie-Vaughns et al., "Social Identity Contingencies: How Diversity Cues Signal Threat or Safety for African Americans in Mainstream Institutions," *Journal of Personality and Social Psychology* 94, no. 4 (2008): 615; Nicole Watkins, Theressa L. LaBarrie, and Lauren M. Appio, "Black Undergraduates' Experience with Perceived Racial Microaggressions in Predominantly White Colleges and Universities," in *Microaggressions and Marginality: Manifestation, Dynamics, and Impact*, ed. D. W. Sue (Hoboken, NJ: John Wiley & Sons, 2010), 25–58.

20. Anne-Marie Núñez, "Counterspaces and Connections in College Transitions: First-Generation Latino Students' Perspectives on Chicano Studies," *Journal of College Student Development* 52, no. 6 (2011): 639–55; Tara Yosso and Corina B. Lopez, "Counterspaces in a Hostile Place," in *Culture Centers in Higher Education: Perspectives on Identity, Theory, and Practice*, ed. L. D. Patton (Sterling, VA: Stylus, 2010), 83–104; Annemarie Vaccaro and Melissa J. Camba-Kelsay, *Centering Women of Color in Academic Counterspaces: A Critical Race Analysis of Teaching, Learning, and Classroom Dynamics* (Lanham, MD: Rowman & Littlefield, 2016).

21. Deborah F. Carter, Angela Mosi Locks, and Rachelle Winkle-Wagner, "From When and Where I Enter: Theoretical and Empirical Considerations of Minority Students' Transition to College," in *Higher Education: Handbook of Theory and Research*, ed. M. B. Paulsen (Dordrecht, Netherlands: Springer, 2013), 93–149; Sean F. Reardon, Joseph P. Robinson, and Ericka S. Weathers, "Patterns and Trends in Racial/Ethnic and Socioeconomic Academic Achievement Gaps," in *Handbook of Research in Education Finance and Policy*, 2nd ed., ed. H. A. Ladd and E. B. Fiske (New York: Lawrence Erlbaum, 2012), 497–516.

22. Vijay Pendakur, *Closing the Opportunity Gap: Identity-Conscious Strategies for Retention and Student Success* (Sterling, VA: Stylus, 2016), 6.

23. Mary J. Fischer, "Settling into Campus Life: Differences by Race/Ethnicity in College Involvement and Outcomes," *Journal of Higher Education* 78, no. 2. (2007): 125–61.

24. Basil Bernstein, *Class Codes and Control: Theoretical Studies towards a Sociology of Language*, 2nd ed. (New York: Schocken Books, 1974); Pierre Bourdieu and Jean-Claude Passeron, *Reproduction in Education, Society and Culture* (London: Sage, 1990).

25. Nicole M. Stephens et al., "Unseen Disadvantage: How American Universities' Focus on Independence Undermines the Academic Performance of First-Generation College Students," *Journal of Personality and Social Psychology* 102, no. 6 (2012): 1178–97.

26. Ibid.

27. Arthur M. Schlesinger, *The Disuniting of America: Reflections on a Multicultural Society* (New York: W. W. Norton, 1998).

28. Alcoff, *Visible Identities*.

29. Ludger Pries, "Ambiguities of Global and Transnational Collective Identities," *Global Networks* 13, no. 1 (2013): 22–40.

30. Alcoff, *Visible Identities*, 36.

31. Derald W. Sue et al., "Racial Microaggressions in Everyday Life: Implications for Clinical Practice," *American Psychologist* 62, no. 4 (2007): 271–86; Micere Keels, Myles Durkee, and Elan Hope, "The Psychological and Academic Costs of School-Based Racial and Ethnic Microaggressions," *American Educational Research Journal* 54, no. 6 (2017): 1316–44.

32. Mary J. Fischer, "Does Campus Diversity Promote Friendship Diversity? A Look at Interracial Friendships in College," *Social Science Quarterly* 89, no. 3 (2008): 631–55.

33. Ray Black and Albert Y. Bimper Jr., "Successful Undergraduate African American Men's Navigation and Negotiation of Academic and Social Counter-Spaces as Adaptation to Racism at Historically White Institutions," *Journal of College Student Retention: Research, Theory & Practice* 0, no. 0 (2017): 1–25.

34. Alison Cook-Sather, "Creating Brave Spaces within and through Student-Faculty Pedagogical Partnerships," *Teaching and Learning Together in Higher Education* 1, no. 18 (2016): 1–5.

35. Andrew D. Case and Carla D. Hunter, "Counterspaces: A Unit of Analysis for Understanding the Role of Settings in Marginalized Individuals' Adaptive Responses to Oppression," *American Journal of Community Psychology* 50, nos. 1–2 (2012): 267.

36. Andrew D. Case and Carla D. Hunter, "Counterspaces and the Narrative Identity Work of Offender-Labeled African American Youth," *Journal of Community Psychology* 42, no. 8 (2014): 907–23.

37. Na'ilah Nasir, *Racialized Identities: Race and Achievement among African American Youth* (Stanford, CA: Stanford University Press, 2011).

38. Beverly D. Tatum, *Why Are All the Black Kids Sitting Together in the Cafeteria? And Other Conversations about Race* (New York: Basic Books, 2017).

39. Daniel Solórzano, Miguel Ceja, and Tara Yosso, "Critical Race Theory, Racial Microaggressions, and Campus Racial Climate: The Experiences of African American College Students," *Journal of Negro Education* 69, nos. 1–2 (2000): 60–73.

40. Richard Delgado and Jean Stefancic, *Critical Race Theory: An Introduction*, 2nd ed. (New York: NYU Press, 2012); Daniel Solórzano and Tara Yosso, "Critical Race Methodology: Counter-Storytelling as an Analytical Framework for Education Research," *Qualitative Inquiry* 8, no. 1 (2002): 23–44.

41. Kristen Renn, "Creating and Re-creating Race: The Emergence of Racial Identity as a Critical Element in Psychological, Sociological, and Ecological Perspectives on Human Development," in *New Perspectives on Racial Identity Development: Integrating Emerging Frameworks*, ed. C. L. Wijeyesinghe and B. W. Jackson (New York: NYU Press, 2012), 11–32.

42. Delgado and Stefancic, *Critical Race Theory*; Berta E. Hernandez-Truyol, "Borders (En)gendered: Normativities, Latinas and a LatCrit Paradigm," *New York University Law Review* 72 (1997): 882–927.

43. Octavio Villalpando, "Practical Considerations of Critical Race Theory and Latino Critical Theory for Latino College Students," *New Directions for Student Services* 105 (2004): 41–50; Francisco Valdes, "Latina/o Ethnicities, Critical Race Theory, and Post-Identity Politics in Postmodern Legal Culture: From Practices to Possibilities," *La Raza Law Journal* 9, no. 1 (1996): 1–31.

44. Lisa Bowleg, "When Black + Lesbian + Woman ≠ Black Lesbian Woman: The Methodological Challenges of Qualitative and Quantitative Intersectionality Research," *Sex Roles* 59, no. 5–6 (2008): 312–25; Kimberle Crenshaw, "Mapping the Margins: Intersectionality, Identity Politics, and Violence against Women of Color," *Stanford Law Review* 43, no. 6 (1991): 1241–99.

45. Chimamanda N. Adichie, "The Danger of a Single Story," TED talk, October 2009.

46. Representative of the Illinois student population, the sample includes significantly more Latinx than Black students (59 percent Latinx vs. 41 percent Black). The sample is also indicative of the dire national gender gap in minority student enrollment and includes significantly more female than male students (64 percent women vs. 36 percent men). Approximately 69 percent of students lived in campus housing, and 26 percent lived with their parents. Students' housing status heavily depended on the institution attended; more than 90 percent of those attending the rural colleges lived in campus housing, compared

to about 50 percent of those attending the urban colleges. Only 9 percent of the sample is foreign born (10 percent of Latino and 7 percent of Black students). Of this 9 percent, only 20 percent came to the United States after age ten, and only four students came after the age of eighteen.

2. THE IMPOSSIBILITY OF A COLOR-BLIND IDENTITY

1. Erik H. Erikson, *Identity: Youth and Crisis* (New York: W. W. Norton, 1994).

2. Sheldon Stryker and Peter J. Burke, "The Past, Present, and Future of an Identity Theory," *Social Psychology Quarterly* 63, no. 4 (2000): 284–97.

3. Henri Tajfel and John Turner, "An Integrative Theory of Intergroup Conflict," *Social Psychology of Intergroup Relations* 33, no. 47 (1979): 56–65.

4. Karolyn Tyson, ed., *Integration Interrupted: Tracking, Black Students, and Acting White after Brown* (New York: Oxford University Press, 2011).

5. Randall Kennedy, "Lifting as We Climb: A Progressive Defense of Respectability Politics," *Harper's Magazine*, October 2015; Ta-Nehisi Coates, "Charles Barkley and the Plague of 'Unintelligent' Blacks," *Atlantic*, October 2014.

6. Keels, Durkee, and Hope, "Psychological and Academic Costs," 1316–44.

7. Myles Durkee and Joanna L. Williams, "Accusations of Acting White: Links to Black Students' Racial Identity and Mental Health," *Journal of Black Psychology* 41, no. 1 (2015): 26–48.

8. Toon Kuppens and Russell Spears, "You Don't Have to Be Well-Educated to Be an Aversive Racist, but It Helps," *Social Science Research* 45 (2014): 211–23.

9. Ibid., 221.

10. Derald W. Sue, *Overcoming Our Racism: The Journey to Liberation* (San Francisco: Jossey-Bass, 2003); I. M. Young, *Justice and the Politics of Difference* (Princeton, NJ: Princeton University Press, 1990).

11. James J. Scheurich and Michelle D. Young, "White Racism among White Faculty: From Critical Understanding to Antiracist Activism," in *The Racial Crisis in American Higher Education: Continuing Challenges for the Twenty-First Century*, ed. W. A. Smith, P. G. Altbach, and K. Lomotey (New York: SUNY Press, 2002), 221–42.

12. Vincent L. Hutchings, "Change or More of the Same? Evaluating Racial Attitudes in the Obama Era," *Public Opinion Quarterly* 73, no 5 (2009): 917–42; Eric D. Knowles, Brian S. Lowery, and Rebecca L. Schaumberg, "Racial Prejudice Predicts Opposition to Obama and His Health Care Reform Plan," *Journal of Experimental Social Psychology* 46, no. 2 (2010): 420–23.

13. Margaret B. Spencer and Carol Markstrom-Adams, "Identity Processes among Racial and Ethnic Minority Children in America," *Child Development* 61, no. 2 (1990): 290–310.

14. Eduardo Bonilla-Silva, "More Than Prejudice: Restatement, Reflections, and New Directions in Critical Race Theory," *Sociology of Race and Ethnicity* 1, no. 1 (2015): 73–87; Karim Murji and John Solomos, *Racialization: Studies in Theory and Practice* (New York: Oxford University Press, 2005).

15. Based on an analysis of IPEDS data for 1980 and 2014, for degree-granting four-year public and private institutions; examining enrollment of full-time freshmen.

16. Dorinda J. Carter, "Why the Black Kids Sit Together at the Stairs: The Role of Identity-Affirming Counter-Spaces in a Predominantly White High School," *Journal of Negro Education* 76, no. 4 (2007): 542–54; Purdie-Vaughns et al., "Social Identity Contingencies," 615.

17. Carter, Locks, and Winkle-Wagner, "From When and Where I Enter."

18. Tatum, *Why Are All the Black Kids Sitting Together?*, 62

19. Massey et al., *Source of the River*.

20. Sharon Fries-Britt and Kimberly Griffin, "The Black Box: How High-Achieving Blacks Resist Stereotypes about Black Americans," *Journal of College Student Development* 48, no. 5 (2007): 509–24.

21. David C. Haak et al., "Increased Structure and Active Learning Reduce the Achievement Gap in Introductory Biology," *Science*, 332, no. 6034 (2011): 1213–16; Lars Ulriksen, Lene M. Madsen, and Henriette T. Holmegaard, "What Do We Know about Explanations for Drop Out / Opt Out among Young People from STM Higher Education Programmes?," *Studies in Science Education* 46, no. 2 (2010): 209–44.

22. Josephine A. Gasiewski et al., "From Gatekeeping to Engagement: A Multicontextual, Mixed Method Study of Student Academic Engagement in Introductory STEM Courses," *Research in Higher Education* 53, no. 2 (2012): 229–61.

23. Karen K. Inkelas et al., "Differences in Student Outcomes by Types of Living-Learning Programs: The Development of an Empirical Typology," *Research in Higher Education* 49, no. 6 (2008): 495–512.

24. Nasir, *Racialized Identities.*

25. Beber Ravji, Resolution draft on university residence housing. Sponsored by Culture and Minority Student Affairs Illinois Student Senate Resolution (11–03–2008–01), November 2008.

26. Tatum, *Why Are All the Black Kids Sitting Together?*, 62.

27. Ibid.

28. Carter, "Why the Black Kids Sit Together."

29. Václav Linkov, "Tokenism in Psychology: Standing on the Shoulders of Small Boys," *Integrative Psychological and Behavioral Science* 48, no. 2 (2014): 143–4.

30. Kelly Danaher and Nyla R. Branscombe, "Maintaining the System with Tokenism: Bolstering Individual Mobility Beliefs and Identification with a Discriminatory Organization," *British Journal of Social Psychology* 49, no. 2 (2010): 343–62.

31. Purdie-Vaughns et al., "Social Identity Contingencies."

32. Kevin O. Cokley, "Testing Cross's Revised Racial Identity Model: An Examination of the Relationship between Racial Identity and Internalized Racialism," *Journal of Counseling Psychology* 49, no. 4 (2002): 476–83.

33. Patricia Gurin et al., "Diversity and Higher Education: Theory and Impact on Educational Outcomes," *Harvard Educational Review* 72, no. 3 (2002): 330–67.

34. Jane Fried, "Multicultural Identities and Shifting Selves among College Students," in *Multiculturalism on Campus: Theory, Models, and Practices for Understanding Diversity and Creating Inclusion*, ed. M. Cuyjet et al. (Sterling, VA: Stylus, 2011), 65–83.

35. Sylvia Hurtado et al., "Enhancing Campus Climates for Racial/Ethnic Diversity: Educational Policy and Practice," *Review of Higher Education* 21, no. 3 (1998): 279–302; Vincent Tinto, "Building Community," *Liberal Education* 79, no. 4 (1993): 16–21.

36. Peter Auer, ed., *Code-Switching in Conversation: Language, Interaction and Identity* (New York: Routledge, 2013); Anna De Fina, "Code-Switching and the Construction of Ethnic Identity in a Community of Practice," *Language in Society* 36, no. 3 (2007): 371–92.

37. Fried, "Multicultural Identities and Shifting Selves," 65–83.

3. AN AMBIVALENT EMBRACE

1. Elizabeth Lee, *Class and Campus Life: Managing and Experiencing Inequality at an Elite College* (Ithaca, NY: Cornell University Press, 2016).

2. Regina Deil-Amen, "The 'Traditional' College Student: A Smaller and Smaller Minority and Its Implications for Diversity and Access Institutions," paper prepared for the conference Mapping Broad-Access Higher Education, Stanford University, November 2011, 15.

3. Kimberly A. Goyette, "College for Some to College for All: Social Background, Occupational Expectations, and Educational Expectations over Time," *Social Science Research* 37, no. 2 (2008): 461–84.

4. Donald E. Heller and Kimberly R. Rogers, "Shifting the Burden: Public and Private Financing of Higher Education in the United States and Implications for Europe," *Tertiary Education & Management* 12, no. 2 (2006): 91–117.

5. Sandy Baum et al., "Trends in College Pricing, 2014." *Trends in Higher Education Series* (New York: College Board, 2014); Tracey King and Ellyne Bannon, *At What Cost? The Price That Working Students Pay for a College Education* (Washington, DC: United States Public Interest Research Group, 2002); Wirt et al., "Financing for Postsecondary Education."

6. Carnevale and Strohl, "How Increasing College Access Is Increasing Inequality."

7. Micere Keels et al., *Financial Distress at the Start of College*, Minority College Cohort Study policy report (Chicago: University of Chicago, 2015).

8. Louise Archer and Merryn Hutchings, "'Bettering Yourself'? Discourses of Risk, Cost and Benefit in Ethnically Diverse, Young Working-Class Non-participants' Constructions of Higher Education," *British Journal of Sociology of Education* 21, no. 4 (2000): 555–74; Amaury Nora, Libby Barlow, and Gloria Crisp, "Examining the Tangible and Psychosocial Benefits of Financial Aid with Student Access, Engagement, and Degree Attainment," *American Behavioral Scientist* 49, no. 12 (2006): 1636–51; Edward P. St. John, Shouping Hu, and Tina Tuttle, "Persistence by Undergraduates in an Urban Public University: Understanding the Effects of Financial Aid," *Journal of Student Financial Aid* 30, no. 2 (2000): 23–37.

9. Alberto F. Cabrera, Amaury Nora, and Maria B. Castaneda, "The Role of Finances in the Persistence Process: A Structural Model," *Research in Higher Education* 33, no. 5 (1992): 571–93; Jenny M. Stuber, *Inside the College Gates: How Class and Culture Matter in Higher Education* (Lanham, MD: Lexington Books, 2011).

10. Mark Kantrowitz, "Why the Student Loan Crisis Is Even Worse Than People Think," *Time*, January 11, 2016; Selena Simmons-Duffin, "For Millions of Millennials, Some College, No Degree, Lots of Debt," National Public Radio, November 19, 2014; Susan Tompor, "College Students' Nightmare: Loan Debt and No Degree," *USA Today*, June 7, 2015.

11. Manfred Wallenborn and Stephen P. Heyneman, "Should Vocational Education Be Part of Secondary Education?," *Journal of Educational Change* 10, no. 4 (2009): 405–13.

12. Steve Lohr, "A New Kind of Tech Job Emphasizes Skills, Not a College Degree," *New York Times*, June 28, 2017.

13. Jennie E. Brand and Yu Xie, "Who Benefits Most from College? Evidence for Negative Selection in Heterogeneous Economic Returns to Higher Education," *American Sociological Review* 75, no. 2 (2010): 273–302.

14. Haley Glatter, "College Is Still the Promised Land for High School Students," *Atlantic*, September 13, 2016; Goldrick-Rab, *Paying the Price.*

15. Jeffrey J. Arnett, "Emerging Adulthood: A Theory of Development from the Late Teens through the Twenties," *American Psychologist* 55, no. 5 (2000): 469–80.

16. Mesmin Destin and Daphna Oyserman, "From Assets to School Outcomes: How Finances Shape Children's Perceived Possibilities and Intentions," *Psychological Science* 20, no. 4 (2009): 417.

17. Dwyer, McCloud, and Hodson, "Debt and Graduation from American Universities."

18. Bettinger, "How Financial Aid Affects Persistence."

19. Joe Cuseo, "Fiscal Benefits of Student Retention and First-Year Retention Initiatives" (Athens: Ohio University, 2010).

20. Gail MarksJarvis, Working during College Doesn't Always Pay, Study Says," *Chicago Tribune*, October 29, 2015.

21. Alicia C. Dowd, "Dynamic Interactions and Intersubjectivity: Challenges to Causal Modeling in Studies of College Student Debt," *Review of Educational Research* 78, no. 2 (2008): 250–51.

22. Deborah M. Warnock and A. L. Hurst, "'The Poor Kids' Table': Organizing around an Invisible and Stigmatized Identity in Flux," *Journal of Diversity in Higher Education* 9, no. 3 (2016): 261–76.

23. Ibid., 271.

4. STRATEGIC DISENGAGEMENT

1. George D. Kuh et al., "Unmasking the Effects of Student Engagement on First-Year College Grades and Persistence," *Journal of Higher Education* 79, no. 5 (2008): 540–63; Vincent Tinto, *Leaving College: Rethinking the Causes and Cures of Student Attrition*, 2nd ed. (Chicago: University of Chicago Press, 1993).

2. Leslie Hausmann, Janet Ward Schofield, and Rochelle L. Woods, "Sense of Belonging as a Predictor of Intentions to Persist among African American and White First-Year College Students," *Research in Higher Education* 48, no. 7 (2007): 803–39.

3. Keels, Durkee, and Hope, "Psychological and Academic Costs"; Jioni A. Lewis et al., "Coping with Gendered Racial Microaggressions among Black Women College Students," *Journal of African American Studies* 17, no. 1 (2013): 51–73; Janice McCabe, "Racial and Gender Microaggressions on a Predominantly-White Campus: Experiences of Black, Latina/o and White Undergraduates," *Race, Gender & Class* 16, nos. 1–2 (2009): 133–51.

4. Elijah Anderson, *The Cosmopolitan Canopy: Race and Civility in Everyday Life* (New York: W. W. Norton, 2011), 33.

5. Research confirms that this emotional support that first-generation students receive is pivotal to their college success. See Douglas Guiffrida, "To Break Away or Strengthen Ties to Home: A Complex Issue for African American College Students Attending a Predominantly White Institution," *Equity & Excellence in Education* 38, no. 1 (2005): 56.

6. Patricia Hill Collins, *Black Feminist Thought: Knowledge, Consciousness, and the Politics of Empowerment* (New York: Routledge, 2002).

7. Joanna L. Williams and Tanya M. Nichols, "Black Women's Experiences with Racial Microaggressions in College: Making Meaning at the Crossroads of Race and Gender," in *Black Female Undergraduates on Campus: Successes and Challenges*, ed. C. Chambers and R. Sharpe (Bingley, UK: Emerald Group, 2012), 75–95.

8. Kimberlé Crenshaw, "Mapping the Margins: Intersectionality, Identity Politics, and Violence against Women of Color," *Stanford Law Review* 43, no. 6 (1991): 1241–99.

9. Collins, *Black Feminist Thought.*

10. Ibid.

11. Keels, Durkee, and Hope, "Psychological and Academic Costs"; Derald W. Sue, ed., *Microaggressions and Marginality: Manifestation, Dynamics, and Impact* (Hoboken, NJ: Wiley, 2010).

12. Rachelle Winkle-Wagner, *The Unchosen Me: Race, Gender, and Identity among Black Women in College* (Baltimore: Johns Hopkins University Press, 2010).

13. Anne W. Rawls, "'Race' as an Interaction Order Phenomenon: W. E. B. Du Bois's 'Double Consciousness' Thesis Revisited," *Sociological Theory* 18, no. 2 (2000): 241–74.

14. Tamara Towles-Schwen and Russell H. Fazio, "Automatically Activated Racial Attitudes as Predictors of the Success of Interracial Roommate Relationships," *Journal of Experimental Social Psychology* 42, no. 5 (2006): 698–705.

15. Kimberlé Crenshaw, "The Urgency of Intersectionality," TED talk, October 2016.

16. Lewis et al., "Coping with Gendered Racial Microaggressions."

17. Dawn M. Szymanski and Jioni A. Lewis, "Gendered Racism, Coping, Identity Centrality, and African American College Women's Psychological Distress," *Psychology of Women Quarterly* 40, no. 2 (2016): 229–43.

18. Lori D. Patton, ed., *Culture Centers in Higher Education: Perspectives on Identity, Theory, and Practice* (Sterling, VA: Stylus, 2010).

19. Case and Hunter, "Counterspaces: A Unit of Analysis."

20. Susan R. Jones and Marylu K. McEwen, "A Conceptual Model of Multiple Dimensions of Identity," *Journal of College Student Development* 41, no. 4 (2000): 405–14; Christa J. Porter and Laura A. Dean, "Making Meaning: Identity Development of Black Undergraduate Women," *NASPA Journal about Women in Higher Education* 8, no. 2 (2015): 125–39.

5. POWER IN THE MIDST OF POWERLESSNESS

1. Robert A. Rhoads, *Freedom's Web: Student Activism in an Age of Cultural Diversity* (Baltimore: Johns Hopkins University Press, 1998).

2. Heather Malin, Parissa J. Ballard, and William Damon, "Civic Purpose: An Integrated Construct for Understanding Civic Development in Adolescence," *Human Development* 58, no. 2 (2015): 103–30.

3. Roderick Watts and Omar Guessous, "Sociopolitical Development: The Missing Link in Research and Policy on Adolescents," in *Beyond Resistance! Youth Activism and Community Change: New Democratic Possibilities for Practice and Policy for America's Youth*, ed. S. Ginwright, P. Noguera, and J. Cammarota (New York: Routledge, 2006), 59–80.

4. Case and Hunter, "Counterspaces: A Unit of Analysis."

5. Christopher Morphew and Matthew Hartley, "Mission Statements: A Thematic Analysis of Rhetoric across Institution Type," *Journal of Higher Education* 77 (2006): 456–71.

6. Nithya Muthuswamy, Timothy R. Levine, and Jeanne Gazel, "Interaction-Based Diversity Initiative Outcomes: An Evaluation of an Initiative Aimed at Bridging the Racial Divide on a College Campus," *Communication Education* 55, no. 1 (2006): 105–21; Nida Denson, "Do Curricular and Cocurricular Diversity Activities Influence Racial Bias? A Meta-analysis," *Review of Educational Research* 79, no. 2 (2009): 805–38.

7. Elan Hope and Margaret B. Spencer, "Civic Engagement as an Adaptive Coping Response to Conditions of Inequality: An Application of Phenomenological Variant of Ecological Systems Theory (PVEST)," in *Handbook of Positive Development of Minority Children*, ed. N. Cabrera and B. Leyendecker (New York: Springer, 2017), 421–35.

8. Sebastián Valenzuela, "Unpacking the Use of Social Media for Protest Behavior: The Roles of Information, Opinion Expression, and Activism," *American Behavioral Scientist*, 57, no. 7 (2013): 920–42.

9. Erikson, *Identity*.

10. Jennifer L. Petriglieri, "Under Threat: Responses to and the Consequences of Threats to Individuals' Identities," *Academy of Management Review* 36, no. 4 (2011): 641–62.

11. Nick Crossley and Joseph Ibrahim, "Critical Mass, Social Networks and Collective Action: Exploring Student Political Worlds," *Sociology* 46, no. 4 (2012): 46.

12. Case and Hunter, "Counterspaces: A Unit of Analysis"; Douglas A. Guiffrida, "African American Student Organizations as Agents of Social Integration," *Journal of College Student Development* 44, no. 3 (2003): 304–19; Shaun R. Harper and Stephen J. Quaye, "Student Organizations as Venues for Black Identity Expression and Development among African American Male Student Leaders," *Journal of College Student Development* 48, no. 2 (2007): 127–44.

13. Joy A. Williamson, "In Defense of Themselves: The Black Student Struggle for Success and Recognition at Predominantly White Colleges and Universities," *Journal of Negro Education* 68, no. 1 (1999): 92–105; Yosso and Lopez, "Counterspaces in a Hostile Place."

14. Garrett D. Hoffman and Tania D. Mitchell, "Making Diversity 'Everyone's Business': A Discourse Analysis of Institutional Responses to Student Activism for Equity and Inclusion," *Journal of Diversity in Higher Education* 9, no. 3 (2016): 278.

15. Watts and Guessous, "Sociopolitical Development."

16. Robert Sellers et al., "The Multidimensional Model of Racial Identity: A Reconceptualization of African American Racial Identity," *Personality and Social Psychology Review* 2, no. 1 (1998): 18–39.

17. Tabbye M. Chavous, "The Relationships among Racial Identity, Perceived Ethnic Fit, and Organization Involvement for African American Students at a Predominately White University," *Journal of Black Psychology* 26, no. 1 (2000): 79–100.

18. Elan C. Hope, Kristen N. Pender, and Kristen N. Riddick, "Measuring Youth Proclivity for Social Action in the Black Community: Development and Validation of the Black Community Activism Orientation Scale (BCAOS)," under review.

19. Ibid.

20. Elan C. Hope, Micere Keels, and Myles I. Durkee, "Participation in Black Lives Matters and Deferred Action for Childhood Arrivals: Modern Activism among Black and Latino College Students," *Journal of Diversity in Higher Education* 9, no. 3 (2016): 203–15.

21. Morphew and Hartley, "Mission Statements."

6. IMPORTANCE OF A CRITICAL MASS

1. Timothy D. Pippert, Laura J. Essenburg, and Edward J. Matchett, "We've Got Minorities, Yes We Do: Visual Representations of Racial and Ethnic Diversity in College Recruitment Materials," *Journal of Marketing for Higher Education* 23, no. 2 (2013): 258–82.

2. Shaun R. Harper and Sylvia Hurtado, "Nine Themes in Campus Racial Climates and Implications for Institutional Transformation," in *Responding to the Realities of Race on Campus: New Directions for Student Services*, vol. 120, ed. S. R. Harper and L. D. Patton (San Francisco: Jossey-Bass, 2007), 7–24; Gary R. Pike and George D. Kuh, "Relationships among Structural Diversity, Informal Peer Interactions and Perceptions of the Campus Environment," *Review of Higher Education* 29, no. 4 (2006): 445.

3. Case and Hunter, "Counterspaces: A Unit of Analysis"; Yosso and Lopez, "Counterspaces in a Hostile Place."

4. Meera Komarraju, Sergey Musulkin, and Gargi Bhattacharya, "Role of Student-Faculty Interactions in Developing College Students' Academic Self-Concept, Motivation, and Achievement," *Journal of College Student Development* 51, no. 3 (2010): 332–42.

5. Mary F. Howard-Hamilton, Rosemary E. Phelps, and Vasti Torres, "Meeting the Needs of All Students and Staff Members: The Challenge of Diversity," *New Directions for Student Services*, no. 82 (1998): 49–64.

6. Barbara Read, Louise Archer, and Carole Leathwood, "Challenging Cultures? Student Conceptions of Belonging and Isolation at a Post-1992 University," *Studies in Higher Education* 28, no. 3 (2003): 261–77.

7. Nasir, *Racialized Identities.*

8. Denson, "Do Curricular and Cocurricular Diversity Activities Influence Racial Bias?," 824; Nida Denson and Mitchell Chang, "Racial Diversity Matters: The Impact of Diversity-Related Student Engagement and Institutional Context," *American Educational Research Journal* 46, no. 2 (2009): 322–353.

9. Pike and Kuh, "Relationships among Structural Diversity."

10. Carter, Locks, and Winkle-Wagner, "From When and Where I Enter"; Laura Perna, "The Key to College Access: Rigorous Academic Preparation," in *Preparing for College:*

Nine Elements of Effective Outreach, ed. W. G. Tierney, Z. B. Corwin, and J. E. Colyar (New York: SUNY Press, 2005), 113–34.

11. Sharon L. Fries-Britt and Bridget Turner, "Facing Stereotypes: A Case Study of Black Students on a White Campus," *Journal of College Student Development* 42, no. 5 (2001): 420–29.

12. Monica Biernat and Diane Kobrynowicz, "Gender-and Race-Based Standards of Competence: Lower Minimum Standards but Higher Ability Standards for Devalued Groups," *Journal of Personality and Social Psychology* 72, no. 3 (1997): 544.

13. Ibid., 555.

14. Mary J. Fischer, "A Longitudinal Examination of the Role of Stereotype Threat and Racial Climate on College Outcomes for Minorities at Elite Institutions," *Social Psychology of Education* 13, no. 1 (2010): 19–40.

15. Komarraju, Musulkin, and Bhattacharya, "Role of Student-Faculty Interactions"; Patrick O'Keeffe, "A Sense of Belonging: Improving Student Retention," *College Student Journal* 47, no. 4 (2013): 605–13; Nicholas A. Bowman, "The Development of Psychological Well-Being among First-Year College Students," *Journal of College Student Development* 51, no. 2 (2010): 180–200.

16. Gregory C. Wolniak and Mark E. Engberg, "Academic Achievement in the First Year of College: Evidence of the Pervasive Effects of the High School Context," *Research in Higher Education* 51, no. 5 (2010): 451–67.

17. Germine H. Awad, "The Role of Racial Identity, Academic Self-Concept, and Self-Esteem in the Prediction of Academic Outcomes for African American Students," *Journal of Black Psychology* 33, no. 2 (2007): 188–207.

18. Roderick J. Watts, Matthew A. Diemer, and Adam M. Voight, "Critical Consciousness: Current Status and Future Directions," *New Directions for Child and Adolescent Development*, no. 134 (2011): 43–57.

19. Catherine Campbell and Catherine MacPhail, "Peer Education, Gender and the Development of Critical Consciousness: Participatory HIV Prevention by South African Youth," *Social Science & Medicine* 55 (2002): 331–45.

20. Marlene Berg, Emil Coman, and Jean J. Schensul, "Youth Action Research for Prevention: A Multi-level Intervention Designed to Increase Efficacy and Empowerment among Urban Youth," *American Journal of Community Psychology* 43, nos. 3–4 (2009): 345–59; Campbell and MacPhail, "Peer Education."

21. Hope, Keels, and Durkee, "Participation in Black Lives Matter," 203; Watts, Diemer, and Voight, "Critical Consciousness."

22. Campbell and MacPhail, "Peer Education."

23. Keisha L. Bentley-Edwards and Collette Chapman-Hilliard, "Doing Race in Different Places: Black Racial Cohesion on Black and White College Campuses," *Journal of Diversity in Higher Education* 8, no. 1 (2015): 43; Adele Lozano, "Latina/o Culture Centers Providing a Sense of Belonging and Promoting Student Success," in *Cultural Centers in Higher Education: Perspectives on Identity, Theory, and Practice*, ed. L. D. Patton (Sterling, VA: Stylus, 2010), 3–25.

24. Tatum, *Why Are All the Black Kids Sitting Together?*

25. Case and Hunter, "Counterspaces: A Unit of Analysis."

26. Alexander W. Astin, "Diversity and Multiculturalism on the Campus: How Are Students Affected?," *Change: The Magazine of Higher Learning* 25, no. 2 (1993): 44–49; Mitchell J. Chang, "Does Racial Diversity Matter? The Educational Impact of a Racially Diverse Undergraduate Population," *Journal of College Student Development* 40, no. 4 (1999): 377.

27. Muthuswamy, Levine, and Gazel, "Interaction-Based Diversity Initiative Outcomes"; Denson, "Do Curricular and Cocurricular Diversity Activities Influence Racial Bias?"

7. FINDING ONE'S PEOPLE AND ONE'S SELF ON CAMPUS

1. Varsity Tutors, "7 Extracurricular Activities That Can Enhance Your College Experience," *USA Today*, September 5, 2014.

2. Susan D. Blum, *"I Love Learning; I Hate School": An Anthropology of College* (Ithaca, NY: Cornell University Press, 2016).

3. Arnett, "Emerging Adulthood."

4. Sylvia Hurtado and Deborah F. Carter, "Latino Students' Sense of Belonging in the College Community: Rethinking the Concept of Integration on Campus," in *College Students: The Evolving Nature of Research*, ed. F.K. Stage et al. (Needham Heights, MA: Simon & Schuster Custom, 1996): 123–36.

5. Arthur W. Chickering and Linda Reisser, *Education and Identity* (San Francisco: Jossey-Bass, 1993).

6. Alexander W. Astin, *What Matters in College? Four Critical Years Revisited* (San Francisco: Jossey-Bass, 1993); Amy M. Bohnert, Julie Wargo Aikins, and Jennifer Edidin, "The Role of Organized Activities in Facilitating Social Adaptation across the Transition to College," *Journal of Adolescent Research* 22, no. 2 (2007): 189–208; Nancy J. Evans et al., *Student Development in College: Theory, Research, and Practice* (San Francisco: Jossey-Bass, 2009); Jim Sidanius et al., "Ethnic Enclaves and the Dynamics of Social Identity on the College Campus: The Good, the Bad, and the Ugly," *Journal of Personality and Social Psychology* 87, no. 1 (2004): 96.

7. Jones and McEwen, "Conceptual Model," 405; Henri Tajfel, ed., *Social Identity and Intergroup Relations* (Cambridge: Cambridge University Press, 2010).

8. Ricardo Montelongo, "Student Participation in College Student Organizations: A Review of Literature," *Journal of the Indiana University Student Personnel Association* 2 (2002): 50–63.

9. Sarah Willie, *Acting Black: College, Identity, and the Performance of Race* (New York: Routledge, 2003).

10. See Octavio Villalpando, "Self-Segregation or Self-Preservation? A Critical Race Theory and Latina/o Critical Theory Analysis of a Study of Chicana/o College Students," *Qualitative Studies in Education* 16, no. 5 (2003): 619–46.

11. James Sidanius et al., *The Diversity Challenge: Social Identity and Intergroup Relations on the College Campus* (New York: Russell Sage Foundation, 2008), 228.

12. Chalsa M. Loo and Gary Rolison, "Alienation of Ethnic Minority Students at a Predominantly White University," *Journal of Higher Education* 57, no. 1 (1986): 58–77; McCabe, "Racial and Gender Microaggressions," 146.

13. Silvia J. Santos et al., "The Relationship between Campus Diversity, Students' Ethnic Identity and College Adjustment: A Qualitative Study," *Cultural Diversity and Ethnic Minority Psychology* 13, no. 2 (2007): 104–10.

14. Ibid., 110.

15. Wayne Brekhus, "A Sociology of the Unmarked: Redirecting Our Focus," *Sociological Theory* 16, no. 1 (1998): 34–51.

16. Susan Svrluga, "OU: Frat Members Learned Racist Chant at National SAE Leadership Event," *Washington Post*, March 27, 2015; Alexandra Samuels, "Leaked Emails from U. of Chicago Fraternity Go after Blacks, Muslims," *USA Today*, February 3, 2016.

17. McCabe, "Racial and Gender Microaggressions"; Daniel Solórzano, Miguel Ceja, and Tara Yosso, "Critical Race Theory, Racial Microaggressions, and Campus Racial Climate: The Experiences of African American College Students," *Journal of Negro Education* 69, nos. 1–2 (2000): 60–73; Derald W. Sue, Christina M. Capodilupo, and Aisha Holder, "Racial Microaggressions in the Life Experience of Black Americans," *Professional Psychology: Research and Practice* 39, no. 3 (2008): 329.

18. James Sidanius et al., "Ethnic Organizations and Ethnic Attitudes on Campus," in *The Diversity Challenge: Social Identity and Intergroup Relations on the College Campus* (New York: Russell Sage Foundation, 2008), 228–49.

19. Ibid., 249.

20. Bentley-Edwards and Chapman-Hilliard, "Doing Race in Different Places"; Sidanius et al., *Diversity Challenge.*

21. Guiffrida, "African American Student Organizations"; Harper and Quaye, "Student Organizations."

22. Sidanius et al., "Ethnic Enclaves," 96.

23. Kathleen A. Ethier and Kay Deaux, "Negotiating Social Identity When Contexts Change: Maintaining Identification and Responding to Threat," *Journal of Personality and Social Psychology* 67, no. 2 (1994): 243–51.

24. Ibid., 250.

25. Solórzano, Ceja, and Yosso, "Critical Race Theory, Racial Microaggressions, and Campus Racial Climate," 60–73.

26. McCabe, "Racial and Gender Microaggressions."

27. Tatum, *Why Are All the Black Kids Sitting Together?*

28. Amaury Nora, "The Role of Habitus and Cultural Capital in Choosing a College: Transitioning from High School to Higher Education, and Persisting in College among Minority and Nonminority Students," *Journal of Hispanic Higher Education* 3, no. 2 (2004): 180–208.

29. McCabe, "Racial and Gender Microaggressions," 146.

30. Victor B. Sáenz, Hoi Ning Ngai, and Sylvia Hurtado, "Factors Influencing Positive Interactions across Race for African American, Asian American, Latino, and White College Students," *Research in Higher Education* 48, no. 1 (2007): 1–38.

31. Case and Hunter, "Counterspaces: A Unit of Analysis," 261.

32. Harper and Quaye, "Student Organizations."

33. Edward Murguia, "Ethnicity and the Concept of Social Integration in Tinto's Model of Institutional Departure," *Journal of College Student Development* 32, no. 5 (1991): 433–39; Samuel D. Museus, "The Role of Ethnic Student Organizations in Fostering African American and Asian American Students' Cultural Adjustment and Membership at Predominantly White Institutions," *Journal of College Student Development* 49, no. 6 (2008): 568–86.

34. Sylvia Hurtado and Deborah F. Carter, "Effects of College Transition and Perceptions of the Campus Racial Climate on Latino College Students' Sense of Belonging," *Sociology of Education* 70, no. 4 (1997): 324–45.

8. SPLIT BETWEEN SCHOOL, HOME, WORK, AND MORE

1. Terry R. Ishitani and Aileen M. Reid, "First-to-Second-Year Persistence Profile of Commuter Students," *New Directions for Student Services*, no. 150 (2015): 13–26.

2. Corinne Kodama, "Supporting Commuter Students of Color," in *Understanding and Addressing Commuter Student Needs: New Directions for Student Services*, no. 150, ed. P. J. Biddix (Hoboken, NJ: Wiley, 2015), 45–56.

3. Ishitani and Reid, "First-to-Second-Year Persistence Profile."

4. Kodama, "Supporting Commuter Students of Color"; Ruth N. López Turley and Geoffrey Wodtke, "College Residence and Academic Performance: Who Benefits from Living on Campus?," *Urban Education* 45, no. 4 (2010): 506–32.

5. Dalia R. Gefen and Marian C. Fish, "Adjustment to College in Nonresidential First-Year Students: The Roles of Stress, Family, and Coping," *Journal of the First-Year Experience & Students in Transition* 25, no. 2 (2013): 95–116; Kodama, "Supporting Commuter Students of Color."

6. Barbara Jacoby and John Garland, "Strategies for Enhancing Commuter Student Success," *Journal of College Student Retention: Research, Theory & Practice* 6, no. 1 (2004): 61–79.

7. George D. Kuh, Robert M. Gonyea, and Megan Palmer, "The Disengaged Commuter Student: Fact or Fiction?," *Commuter Perspectives* 27, no. 1 (2001): 2–5.

8. Crystal L. Park and Juliane R. Fenster, "Stress-Related Growth: Predictors of Occurrence and Correlates with Psychological Adjustment," *Journal of Social and Clinical Psychology* 23, no. 2 (2004): 195–215.

9. So-Hyun Joo, Dorothy Bagwell Durband, and John Grable, "The Academic Impact of Financial Stress on College Students," *Journal of College Student Retention: Research, Theory & Practice* 10, no. 3 (2008): 287–305.

10. Mary B. Burlison, "Nonacademic Commitments Affecting Commuter Student Involvement and Engagement," *New Directions for Student Services*, no. 150 (2015): 27–34.

11. Norma Rodriguez et al., "Family or Friends: Who Plays a Greater Supportive Role for Latino College Students?," *Cultural Diversity and Ethnic Minority Psychology* 9, no. 3 (2003): 236–50; Jean S. Phinney and Kumiko Haas, "The Process of Coping among Ethnic Minority First-Generation College Freshmen: A Narrative Approach," *Journal of Social Psychology* 143, no. 6 (2003): 707–26.

12. Ernest T. Pascarella, "The Influence of On-Campus Living versus Commuting to College on Intellectual and Interpersonal Self-Concept," *Journal of College Student Personnel* 26, no. 4 (1985): 292–99.

13. Ishitani and Reid, "First-to-Second-Year Persistence Profile."

9. OUT OF THIN AIR

1. Kristen C. Elmore and Daphna Oyserman, "If 'We' Can Succeed, 'I' Can Too: Identity-Based Motivation and Gender in the Classroom," *Contemporary Educational Psychology* 37, no. 3 (2012): 176–85; Meera Komarraju and C. Dial, "Academic Identity, Self-Efficacy, and Self-Esteem Predict Self-Determined Motivation and Goals," *Learning and Individual Differences* 32 (2014): 1–8; John W. Lounsbury et al., "Sense of Identity and Collegiate Academic Achievement," *Journal of College Student Development* 46, no. 5 (2005): 501–14; Stryker and Burke, "Past, Present, and Future."

2. Daphna Oyserman and Mesmin Destin, "Identity-Based Motivation: Implications for Intervention," *Counseling Psychologist* 38, no. 7 (2010): 1001–43; Ernest T. Pascarella and Patrick T. Terenzini, *How College Affects Students*, vol. 2 (San Francisco: Jossey-Bass, 2005).

3. Stryker and Burke, "Past, Present, and Future."

4. Petriglieri, "Under Threat"; Keels, Durkee, and Hope, "Psychological and Academic Costs of Microaggressions."

5. Ethier and Deaux, "Negotiating Social Identity," 243; Stryker and Burke, "Past, Present, and Future."

6. Sue, *Microaggressions and Marginality*; Gloria Wong et al., "The What, the Why, and the How: A Review of Racial Microaggressions Research in Psychology," *Race and Social Problems* 6, no. 2 (2014): 181–200.

7. Irvin J. Lehmann, Birendra K. Sinha, and Rodney T. Hartnett, "Changes in Attitudes and Values Associated with College Attendance," *Journal of Educational Psychology* 57, no. 2 (1966): 89; Ilsa L. Lottes and Peter J. Kuriloff, "The Impact of College Experience on Political and Social Attitudes," *Sex Roles* 31, no. 1 (1994): 31–54; Pascarella and Terenzini, *How College Affects Students*.

8. Yolanda Vasquez-Salgado, Patricia M. Greenfield, and Rocio Burgos-Cienfuegos, "Exploring Home-School Value Conflicts: Implications for Academic Achievement and

Well-Being among Latino First-Generation College Students," *Journal of Adolescent Research* 30, no. 3 (2015): 271–305.

9. Laura I. Rendon, "From the Barrio to the Academy: Revelations of a Mexican American 'Scholarship Girl,'" *New Directions for Community Colleges* 80 (1992): 55–64.

10. Elizabeth Aries and Maynard Seider, "The Interactive Relationship between Class Identity and the College Experience: The Case of Lower Income Students," *Qualitative Sociology* 28, no. 4 (2005): 419–43.

11. Mark P. Orbe and Christopher R. Groscurth, "A Co-cultural Theoretical Analysis of Communicating on Campus and at Home: Exploring the Negotiation Strategies of First Generation College (FGC) Students," *Qualitative Research Reports in Communication* 5 (2004): 41–47.

12. Sarah M. Ovink, "'They Always Call Me an Investment': Gendered Familism and Latino/a College Pathways," *Gender & Society* 28, no. 2 (2014): 265–88; Roberta Espinoza, "The Good Daughter Dilemma: Latinas Managing Family and School Demands," *Journal of Hispanic Higher Education* 9, no. 4 (2010): 317–30.

13. Susan R. Sy, "Family and Work Influences on the Transition to College among Latina Adolescents," *Hispanic Journal of Behavioral Development* 28, no. 3 (2006): 368–86; Ovink, "They Always Call Me an Investment," 265–288; Espinoza, "Good Daughter Dilemma," 317–330; Melissa Consoli, Jasmín Llamas, and Andrés J. Consoli, "'What's Values Got to Do with It?' Thriving among Mexican/Mexican American College Students," *Journal of Multicultural Counseling and Development* 44, no. 1 (2016): 49–64.

14. Espinoza, "Good Daughter Dilemma," 319.

15. Kristen W. Springer, Brenda K. Parker, and Catherine Leviten-Reid, "Making Space for Graduate Student Parents: Practice and Politics," *Journal of Family Issues* 30, no. 4 (2009): 435–57; Guiffrida, "To Break Away," 56.

16. Espinoza, "Good Daughter Dilemma," 319.

17. Robert Agnew and Diane H. Jones, "Adapting to Deprivation: An Examination of Inflated Educational Expectations," *Sociological Quarterly* 29, no. 2 (1988): 315–37; Laura Horn, "Confronting the Odds: Students at Risk and the Pipeline to Higher Education," NCES 98–094 (Washington, DC: National Center for Education Statistics, US Department of Education, Government Printing Office, 1997).

18. Victor B. Sáenz and Luis Ponjuan, "The Vanishing Latino Male in Higher Education," *Journal of Hispanic Higher Education* 8, no. 1 (2009): 54–89.

19. Ovink, "They Always Call Me an Investment," 275; Guiffrida, "To Break Away."

20. Guiffrida, "To Break Away."

21. Espinoza, "Good Daughter Dilemma," 319.

22. Guiffrida, "To Break Away"; Douglas A. Guiffrida, "Friends from Home: Asset and Liability to African American Students Attending a Predominantly White Institution," *NASPA Journal* 41, no. 4 (2004): 693–708.

23. Astin, *What Matters in College*; Wolfgang Lehmann, "University as Vocational Education: Working-Class Students' Expectations for University," *British Journal of Sociology of Education* 30, no. 2 (2009): 137–49; Robert Longwell-Grice, "Get a Job: Working Class Students Discuss the Purpose of College," *College Student Affairs Journal* 23, no. 1 (2003): 40.

24. Tinto, *Leaving College*; Douglas A. Guiffrida, "Toward a Cultural Advancement of Tinto's Theory," *Review of Higher Education* 29, no. 4 (2006): 451–72.

25. Guiffrida, "To Break Away."

26. Case and Hunter, "Counterspaces: A Unit of Analysis," 258.

27. Petriglieri, "Under Threat."

10. A GUIDING HAND

1. Micere Keels, "Getting Them Enrolled Is Only Half the Battle: College Success as a Function of Race or Ethnicity, Gender, and Class," *American Journal of Orthopsychiatry* 83, nos. 2–3 (2013): 310.

2. Shaun R. Harper, *Black Male Student Success in Higher Education: A Report from the National Black Male College Achievement Study* (Philadelphia: University of Pennsylvania, Graduate School of Education, Center for the Study of Race and Equity in Education, 2012).

3. Elizabeth Redden, "Reaching Black Men," *Inside Higher Ed*, July 14, 2009.

4. Victor B. Sáenz and Luis Ponjuan, "The Vanishing Latino Male in Higher Education," *Journal of Hispanic Higher Education* 8, no. 1 (2009): 54–89.

5. Digest of Education Statistics, "Table 306.10: Total Fall Enrollment in Degree-Granting Postsecondary Institutions, by Level of Enrollment, Sex, Attendance Status, and Race/Ethnicity of Student: Selected Years 1976 through 2015" (Washington, DC: National Center for Educational Statistics, 2016).

6. Ibid.

7. Sáenz and Ponjuan, "Vanishing Latino Male," 54.

8. Julio Cammarota, "The Gendered and Racialized Pathways of Latina and Latino Youth: Different Struggles, Different Resistances in the Urban Context," *Anthropology & Education Quarterly* 35, no. 1 (2004): 53–74; Heidi L. Barajas and Jennifer L. Pierce, "The Significance of Race and Gender in School Success among Latinas and Latinos in College," *Gender & Society* 15, no. 6 (2001): 859–78.

9. Anne-Marie Núñez, "Employing Multilevel Intersectionality in Educational Research: Latino Identities, Contexts, and College Access," *Educational Researcher* 43, no. 2 (2014): 85–92.

10. Stephens et al., "Unseen Disadvantage."

11. V. Scott Solberg and Pete Villareal, "Examination of Self-Efficacy, Social Support, and Stress as Predictors of Psychological and Physical Distress among Hispanic College Students," *Hispanic Journal of Behavioral Sciences* 19, no. 2 (1997): 182–201.

12. Vincent Tinto, "Taking Retention Seriously: Rethinking the First Year of College," *NACADA Journal* 19, no. 2: 5–10.

13. Keels, "Getting Them Enrolled," 310; Nicole M. Stephens et al., "Feeling at Home in College: Fortifying School-Relevant Selves to Reduce Social Class Disparities in Higher Education," *Social Issues and Policy Review* 9, no. 1 (2015): 1–24.

14. David Pérez and Victor B. Sáenz, "Thriving Latino Males in Selective Predominantly White Institutions," *Journal of Hispanic Higher Education* 16, no. 2 (2017): 164.

15. Pérez and Sáenz, "Thriving Latino Males."

16. Terrell L. Strayhorn, "When Race and Gender Collide: Social and Cultural Capital's Influence on the Academic Achievement of African American and Latino Males," *Review of Higher Education* 33, no. 3 (2010): 312.

17. Stephens et al. "Unseen Disadvantage."

18. Sáenz and Ponjuan, "Vanishing Latino Male"; Edward Fergus and Mellie Torres, "Social Mobility and the Complex Status of Latino Males," in *Invisible No More: Understanding the Disenfranchisement of Latino Men and Boys*, ed. N. Pedro, A. Hurtado, and E. Fergus (Abingdon, UK: Routledge, 2013), 19–40.

19. Stephens et al., "Unseen Disadvantage."

20. Richard Rodriguez, "Going Home Again: The New American Scholarship Boy," *American Scholar* (1974): 15.

21. Shaun R. Harper and Frank Harris III, *College Men and Masculinities: Theory, Research, and Implications for Practice* (New York: John Wiley & Sons, 2010).

22. Victor B. Sáenz and Beth E. Bukoski, "Masculinity: Through a Latino Male Lens," in *Men of Color in Higher Education: New Foundations for Developing Models for Success*, ed. R. A. Williams (Sterling, VA: Stylus, 2014), 99.

23. Lizette Ojeda, Rachel L. Navarro, and Alejandro Morales, "The Role of *la Familia* on Mexican American Men's College Persistence Intentions," *Psychology of Men & Masculinity* 12, no. 3 (2011): 216–229.

24. Stephens et al., "Unseen Disadvantage."

25. Ovink, "They Always Call Me an Investment"; Espinoza, "Good Daughter Dilemma."

26. Norma González, Luis C. Moll, and Cathy Amanti, eds. *Funds of Knowledge: Theorizing Practices in Households, Communities, and Classrooms* (New York: Routledge, 2006).

27. Harper and Harris, *College Men and Masculinities*.

28. Mary W. Pritchard and Gregory S. Wilson, "Using Emotional and Social Factors to Predict Student Success," *Journal of College Student Development* 44, no. 1 (2003): 18–28.

29. Sylvia Hurtado, Deborah Faye Carter, and Albert Spuler, "Latino Student Transition to College: Assessing Difficulties and Factors in Successful College Adjustment," *Research in Higher Education* 37, no. 2 (1996): 135–57.

30. Adele R. Arellano and Amado M. Padilla, "Academic Invulnerability among a Select Group of Latino University Students," *Hispanic Journal of Behavioral Sciences* 18, no. 4 (1996): 485–507.

31. Richard C. Richardson Jr. and Elizabeth F. Skinner, "Helping First-Generation Minority Students Achieve Degrees," *New Directions for Community Colleges*, no. 80 (1992): 29–43.

32. Jennifer Hefner and Daniel Eisenberg, "Social Support and Mental Health among College Students," *American Journal of Orthopsychiatry* 79, no. 4 (2009): 491–99; Ruth C. L. Chao, "Managing Stress and Maintaining Well-Being: Social Support, Problem-Focused Coping, and Avoidant Coping," *Journal of Counseling & Development* 89, no. 3 (2011): 338–48.

33. Pendakur, *Closing the Opportunity Gap*, 6.

11. (DIS)INTEGRATION

1. John Bound, Michael F. Lovenheim, and Sarah Turner, "Why Have College Completion Rates Declined? An Analysis of Changing Student Preparation and Collegiate Resources," *American Economic Journal: Applied Economics* 2, no. 3 (2010): 129–57; Jeanne M. Reid and James L. Moore III, "College Readiness and Academic Preparation for Postsecondary Education: Oral Histories of First-Generation Urban College Students," *Urban Education* 43, no. 2 (2008): 240–61.

2. Jason Fletcher and Marta Tienda, "Race and Ethnic Differences in College Achievement: Does High School Attended Matter?," *Annals of the American Academy of Political and Social Science* 627, no. 1 (2010): 144–66.

3. Douglas A. Guiffrida and Kathryn Z. Douthit, "The Black Student Experience at Predominantly White Colleges: Implications for School and College Counselors," *Journal of Counseling & Development* 88, no. 3 (2010): 311–18.

4. Bowen and Bok, *Shape of the River*; Keels, "Getting Them Enrolled," 310.

5. Massey et al., *Source of the River*.

6. Nicole M. Stephens, MarYam G. Hamedani, and Mesmin Destin, "Closing the Social-Class Achievement Gap: A Difference-Education Intervention Improves First-Generation Students' Academic Performance and All Students' College Transition," *Psychological Science* 25, no. 4 (2014): 943–53.

7. Steven W. Bender, "Campus Racial Unrest and the Diversity Bargain," *Indiana Journal of Law and Social Equity* 5, no. 1 (2016): 47–56.

8. Ebony O. McGee and David Stovall, "Reimagining Critical Race Theory in Education: Mental Health, Healing, and the Pathway to Liberatory Praxis," *Educational Theory* 65, no. 5 (2015): 491–511.

9. Jeffrey F. Milem, Mitchell J. Chang, and Anthony L. Antonio, *Making Diversity Work on Campus: A Research-Based Perspective* (Washington, DC: Association of American Colleges and Universities, 2005).

10. Ibid.

11. Stanley Rothman, Seymour Martin Lipset, and Neil Nevitte, "Does Enrollment Diversity Improve University Education?," *International Journal of Public Opinion Research* 15 (2002): 8–26.

12. Milem, Chang, and Antonio, *Making Diversity Work on Campus*, 16.

13. Derald W. Sue et al., "Racial Microaggressions and Difficult Dialogues on Race in the Classroom," *Cultural Diversity and Ethnic Minority Psychology* 15, no. 2 (2009): 183–90.

14. Santos et al., "Relationship between Campus Diversity."

15. B. Afeni Cobham and Tara L. Parker, "Resituating Race into the Movement toward Multiculturalism and Social Justice," *New Directions for Student Services*, no. 120 (2007): 85–93.

16. Harper and Hurtado, "Nine Themes."

17. Patricia Gurin and Biren (Ratnesh) A. Nagda, "Getting to the What, How, and Why of Diversity on Campus," *Educational Researcher* 35, no. 1 (2006): 20–24.

18. Jodi L. Linley, "We Are (Not) All Bulldogs: Minoritized Peer Socialization Agents' Meaning-Making about Collegiate Contexts," *Journal of College Student Development* 58, no. 5 (2017): 643–56.

19. Samuel L. Gaertner and John F. Dovidio, *Reducing Intergroup Bias: The Common Ingroup Identity Model* (Ann Arbor, MI: Sheridan Books, 2000).

20. Patricia Gurin, Biren Ratnesh A. Nagda, and Ximena Zuniga, *Dialogue Across Difference: Practice, Theory, and Research on Intergroup Dialogue* (New York: Russell Sage Foundation, 2013).

21. Oyserman and Destin, "Identity-Based Motivation"; Stephens et al., "Closing the Social-Class Achievement Gap"; Gregory M. Walton and Geoffrey L. Cohen "A Brief Social-Belonging Intervention Improves Academic and Health Outcomes of Minority Students," *Science* 331 (2011): 1447–51.

22. Stephens, Hamedani, and Destin, "Closing the Social-Class Achievement Gap," 949–50.

23. Ginger Hervey, "Yale Undergraduates Aim to 'Decolonize' the English Department's Curriculum," *USA Today*, June 10, 2016).

24. Nuñez, "Counterspaces and Connections."

25. Gurin et al., "Diversity and Higher Education"; Harper and Hurtado, "Nine Themes."

26. Milem, Chang, and Antonio, *Making Diversity Work*; Nicholas A. Bowman, "College Diversity Experiences and Cognitive Development: A Meta-Analysis," *Review of Educational Research* 80, no. 1 (2010): 4–33.

27. Harper and Hurtado, "Nine Themes."

28. Hurtado et al., "Enhancing Campus Climates for Racial/Ethnic Diversity."

29. Angela M. Locks et al., "Extending Notions of Campus Climate and Diversity to Students' Transition to College," *Review of Higher Education* 31, no. 3 (2008): 257–85.

30. Denson and Chang, "Racial Diversity Matters"

31. Anthony L. Antonio, "When Does Race Matter in College Friendships? Exploring Men's Diverse and Homogeneous Friendship Groups," *Review of Higher Education* 27, no. 4 (2004): 553–75.

32. Bowman, "College Diversity Experiences."

33. Kilgo Roksa et al., "Engaging with Diversity: How Positive and Negative Diversity Interactions Influence Students' Cognitive Outcomes," *Journal of Higher Education* 88, no. 3 (2017): 297–322.

34. Deborah S. Holoien, "Do Differences Make a Difference? The Effects of Diversity on Learning, Intergroup Outcomes, and Civic Engagement" (Princeton, NJ: Princeton University: Trustee Ad Hoc Committee on Diversity, 2013), 4.

35. Muthuswamy, Levine, and Gazel, "Interaction-Based Diversity Initiative Outcomes."

36. Nicholas A. Bowman and Jay W. Brandenberger, "Experiencing the Unexpected: Toward a Model of College Diversity Experiences and Attitude Change," *Review of Higher Education* 35, no. 2 (2012): 179–205.

37. Tabitha L. Grier-Reed, "The African American Student Network: Creating Sanctuaries and Counterspaces for Coping with Racial Microaggressions in Higher Education Settings," *Journal of Humanistic Counseling* 49, no. 2 (2010): 181–88.

38. Charles Lawrence, "Foreword: Who Are We? Why Are We Here? Doing Critical Race Theory in Hard Times," in *Crossroads, Directions and a New Critical Race Theory*, ed. F. Valdes, J. M. Culp, and A. Harris (Philadelphia: Temple University Press, 2002), xvii.

39. Lori D. Patton, "A Call to Action: Historical and Contemporary Reflections on the Relevance of Campus Culture Centers in Higher Education," in *Cultural Centers in Higher Education: Perspectives on Identity, Theory, and Practice*, ed. L. D. Patton (Sterling, VA: Stylus, 2010).

40. Case and Hunter, "Counterspaces: A Unit of Analysis"; Museus, "Role of Ethnic Student Organizations"; Susana Muñoz, Michelle M. Espino, and Rene Antrop-Gonzalez, "Creating Counter-Spaces of Resistance and Sanctuaries of Learning and Teaching: An Analysis of Freedom University," *Teachers College Record* 116 (2014): 1–32; Núñez, "Counterspaces and Connections"; Yosso and Lopez, "Counterspaces in a Hostile Place."

41. Claire S. Blyth, Guillermo A. Alvarado, and Sandi K. Nenga, "'I Kind of Found My People': Latino/a College Students' Search for Social Integration on Campus," in *College Students' Experiences of Power and Marginality: Sharing Spaces and Negotiating Differences*, ed. E. Lee and C. LaDousa (New York: Routledge, 2015), 29–45.

42. Villalpando, "Self-Segregation or Self-Preservation?," 619.

43. Mitchell J. Chang, Alexander W. Astin, and Dongbin Kim, "Cross-Racial Interaction among Undergraduates: Some Consequences, Causes, and Patterns," *Research in Higher Education* 45 (2004): 529–53; Julie J. Park and Young K. Kim, "Interracial Friendship, Structural Diversity, and Peer Groups: Patterns in Greek, Religious, and Ethnic Student Organizations," *Review of Higher Education* 37, no. 1 (2013): 1–24.

44. Hurtado et al., "Enhancing Campus Climates"; Santos et al., "Relationship between Campus Diversity."

45. Milem, Chang, and Antonio, *Making Diversity Work*, 16.

46. Ong, Smith, and Ko, "Counterspaces for Women of Color."

47. Derald W. Sue, *Microaggressions in Everyday Life: Race, Gender, and Sexual Orientation* (New York: John Wiley & Sons, 2010).

48. Derrick R. Brooms, "'Building Us Up': Supporting Black Male College Students in a Black Male Initiative Program," *Critical Sociology* 44, no. 1 (2018): 141–55.

49. Michelle Samura, "Remaking Selves, Repositioning Selves, or Remaking Space: An Examination of Asian American College Students' Processes of" Belonging," *Journal of College Student Development* 57, no. 2 (2016): 135–50.

50. Benjamin Bowser, Gale S. Auletta, and Terry Jones, *Confronting Diversity Issues on Campus*. vol. 6 (Newbury Park, CA: Sage, 1993).

51. Collins, *Black Sexual Politics*, 55.

METHODOLOGICAL APPENDIX

1. Stryker and Burke, "Past, Present, and Future of an Identity Theory"; Case and Hunter, "Counterspaces: A Unit of Analysis."

2. Judith Shulevitz, "In College and Hiding from Scary Ideas," *New York Times*, March 21, 2015; Matthew P. Guterl, "Students Deserve Safe Spaces on Campus," *Inside Higher Ed*, August 29, 2016.

3. Thomas D. Snyder, Cristobal de Brey, and Sally A. Dillow, *Digest of Education Statistics 2014, NCES 2016–006* (Washington, DC: National Center for Education Statistics, 2015).

4. Stephanie Fade, "Using Interpretative Phenomenological Analysis for Public Health Nutrition and Dietetic Research: A Practical Guide," *Proceedings of the Nutrition Society* 63, no. 4 (2004): 647–53; Jonathan A. Smith, Paul Flowers, and Michael Larkin, *Interpretative Phenomenological Analysis: Theory, Method and Research* (Los Angeles: Sage, 2009).

5. Irving Seidman, *Interviewing as Qualitative Research: A Guide for Researchers in Education and the Social Sciences* (New York: Teachers College Press, 2013).

6. Iddo Tavory and Stefan Timmermans, *Abductive Analysis: Theorizing Qualitative Research* (Chicago: University of Chicago Press, 2014).

7. Tavory and Timmermans, *Abductive Analysis.*

8. Barney G. Glaser, "The Constant Comparative Method of Qualitative Analysis," *Social Problems* 12, no. 4 (1965): 436–45.

9. Laura Krefting, "Rigor in Qualitative Research: The Assessment of Trustworthiness," *American Journal of Occupational Therapy* 45, no. 3 (1991): 214–22.

Bibliography

Adichie, Chimamanda N. "The Danger of a Single Story." TED talk, October 2009. https://www.ted.com/talks/chimamanda_adichie_the_danger_of_a_single_story/transcript.

Agnew, Robert, and Diane H. Jones. "Adapting to Deprivation: An Examination of Inflated Educational Expectations." *Sociological Quarterly* 29, no. 2 (1988): 315–37. doi:10.1111/j.1533–8525.1988.tb01256.x.

Alcoff, Linda M. *Visible Identities: Race, Gender, and the Self.* New York: Oxford University Press, 2005.

Anderson, Elijah. *The Cosmopolitan Canopy: Race and Civility in Everyday Life.* New York: W.W. Norton, 2011.

Antonio, Anthony L. "When Does Race Matter in College Friendships? Exploring Men's Diverse and Homogeneous Friendship Groups." *Review of Higher Education* 27, no. 4 (2004): 553–75. doi:10.1353/rhe.2004.0007.

Archer, Louise, and Merryn Hutchings. "'Bettering Yourself'? Discourses of Risk, Cost and Benefit in Ethnically Diverse, Young Working-Class Non-participants' Constructions of Higher Education." *British Journal of Sociology of Education* 21, no. 4 (2000): 555–74. doi:10.1080/713655373.

Arellano, Adele R., and Amado M. Padilla. "Academic Invulnerability among a Select Group of Latino University Students." *Hispanic Journal of Behavioral Sciences* 18, no. 4 (1996): 485–507. doi:10.1177/07399863960184004.

Aries, Elizabeth, and Maynard Seider. "The Interactive Relationship between Class Identity and the College Experience: The Case of Lower Income Students." *Qualitative Sociology* 28, no. 4 (2005): 419–43. doi: 10.1007/s11133-005-8366-1.

Arnett, Jeffrey J. "Emerging Adulthood: A Theory of Development from the Late Teens through the Twenties." *American Psychologist* 55, no. 5 (2000): 469–80. doi:10.1037/0003–066X.55.5.469.

Astin, Alexander W. "Diversity and Multiculturalism on the Campus: How Are Students Affected?" *Change: The Magazine of Higher Learning* 25, no. 2 (1993): 44–49. doi:10.1080/00091383.1993.9940617.

——. *What Matters in College? Four Critical Years Revisited.* San Francisco: Jossey-Bass, 1993.

Auer, Peter, ed. *Code-Switching in Conversation: Language, Interaction and Identity.* New York: Routledge, 2013.

Awad, Germine H. "The Role of Racial Identity, Academic Self-Concept, and Self-Esteem in the Prediction of Academic Outcomes for African American Students." *Journal of Black Psychology* 33, no. 2 (2007): 188–207. doi:10.1177/0095798407299513.

Barajas, Heidi L., and Jennifer L. Pierce. "The Significance of Race and Gender in School Success among Latinas and Latinos in College." *Gender & Society* 15, no. 6 (2001): 859–78. doi:10.1177/089124301015006005.

Baum, Sandy, Jennifer Ma, D'Wayne Bell, and Diane Cardenas Elliott. "Trends in College Pricing, 2014." *Trends in Higher Education Series.* New York: College Board, 2014.

Bender, Steven W. "Campus Racial Unrest and the Diversity Bargain." *Indiana Journal of Law and Social Equity* 5, no. 1 (2016): 47–56. https://www.repository.law.indiana.edu/ijlse/.

Bentley-Edwards, Keisha L., and Collette Chapman-Hilliard. "Doing Race in Different Places: Black Racial Cohesion on Black and White College Campuses." *Journal of Diversity in Higher Education* 8, no. 1 (2015): 43. doi:10.1037/a0038293.

Berg, Marlene, Emil Coman, and Jean J. Schensul. "Youth Action Research for Prevention: A Multi-level Intervention Designed to Increase Efficacy and Empowerment among Urban Youth." *American Journal of Community Psychology* 43, nos. 3–4 (2009): 345–59. doi:10.1007/s10464-009-9231-2.

Bernstein, Basil. *Class Codes and Control: Theoretical Studies towards a Sociology of Language*. 2nd ed. New York: Schocken Books, 1974.

Bettinger, Eric. "How Financial Aid Affects Persistence." In *College Choices: The Economics of Where to Go, When to Go, and How to Pay for It*, edited by C. Hoxby, 207–38. Chicago: University of Chicago Press, 2004.

Biernat, Monica, and Diane Kobrynowicz. "Gender- and-Race-Based Standards of Competence: Lower Minimum Standards but Higher Ability Standards for Devalued Groups." *Journal of Personality and Social Psychology* 72, no. 3 (1997): 544–57. doi:10.1037/0022–3514.72.3.544.

Black, Ray, and Albert Y. Bimper Jr. "Successful Undergraduate African American Men's Navigation and Negotiation of Academic and Social Counter-Spaces as Adaptation to Racism at Historically White Institutions." *Journal of College Student Retention: Research, Theory & Practice* 0, no. 0 (2017): 1–25. doi:10.1177/1521025117747209.

Blum, Susan D. *"I Love Learning; I Hate School": An Anthropology of College*. Ithaca, NY: Cornell University Press, 2016.

Blyth, Claire S., Guillermo A. Alvarado, and Sandi K. Nenga. "'I Kind of Found My People': Latino/a College Students' Search for Social Integration on Campus." In *College Students' Experiences of Power and Marginality: Sharing Spaces and Negotiating Differences*, edited by E. Lee and C. LaDousa, 29–45. New York: Routledge, 2015.

Bohnert, Amy M., Julie Wargo Aikins, and Jennifer Edidin. "The Role of Organized Activities in Facilitating Social Adaptation across the Transition to College." *Journal of Adolescent Research* 22, no. 2 (2007): 189–208. doi:10.1177/0743558406297940.

Bonilla-Silva, Eduardo. "More than Prejudice: Restatement, Reflections, and New Directions in Critical Race Theory." *Sociology of Race and Ethnicity* 1, no. 1 (2015): 73–87. doi:10.1177/2332649214557042.

——. "Rethinking Racism: Toward a Structural Interpretation." *American Sociological Review* 62, no. 3 (1997): 465–80. doi:10.2307/2657316.

Bound, John, Michael F. Lovenheim, and Sarah Turner. "Why Have College Completion Rates Declined? An Analysis of Changing Student Preparation and Collegiate Resources." *American Economic Journal: Applied Economics* 2, no. 3 (2010): 129–57. doi:10.1257/app.2.3.129.

Bourdieu, Pierre, and Jean-Claude Passeron. *Reproduction in Education, Society and Culture*. London: Sage, 1990.

Bowen, William G., and Derek Bok. *The Shape of the River: Long-Term Consequences of Considering Race in College and University Admissions*. Princeton, NJ: Princeton University Press, 2016.

Bowleg, Lisa. "When Black + Lesbian + Woman ≠ Black Lesbian Woman: The Methodological Challenges of Qualitative and Quantitative Intersectionality

Research." *Sex Roles* 59, no 5–6 (2008): 312–25. doi:10.1007/s11199–008–9400-z.

Bowman, Nicholas A. "College Diversity Experiences and Cognitive Development: A Meta-analysis." *Review of Educational Research* 80, no. 1 (2010): 4–33. doi:10.3102/0034654309352495.

——. "The Development of Psychological Well-Being among First-Year College Students." *Journal of College Student Development* 51, no. 2 (2010): 180–200. doi:10.1353/csd.0.0118.

Bowman, Nicholas A., and Jay W. Brandenberger. "Experiencing the Unexpected: Toward a Model of College Diversity Experiences and Attitude Change." *Review of Higher Education* 35, no. 2 (2012): 179–205. doi:10.1353/rhe.2012.0016.

Bowser, Benjamin, Gale S. Auletta, and Terry Jones. *Confronting Diversity Issues on Campus*. Vol. 6. Newbury Park, CA: Sage, 1993.

Brand, Jennie E., and Yu Xie. "Who Benefits Most from College? Evidence for Negative Selection in Heterogeneous Economic Returns to Higher Education." *American Sociological Review* 75, no. 2 (2010): 273–302. doi:10.1177/0003122410363567.

Brekhus, Wayne. "A Sociology of the Unmarked: Redirecting our Focus." *Sociological Theory* 16, no. 1 (1998): 34–51.

Brooms, Derrick R. "'Building Us Up': Supporting Black Male College Students in a Black Male Initiative Program." *Critical Sociology* 44, no. 1 (2018): 141–55. doi:10.1177/0896920516658940.

Burlison, Mary B. "Nonacademic Commitments Affecting Commuter Student Involvement and Engagement." *New Directions for Student Services*, no. 150 (2015): 27–34. doi:10.1002/ss.20124.

Cabrera, Alberto F., Amaury Nora, and Maria B. Castaneda. "The Role of Finances in the Persistence Process: A Structural Model." *Research in Higher Education* 33, no. 5 (1992): 571–93. doi:10.1007/BF00973759.

Cahalan, Margaret, and Laura Perna. *Indicators of Higher Education Equity in the United States: 45-Year Trend Report*. Washington, DC: Pell Institute for the Study of Opportunity in Education, 2015.

Cammarota, Julio. "The Gendered and Racialized Pathways of Latina and Latino Youth: Different Struggles, Different Resistances in the Urban Context." *Anthropology & Education Quarterly* 35, no. 1 (2004): 53–74. doi:10.1525/aeq.2004.35.1.53.

Campbell, Catherine, and Catherine MacPhail. "Peer Education, Gender and the Development of Critical Consciousness: Participatory HIV Prevention by South African Youth." *Social Science & Medicine* 55 (2002): 331–45. doi:10.1016/S0277–9536(01)00289–1.

Carnevale, Anthony P., and Jeff Strohl. "How Increasing College Access Is Increasing Inequality, and What to Do about It." In *Rewarding Strivers: Helping Low-Income Students Succeed in College*, edited by R. D. Kahlenberg, 71–190. New York: Century Foundation, 2010.

Carter, Deborah F., Angela Mosi Locks, and Rachelle Winkle-Wagner. "From When and Where I Enter: Theoretical and Empirical Considerations of Minority Students' Transition to College." In *Higher Education: Handbook of Theory and Research*, edited by M. B. Paulsen, 93–149. Dordrecht, Netherlands: Springer, 2013.

Carter, Dorinda J. "Why the Black Kids Sit Together at the Stairs: The Role of Identity-Affirming Counter-Spaces in a Predominantly White High School." *Journal of Negro Education* 76, no. 4 (2007): 542–54. http://www.journalnegroed.org/.

Case, Andrew D., and Carla D. Hunter, "Counterspaces and the Narrative Identity Work of Offender-Labeled African American Youth." *Journal of Community Psychology* 42, no. 8 (2014): 907–23. doi:10.1002/jcop.21661.

——. "Counterspaces: A Unit of Analysis for Understanding the Role of Settings in Marginalized Individuals' Adaptive Responses to Oppression." *American Journal of Community Psychology* 50, nos. 1–2 (2012): 257–70. doi:10.1007/s10464-012-9497-7.

Chang, Mitchell J. "Does Racial Diversity Matter? The Educational Impact of a Racially Diverse Undergraduate Population." *Journal of College Student Development* 40, no. 4 (1999): 377. https://muse.jhu.edu/journal/238.

Chang, Mitchell J., Alexander W. Astin, and Dongbin Kim. "Cross-Racial Interaction among Undergraduates: Some Consequences, Causes, and Patterns." *Research in Higher Education 45* (2004): 529–53. doi:10.1023/B:RIHE.0000032327.45961.33.

Chao, Ruth C. L. "Managing Stress and Maintaining Well-Being: Social Support, Problem-Focused Coping, and Avoidant Coping." *Journal of Counseling & Development* 89, no. 3 (2011): 338–48. doi:10.1002/j.1556–6678.2011.tb00098.x.

Chavous, Tabbye M. "The Relationships among Racial Identity, Perceived Ethnic Fit, and Organization Involvement for African American Students at a Predominately White University." *Journal of Black Psychology* 26, no. 1 (2000): 79–100. doi:10.1177/0095798400026001005.

Chickering, Arthur W., and Linda Reisser. *Education and Identity*. San Francisco: Jossey Bass, 1993.

Coates, Ta-Nehisi. "Charles Barkley and the Plague of 'Unintelligent' Blacks." *Atlantic*, October 2014. https://www.theatlantic.com/politics/archive/2014/10/charles-barkley-and-the-plague-of-unintelligent-blacks/382022/.

Cobham, B. Afeni, and Tara L. Parker. "Resituating Race into the Movement toward Multiculturalism and Social Justice." *New Directions for Student Services*, no. 120 (2007): 85–93. doi:10.1002/ss.260.

Cokley, Kevin O. "Testing Cross's Revised Racial Identity Model: An Examination of the Relationship between Racial Identity and Internalized Racialism." *Journal of Counseling Psychology* 49, no. 4 (2002): 476–83. doi:10.1037/0022–0167.49.4.476.

College Board. *Trends in Student Aid 2017*. Washington, DC: College Board, 2017.

Cook-Sather, Alison. "Creating Brave Spaces within and through Student-Faculty Pedagogical Partnerships." *Teaching and Learning Together in Higher Education* 1, no. 18 (2016): 1–5. https://repository.brynmawr.edu/tlthe/.

Collins, Patricia Hill. *Black Feminist Thought: Knowledge, Consciousness, and the Politics of Empowerment*. New York: Routledge, 2002.

——. *Black Sexual Politics: African Americans, Gender, and the New Racism*. New York: Routledge, 2004.

Consoli, Melissa, Jasmín Llamas, and Andrés J. Consoli. "What's Values Got to Do with It? Thriving among Mexican / Mexican American College Students." *Journal of Multicultural Counseling and Development* 44, no. 1 (2016): 49–64. doi:10.1002/jmcd.12036.

Crenshaw, Kimberlé. "Mapping the Margins: Intersectionality, Identity Politics, and Violence against Women of Color." *Stanford Law Review* 43, no. 6 (1991): 1241–99. doi:10.2307/1229039.

——. "The Urgency of Intersectionality." TED talk, October 2016. https://www.ted.com/talks/kimberle_crenshaw_the_urgency_of_intersectionality.

Crossley, Nick, and Joseph Ibrahim. "Critical Mass, Social Networks and Collective Action: Exploring Student Political Worlds." *Sociology* 46, no. 4 (2012): 596–612. doi:10.1177/0038038511425560.

Cuseo, Joe. "Fiscal Benefits of Student Retention and First-Year Retention Initiatives." Athens: Ohio University, 2010. https://www.researchgate.net/publication/252903476_Fiscal_Benefits_of_Student_Retention_and_First-Year_Retention_Initiatives.

Danaher, Kelly, and Nyla R. Branscombe. "Maintaining the System with Tokenism: Bolstering Individual Mobility Beliefs and Identification with a Discriminatory Organization." *British Journal of Social Psychology* 49, no. 2 (2010): 343–62. doi:10.1348/014466609X457530.

De Fina, Anna. "Code-Switching and the Construction of Ethnic Identity in a Community of Practice." *Language in Society* 36, no. 3 (2007): 371–92. doi:10.1017/S0047404507070182.

Deil-Amen, Regina. "The 'Traditional' College Student: A Smaller and Smaller Minority and Its Implications for Diversity and Access Institutions." Paper prepared for the conference Mapping Broad-Access Higher Education, Stanford University, November 2011.

Delgado, Richard, and Jean Stefancic. *Critical Race Theory: An Introduction*. 2nd ed. New York: NYU Press, 2012.

Denson, Nida. "Do Curricular and Cocurricular Diversity Activities Influence Racial Bias? A Meta-analysis." *Review of Educational Research* 79, no. 2 (2009): 805–38. doi:10.3102/0034654309331551.

Denson, Nida, and Mitchell J. Chang. "Racial Diversity Matters: The Impact of Diversity-Related Student Engagement and Institutional Context." *American Educational Research Journal* 46, no. 2 (2009): 322–353. doi:10.3102/0002831208323278.

Digest of Education Statistics. "Table 306.10: Total Fall Enrollment in Degree-Granting Postsecondary Institutions, by Level of Enrollment, Sex, Attendance Status, and Race/Ethnicity of Student: Selected Years 1976 through 2015." Washington, DC: National Center for Educational Statistics, 2016.

Dovidio, John F., and Samuel L. Gaertner. "Aversive Racism." *Advances in Experimental Social Psychology* 36 (2004): 1–52. https://www.elsevier.com/.

Dowd, Alicia C. "Dynamic Interactions and Intersubjectivity: Challenges to Causal Modeling in Studies of College Student Debt." *Review of Educational Research* 78, no. 2 (2008): 232–59, 250–51. doi:10.3102/0034654308317252.

Durkee, Myles, and Joanna L. Williams. "Accusations of Acting White: Links to Black Students' Racial Identity and Mental Health." *Journal of Black Psychology* 41, no. 1 (2015): 26–48. doi:10.1177/0095798413505323.

Dwyer, Rachel, Laura McCloud, and Randy Hodson. "Debt and Graduation from American Universities." *Social Forces* 90, no. 4 (2012): 1133–55. doi:10.1093/sf/sos072.

Elmore, Kristen C., and Daphna Oyserman. "If 'We' Can Succeed, 'I' Can Too: Identity-Based Motivation and Gender in the Classroom." *Contemporary Educational Psychology* 37, no. 3 (2012): 176–85. doi:10.1016/j.cedpsych.2011.05.003.

Erikson, Erik H. *Identity: Youth and Crisis*. New York: W. W. Norton, 1994.

Espinoza, Roberta. "The Good Daughter Dilemma: Latinas Managing Family and School Demands." *Journal of Hispanic Higher Education* 9, no. 4 (2010): 317–30. doi:10.1177/1538192710380919.

Ethier, Kathleen A., and Kay Deaux. "Negotiating Social Identity When Contexts Change: Maintaining Identification and Responding to Threat." *Journal of*

Personality and Social Psychology 67, no. 2 (1994): 243–51. doi:10.1037//0022-3514.67.2.243.

Evans, Nancy J., Deanna S. Forney, Florence M. Guido, Lori D. Patton, and Kristen A. Renn. *Student Development in College: Theory, Research, and Practice*. San Francisco: Jossey-Bass, 2009.

Fade, Stephanie. "Using Interpretative Phenomenological Analysis for Public Health Nutrition and Dietetic Research: A Practical Guide." *Proceedings of the Nutrition Society* 63, no. 4 (2004): 647–53. doi:10.1079/PNS2004398.

Fergus, Edward, and Mellie Torres. "Social Mobility and the Complex Status of Latino Males."

In *Invisible No More: Understanding the Disenfranchisement of Latino Men and Boys*, edited by N. Pedro, A. Hurtado, and E. Fergus, 19–40. Abingdon, UK: Routledge, 2013.

Fischer, Mary J. "Does Campus Diversity Promote Friendship Diversity? A Look at Interracial Friendships in College." *Social Science Quarterly* 89, no. 3 (2008): 631–55. doi:10.1111/j.1540-6237.2008.00552.x.

——. "A Longitudinal Examination of the Role of Stereotype Threat and Racial Climate on College Outcomes for Minorities at Elite Institutions." *Social Psychology of Education* 13, no. 1 (2010): 19–40. doi:10.1007/s11218-009-9105-3.

——. "Settling into Campus Life: Differences by Race/Ethnicity in College Involvement and Outcomes." *Journal of Higher Education* 78, no. 2 (2007): 125–61. doi:10.1080/00221546.2007.11780871.

Fletcher, Jason, and Marta Tienda. "Race and Ethnic Differences in College Achievement: Does High School Attended Matter?" *Annals of the American Academy of Political and Social Science* 627, no. 1 (2010): 144–66. doi:10.1177/0002716209348749.

Fried, Jane. "Multicultural Identities and Shifting Selves among College Students." In *Multiculturalism on Campus: Theory, Models, and Practices for Understanding Diversity and Creating Inclusion*, edited by Michael J. Cuyjet, Mary F. Howard-Hamilton, and Diane L. Cooper, 65–83. Sterling, VA: Stylus, 2011.

Fries-Britt, Sharon, and Kimberly Griffin. "The Black Box: How High-Achieving Blacks Resist Stereotypes about Black Americans." *Journal of College Student Development* 48, no. 5 (2007): 509–24. doi:10.1353/csd.2007.0048.

Fries-Britt, Sharon, and Bridget Turner. "Facing Stereotypes: A Case Study of Black Students on a White Campus." *Journal of College Student Development* 42, no. 5 (2001): 420–29. http://muse.jhu.edu/journal/238.

Gaertner, Samuel L., and John F. Dovidio. *Reducing Intergroup Bias: The Common Ingroup Identity Model*. Ann Arbor, MI: Sheridan Books, 2000.

Gasiewski, Josephine A., M. Kevin Eagan, Gina A. Garcia, Sylvia Hurtado, and Mitchell J. Chang. "From Gatekeeping to Engagement: A Multicontextual, Mixed Method Study of Student Academic Engagement in Introductory STEM Courses." *Research in Higher Education* 53, no. 2 (2012): 229–61. doi:10.1007/s11162-011-9247-y.

Gefen, Dalia R., and Marian C. Fish. "Adjustment to College in Nonresidential First-Year Students: The Roles of Stress, Family, and Coping." *Journal of the First-Year Experience & Students in Transition* 25, no. 2 (2013): 95–116. https://sc.edu/about/offices_and_divisions/national_resource_center/publications/journal/index.php.

Gladieux, Lawrence, and Laura Perna. *Borrowers Who Drop Out: A Neglected Aspect of the College Student Loan Trend*. San Jose, CA: National Center for Public Policy and Higher Education, 2005.

Glaser, Barney G. "The Constant Comparative Method of Qualitative Analysis." *Social Problems* 12, no. 4 (1965): 436–45.

Glatter, Haley. "College Is Still the Promised Land for High School Students." *Atlantic*, September 13, 2016. https://www.theatlantic.com/education/archive/2016/09/college-is-still-the-promised-land-for-high-school-students/499865/.

Golash-Boza, Tanya. "A Critical and Comprehensive Sociological Theory of Race and Racism." *Sociology of Race and Ethnicitynicity* 2, no. 2 (2016): 129–41. doi:10.1177/2332649216632242.

Goldrick-Rab, Sara. *Paying the Price: College Costs, Financial Aid, and the Betrayal of the American Dream*. Chicago: University of Chicago Press, 2016.

Goldrick-Rab, Sara, Robert Kelchen, and Jason Houle. *The Color of Student Debt: Implications of Federal Loan Program Reforms for Black Students and Historically Black Colleges and Universities*. Madison: Hope Lab, University of Wisconsin–Madison, 2014.

González, Norma, Luis C. Moll, and Cathy Amanti, eds. *Funds of Knowledge: Theorizing Practices in Households, Communities, and Classrooms*. New York: Routledge, 2006.

Goyette, Kimberly A. "College for Some to College for All: Social Background, Occupational Expectations, and Educational Expectations over Time." *Social Science Research* 37, no. 2 (2008): 461–84. doi:10.1016/j.ssresearch.2008.02.002.

Grable, John E., and So-Hyun Joo. "Student Racial Differences in Credit Card Debt and Financial Behaviors and Stress." *College Student Journal* 40, no. 2 (2006): 400–408. https://www.projectinnovation.com/college-student-journal.html.

Grier-Reed, Tabitha L. "The African American Student Network: Creating Sanctuaries and Counterspaces for Coping with Racial Microaggressions in Higher Education Settings." *Journal of Humanistic Counseling* 49, no. 2 (2010): 181–88. doi:10.1002/j.2161–1939.2010.tb00096.x.

Gross, Jacob P. K., Osman Cekic, Don Hossler, and Nick Hillman. "What Matters in Student Loan Default: A Review of the Research Literature." *Journal of Student Financial Aid* 39, no. 1 (2009): 19–29. https://www.nasfaa.org/journal_of_student_financial_aid.

Guiffrida, Douglas A. "African American Student Organizations as Agents of Social Integration." *Journal of College Student Development* 44, no. 3 (2003): 304–19. doi:10.1353/csd.2003.0024.

——. "Friends from Home: Asset and Liability to African American Students Attending a Predominantly White Institution." *NASPA Journal* 41, no. 4 (2004): 693–708. doi:10.2202/1949–6605.1394.

——. "To Break Away or Strengthen Ties to Home: A Complex Issue for African American College Students Attending a Predominantly White Institution." *Equity & Excellence in Education* 38, no. 1 (2005): 49–60. doi:10.1080/10665680590907864.

——. "Toward a Cultural Advancement of Tinto's Theory." *Review of Higher Education* 29, no. 4 (2006): 451–72. doi:10.1353/rhe.2006.0031.

Guiffrida, Douglas A., and Kathryn Z. Douthit. "The Black Student Experience at Predominantly White Colleges: Implications for School and College Counselors." *Journal of Counseling & Development* 88, no. 3 (2010): 311–18. doi:10.1002/j.1556–6678.2010.tb00027.x.

Gurin, Patricia, Eric Dey, Sylvia Hurtado, and Gerald Gurin. "Diversity and Higher Education: Theory and Impact on Educational Outcomes." *Harvard Educational Review* 72, no. 3 (2002): 330–67. doi:10.17763/haer.72.3.01151786u134n051.

Gurin, Patricia, and Biren (Ratnesh) A. Nagda. "Getting to the What, How, and Why of Diversity on Campus." *Educational Researcher* 35, no. 1 (2006): 20–24. doi10.3102/0013189X035001020.

Gurin, Patricia, Biren (Ratnesh) A. Nagda, and Ximena Zuniga. *Dialogue across Difference: Practice, Theory, and Research on Intergroup Dialogue*. New York: Russell Sage Foundation, 2013.

Guterl, Matthew P. "Students Deserve Safe Spaces on Campus." *Inside Higher Ed*, August 29, 2016. https://www.insidehighered.com/views/2016/08/29/students-deserve-safe-spaces-campus-essay.

Haak, David C., Janneke HilleRisLambers, Emile Pitre, and Scott Freeman. "Increased Structure and Active Learning Reduce the Achievement Gap in Introductory Biology." *Science* 332, no. 6034 (2011): 1213–16. doi:10.1126/science.1204820.

Harper, Shaun R. *Black Male Student Success in Higher Education: A Report from the National Black Male College Achievement Study*. Philadelphia: University of Pennsylvania, Graduate School of Education, Center for the Study of Race and Equity in Education, 2012.

Harper, Shaun R., and Frank Harris III. *College Men and Masculinities: Theory, Research, and Implications for Practice*. New York: John Wiley & Sons, 2010.

Harper, Shaun R., and Sylvia Hurtado. "Nine Themes in Campus Racial Climates and Implications for Institutional Transformation." In *Responding to the Realities of Race on Campus: New Directions for Student Services*. Vol. 120, edited by S. R. Harper and L. D. Patton, 7–24. San Francisco: Jossey-Bass, 2007.

Harper, Shaun R., and Stephen J. Quaye. "Student Organizations as Venues for Black Identity Expression and Development among African American Male Student Leaders." *Journal of College Student Development* 48, no. 2 (2007): 127–44. doi:10.1353/csd.2007.0012.

Hausmann, Leslie, Janet Ward Schofield, and Rochelle L. Woods. "Sense of Belonging as a Predictor of Intentions to Persist among African American and White First-Year College Students." *Research in Higher Education* 48, no. 7 (2007): 803–39. doi:10.1007/s11162-007-9052-9.

Hefner, Jennifer, and Daniel Eisenberg. "Social Support and Mental Health among College Students." *American Journal of Orthopsychiatry* 79, no. 4 (2009): 491–99. doi:10.1037/a0016918.

Heller, Donald E., and Kimberly R. Rogers. "Shifting the Burden: Public and Private Financing of Higher Education in the United States and Implications for Europe." *Tertiary Education & Management* 12, no. 2 (2006): 91–117. doi:10.1080/13583883.2006.9967162.

Hernandez-Truyol, Berta E. "Borders (En)gendered: Normativities, Latinas and a LatCrit Paradigm." *New York University Law Review* 72 (1997): 882–927.

Hervey, Ginger. "Yale Undergraduates Aim to 'Decolonize' the English Department's Curriculum." *USA Today*, June 10, 2016. http://college.usatoday.com/2016/06/10/yale-undergraduates-aim-to-decolonize-the-english-departments-curriculum/.

Hirsch, Deborah. "Access to a College Degree or Just College Debt? Moving beyond Admission to Graduation." *New England Journal of Higher Education* 23, no. 2 (2008): 17–18. https://nebhe.org/nejhe.

Hoffman, John L., and Katie E. Lowitzki. "Predicting College Success with High School Grades and Test Scores: Limitations for Minority Students." *Review of Higher Education* 28, no. 4 (2005): 455–74. doi:10.1353/rhe.2005.0042.

Hoffman, Garrett D., and Tania D. Mitchell. "Making Diversity 'Everyone's Business': A Discourse Analysis of Institutional Responses to Student Activism for Equity and Inclusion." *Journal of Diversity in Higher Education* 9, no. 3 (2016): 277–89. doi:10.1037/dhe0000037.

Holoien, Deborah S. "Do Differences Make a Difference? The Effects of Diversity on Learning, Intergroup Outcomes, and Civic Engagement." Princeton, NJ: Princeton University, Trustee Ad Hoc Committee on Diversity, 2013.

Hope, Elan C., and Margaret B. Spencer. "Civic Engagement as an Adaptive Coping Response to Conditions of Inequality: An Application of Phenomenological Variant of Ecological Systems Theory (PVEST)." In *Handbook of Positive Development of Minority Children*, edited by N. Cabrera and B. Leyendecker, 421–35. New York: Springer, 2017.

Hope, Elan C., Micere Keels, and Myles I. Durkee. "Participation in Black Lives Matter and Deferred Action for Childhood Arrivals: Modern Activism among Black and Latino College Students." *Journal of Diversity in Higher Education* 9, no. 3 (2016): 203–15. doi:10.1037/dhe0000032.

Hope, Elan C., Kristen N. Pender, and Kristen N. Riddick. "Measuring Youth Proclivity for Social Action in the Black Community: Development and Validation of the Black Community Activism Orientation Scale (BCAOS)." Under review.

Horn, Laura. "Confronting the Odds: Students at Risk and the Pipeline to Higher Education." NCES 98–094. Washington, DC: National Center for Education Statistics, US Department of Education, Government Printing Office, 1997.

Howard-Hamilton, Mary F., Rosemary E. Phelps, and Vasti Torres. "Meeting the Needs of All Students and Staff Members: The Challenge of Diversity." *New Directions for Student Services*, no. 82 (1998): 49–64. doi:10.1002/ss.8205.

Huelsman, Mark. *The Debt Divide: The Racial and Class Bias behind the "New Normal" of Student Borrowing*. New York: Demos, 2015.

Hurtado, Sylvia, and Deborah F. Carter. "Effects of College Transition and Perceptions of the Campus Racial Climate on Latino College Students' Sense of Belonging." *Sociology of Education* 70, no. 4 (1997): 324–45. doi:10.2307/2673270.

——. "Latino Students' Sense of Belonging in the College Community: Rethinking the Concept of Integration on Campus." In *College Students: The Evolving Nature of Research*, edited by F. K. Stage et al., 123–36. Needham Heights, MA: Simon & Schuster Custom, 1996.

Hurtado, Sylvia, Deborah F. Carter, and Albert Spuler. "Latino Student Transition to College: Assessing Difficulties and Factors in Successful College Adjustment." *Research in Higher Education* 37, no. 2 (1996): 135–57. doi:10.1007/BF01730113.

Hurtado, Sylvia, Alma R. Clayton-Pedersen, Walter Recharde Allen, and Jeffrey F. Milem. "Enhancing Campus Climates for Racial/Ethnic Diversity: Educational Policy and Practice." *Review of Higher Education* 21, no. 3 (1998): 279–302. doi:10.1353/rhe.1998.003.

Hutchings, Vincent L. "Change or More of the Same? Evaluating Racial Attitudes in the Obama Era." *Public Opinion Quarterly* 73, no 5 (2009): 917–42. doi:10.1093/poq/nfp080.

Inkelas, Karen K., Zaneeta E. Daver, Kristen E. Vogt, and Jeannie Brown Leonard. "Living-Learning Programs and First-Generation College Students' Academic and Social Transition to College." *Research in Higher Education* 48, no. 4 (2007): 403–34. doi:10.1007/s11162–006–9031-.

Inkelas, Karen K., Matthew Soldner, Susan D. Longerbeam, and Jeannie Brown Leonard. "Differences in Student Outcomes by Types of Living-Learning Programs: The Development of an Empirical Typology." *Research in Higher Education* 49, no. 6 (2008): 495–512.

Ishitani, Terry R., and Aileen M. Reid. "First-to-Second-Year Persistence Profile of Commuter Students." *New Directions for Student Services*, no. 150 (2015): 13–26. doi:10.1002/ss.20123.

Jacoby, Barbara, and John Garland. "Strategies for Enhancing Commuter Student Success." *Journal of College Student Retention: Research, Theory & Practice* 6, no. 1 (2004): 61–79. doi:10.2190/567C-5TME-Q8F4–8FRG.

Jones, Susan R., and Marylu K. McEwen. "A Conceptual Model of Multiple Dimensions of Identity." *Journal of College Student Development* 41, no. 4 (2000): 405–14. http://muse.jhu.edu/journal/238.

Joo, So-Hyun, Dorothy Bagwell Durband, and John Grable. "The Academic Impact of Financial Stress on College Students." *Journal of College Student Retention: Research, Theory & Practice* 10, no. 3 (2008): 287–305. doi:10.2190/CS.10.3.c.

Kantrowitz, Mark. "Why the Student Loan Crisis Is Even Worse Than People Think." *Time*, January 11, 2016. http://time.com/money/4168510/why-student-loan-crisis-is-worse-than-people-think/.

Keels, Micere. "Getting Them Enrolled Is Only Half the Battle: College Success as a Function of Race or Ethnicity, Gender, and Class." *American Journal of Orthopsychiatry* 83, nos. 2–3 (2013): 310. doi:10.1111/ajop.12033.

Keels, Micere, Myles Durkee, and Elan Hope. *Financial Distress at the Start of College*. Minority College Cohort Study policy report, Chicago: University of Chicago, 2015.

——. "The Psychological and Academic Costs of School-Based Racial and Ethnic Microaggressions." *American Educational Research Journal* 54, no. 6 (2017): 1316–44. doi:10.3102/0002831217722120.

Kennedy, Randall. "Lifting as We Climb: A Progressive Defense of Respectability Politics." *Harper's Magazine*, October 2015.

King, Tracey, and Ellyne Bannon. *At What Cost? The Price That Working Students Pay for a College Education*. Washington, DC: United States Public Interest Research Group, 2002.

——. *The Burden of Borrowing: A Report on the Rising Rates of Student Loan Debt*. Boston: Public Interest Research Group, 2002.

Knowles, Eric D., Brian S. Lowery, and Rebecca L. Schaumberg. "Racial Prejudice Predicts Opposition to Obama and His Health Care Reform Plan." *Journal of Experimental Social Psychology* 46, no. 2 (2010): 420–23. doi:10.1016/j.jesp.2009.10.011.

Kodama, Corinne. "Supporting Commuter Students of Color." In *Understanding and Addressing Commuter Student Needs: New Directions for Student Services*, no. 150, edited by P. J. Biddix, 45–56. Hoboken, NJ: Wiley, 2015.

Komarraju, Meera, and C. Dial. "Academic Identity, Self-Efficacy, and Self-Esteem Predict Self-Determined Motivation and Goals." *Learning and Individual Differences* 32 (2014): 1–8. doi:10.1016/j.lindif.2014.02.004.

Komarraju, Meera, Sergey Musulkin, and Gargi Bhattacharya. "Role of Student-Faculty Interactions in Developing College Students' Academic Self-Concept, Motivation, and Achievement." *Journal of College Student Development* 51, no. 3 (2010): 332–42. doi:10.1353/csd.0.0137.

Krefting, Laura. "Rigor in Qualitative Research: The Assessment of Trustworthiness." *American Journal of Occupational Therapy* 45, no. 3 (1991): 214–22.

Krogstad, Jens Manuel, and Richard Fry. "More Hispanics, Blacks Enrolling in College but Lag in Bachelor's Degrees." Washington, DC: Pew Research Center, 2014. http://www.pewresearch.org/fact-tank/2014/04/24/more-hispanics-blacks-enrolling-in-college-but-lag-in-bachelors-degrees/.

Kuh, George D., Ty M. Cruce, Rick Shoup, Jillian Kinzie, and Robert M. Gonyea. "Unmasking the Effects of Student Engagement on First-Year College Grades and Persistence." *Journal of Higher Education* 79, no. 5 (2008): 540–63. doi:10.1080/00221546.2008.11772116.

Kuh, George D., Robert M. Gonyea, and Megan Palmer. "The Disengaged Commuter Student: Fact or Fiction?." *Commuter Perspectives* 27, no. 1 (2001): 2–5. https://www.researchgate.net.

Kuppens, Toon, and Russell Spears. "You Don't Have to Be Well-Educated to Be an Aversive Racist, but It Helps." *Social Science Research* 45 (2014): 211–23. doi:10.1016/j.ssresearch.2014.01.006.

Lawrence, Charles. "Foreword: Who Are We? Why Are We Here? Doing Critical Race Theory in Hard Times." In *Crossroads, Directions and a New Critical Race Theory*, edited by F. Valdes, J. M. Culp, and A. Harris, xi–xxi Philadelphia: Temple University Press, 2002.

Lee, Elizabeth. *Class and Campus Life: Managing and Experiencing Inequality at an Elite College*. Ithaca, NY: Cornell University Press, 2016.

Lehmann, Irvin J., Birendra K. Sinha, and Rodney T. Hartnett. "Changes in Attitudes and Values Associated with College Attendance." *Journal of Educational Psychology* 57, no. 2 (1966): 89.

Lehmann, Wolfgang. "University as Vocational Education: Working-Class Students' Expectations for University." *British Journal of Sociology of Education* 30, no. 2 (2009): 137–49. doi:10.1080/01425690802700164.

Lewis, Jioni A., Ruby Mendenhall, Stacey A. Harwood, and Margaret Browne Huntt. "Coping with Gendered Racial Microaggressions among Black Women College Students." *Journal of African American Studies* 17, no. 1 (2013): 51–73. doi:10.1007/s12111-012-9219-0.

Linley, Jodi L. "We Are (Not) All Bulldogs: Minoritized Peer Socialization Agents' Meaning-Making about Collegiate Contexts." *Journal of College Student Development* 58, no. 5 (2017): 643–56. doi:10.1353/csd.2017.0051.

Locks, Angela M., Sylvia Hurtado, Nicholas A. Bowman, and Leticia Oseguera. "Extending Notions of Campus Climate and Diversity to Students' Transition to College," *Review of Higher Education* 31, no. 3 (2008): 257–85. doi:10.1353/rhe.2008.0011.

Lohr, Steve. "A New Kind of Tech Job Emphasizes Skills, Not a College Degree." *New York Times*, June 28, 2017. https://www.nytimes.com/2017/06/28/technology/tech-jobs-skills-college-degree.html?mcubz=3.

Longwell-Grice, Robert. "Get a Job: Working Class Students Discuss the Purpose of College." *College Student Affairs Journal* 23, no. 1 (2003): 40. http://muse.jhu.edu/journal/689.

Loo, Chalsa M., and Gary Rolison. "Alienation of Ethnic Minority Students at a Predominantly White University." *Journal of Higher Education* 57, no. 1 (1986): 58–77. doi:10.1080/00221546.1986.11778749.

López Turley, Ruth N., and Geoffrey Wodtke. "College Residence and Academic Performance: Who Benefits from Living on Campus?" *Urban Education* 45, no. 4 (2010): 506–32. doi:10.1177/0042085910372351.

Lottes, Ilsa L., and Peter J. Kuriloff. "The Impact of College Experience on Political and Social Attitudes." *Sex Roles* 31, no. 1 (1994): 31–54. doi:10.1007/BF01560276.

Lounsbury, John W., Beverly C. Huffstetler, Frederick T. L. Leong, and Lucy W. Gibson. "Sense of Identity and Collegiate Academic Achievement." *Journal of College Student Development* 46, no. 5 (2005): 501–14. doi:10.1353/csd.2005.0051.

Lozano, Adele. "Latina/o Culture Centers Providing a Sense of Belonging and Promoting Student Success." In *Cultural Centers in Higher Education: Perspectives on Identity, Theory, and Practice*, edited by L. D. Patton, 3–25. Sterling, VA: Stylus, 2010.

Malin, Heather, Parissa J. Ballard, and William Damon. "Civic Purpose: An Integrated Construct for Understanding Civic Development in Adolescence." *Human Development* 58, no. 2 (2015): 103–30. doi:10.1159/000381655.

MarksJarvis, Gail. "Working during College Doesn't Always Pay, Study Says." *Chicago Tribune*, Oct. 29, 2015. http://www.chicagotribune.com/business/ct-working-through-college-costs-1030-biz-20151029-story.html.

Massey, Douglas, Camille Z. Charles, Garvey F. Lundy, and Mary J. Fisher. *The Source of the River: The Social Origins of Freshmen at America's Selective Colleges and Universities*. Princeton, NJ: Princeton University Press, 2011.

McCabe, Janice. "Racial and Gender Microaggressions on a Predominantly-White Campus: Experiences of Black, Latina/o and White Undergraduates." *Race, Gender & Class* 16, nos. 1–2 (2009): 133–51. https://www.jstor.org/journal/racegenderclass.

McGee, Ebony O., and David Stovall. "Reimagining Critical Race Theory in Education: Mental Health, Healing, and the Pathway to Liberatory Praxis." *Educational Theory* 65, no. 5 (2015): 491–511. doi:10.1111/edth.12129.

Milem, Jeffrey F., Mitchell J. Chang, and Anthony L. Antonio. *Making Diversity Work on Campus: A Research-Based Perspective*. Washington, DC: Association of American Colleges and Universities, 2005.

Montelongo, Ricardo. "Student Participation in College Student Organizations: A Review of Literature." *Journal of the Indiana University Student Personnel Association* 2 (2002): 50–63. https://scholarworks.iu.edu/journals/index.php/jiuspa.

Morphew, Christopher, and Matthew Hartley. "Mission Statements: A Thematic Analysis of Rhetoric across Institution Type." *Journal of Higher Education* 77 (2006): 456–71. doi:10.1080/00221546.2006.11778934.

Muñoz, Susana, Michelle M. Espino, and Rene Antrop-Gonzalez. "Creating Counter-Spaces of Resistance and Sanctuaries of Learning and Teaching: An Analysis of Freedom University." *Teachers College Record* 116 (2014): 1–32. http://www.tcrecord.org.

Murguia, Edward. "Ethnicity and the Concept of Social Integration in Tinto's Model of Institutional Departure." *Journal of College Student Development* 32, no. 5(1991): 433–39.

Murji, Karim, and John Solomos. *Racialization: Studies in Theory and Practice*. New York: Oxford University Press, 2005.

Museus, Samuel D. "The Role of Ethnic Student Organizations in Fostering African American and Asian American Students' Cultural Adjustment and Membership at Predominantly White Institutions." *Journal of College Student Development* 49, no. 6 (2008): 568–86. doi:10.1353/csd.0.0039.

Muthuswamy, Nithya, Timothy R. Levine, and Jeanne Gazel. "Interaction-Based Diversity Initiative Outcomes: An Evaluation of an Initiative Aimed at Bridging the Racial Divide on a College Campus." *Communication Education* 55, no. 1 (2006): 105–21. doi:10.1080/03634520500489690.

Nasir, Na'ilah. *Racialized Identities: Race and Achievement among African American Youth*. Stanford, CA: Stanford University Press, 2011.

Nora, Amaury. "The Role of Habitus and Cultural Capital in Choosing a College: Transitioning from High School to Higher Education, and Persisting in College among Minority and Nonminority Students." *Journal of Hispanic Higher Education* 3, no. 2 (2004): 180–208. doi:10.1177/1538192704263189.

Nora, Amaury, Libby Barlow, and Gloria Crisp. "Examining the Tangible and Psychosocial Benefits of Financial Aid with Student Access, Engagement, and Degree Attainment." *American Behavioral Scientist* 49, no. 12 (2006): 1636–51. doi:10.1177/0002764206289143.

Núñez, Anne-Marie. "Counterspaces and Connections in College Transitions: First-Generation Latino Students' Perspectives on Chicano Studies." *Journal of College Student Development*, 52, no. 6 (2011): 639–55. doi:10.1353/csd.2011.0077.

——. "Employing Multilevel Intersectionality in Educational Research: Latino Identities, Contexts, and College Access." *Educational Researcher* 43, no. 2 (2014): 85–92. doi:10.3102/0013189X14522320.

Ojeda, Lizette, Rachel L. Navarro, and Alejandro Morales. "The Role of *la Familia* on Mexican American Men's College Persistence Intentions." *Psychology of Men & Masculinity* 12, no. 3 (2011): 216–229. doi:10.1037/a0020091.

O'Keeffe, Patrick. "A Sense of Belonging: Improving Student Retention." *College Student Journal* 47, no. 4 (2013): 605–13. https://www.projectinnovation.com/college-student-journal.html.

Ong, Maria, Janet M. Smith, and Lily T. Ko. "Counterspaces for Women of Color in STEM Higher Education: Marginal and Central Spaces for Persistence and Success." *Journal of Research in Science Teaching* 55, no. 2 (2018): 206–45. doi:10.1002/tea.21417.

Orbe, Mark P., and Christopher R. Groscurth. "A Co-cultural Theoretical Analysis of Communicating on Campus and at Home: Exploring the Negotiation Strategies of First Generation College (FGC) Students." *Qualitative Research Reports in Communication* 5 (2004): 41–47. https://www.tandfonline.com/loi/rqrr20.

Ovink, Sarah M. "'They Always Call Me an Investment': Gendered Familism and Latino/a College Pathways." *Gender & Society* 28, no. 2 (2014): 265–88. doi:10.1177/0891243213508308.

Oyserman, Daphna, and Mesmin Destin. "Identity-Based Motivation: Implications for Intervention." *Counseling Psychologist* 38, no. 7 (2010): 1001–43. doi:10.1177/0011000010374775.

Park, Crystal L., and Juliane R. Fenster. "Stress-Related Growth: Predictors of Occurrence and Correlates with Psychological Adjustment." *Journal of Social and Clinical Psychology* 23, no. 2 (2004): 195–215. doi:10.1521/jscp.23.2.195.31019.

Park, Julie J., and Young K. Kim. "Interracial Friendship, Structural Diversity, and Peer Groups: Patterns in Greek, Religious, and Ethnic Student Organizations." *Review of Higher Education* 37, no. 1 (2013): 1–24. doi:10.1353/rhe.2013.0061.

Pascarella, Ernest T. "The Influence of On-Campus Living versus Commuting to College on Intellectual and Interpersonal Self-Concept." *Journal of College Student Personnel* 26, no. 4 (1985): 292–99. doi:10.2307/1162852.

Pascarella, Ernest T., and Patrick T. Terenzini. *How College Affects Students*. Vol. 2. San Francisco: Jossey-Bass, 2005.

Patton, Lori D. "A Call to Action: Historical and Contemporary Reflections on the Relevance of Campus Culture Centers in Higher Education." In *Cultural Centers in Higher Education: Perspectives on Identity, Theory, and Practice*, edited by L. D. Patton, xiii–xvi. Sterling, VA: Stylus, 2010.

——, ed. *Culture Centers in Higher Education: Perspectives on Identity, Theory, and Practice*. Sterling, VA: Stylus, 2010.

Pendakur, Vijay. *Closing the Opportunity Gap: Identity-Conscious Strategies for Retention and Student Success*. Sterling, VA: Stylus, 2016.

Pérez, David, and Victor B. Sáenz. "Thriving Latino Males in Selective Predominantly White Institutions." *Journal of Hispanic Higher Education* 16, no. 2 (2017): 162–86. doi:10.1177/1538192717697754.

Perna, Laura. "The Key to College Access: Rigorous Academic Preparation." In *Preparing for College: Nine Elements of Effective Outreach*, edited by W. G. Tierney, Z. B. Corwin, and J. E. Colyar, 113–34. New York: SUNY Press, 2005.

Petriglieri, Jennifer L. "Under Threat: Responses to and the Consequences of Threats to Individuals' Identities." *Academy of Management Review* 36, no. 4 (2011): 641–62. doi:10.5465/amr.2009.0087.

Phinney, Jean S., and Kumiko Haas. "The Process of Coping among Ethnic Minority First-Generation College Freshmen: A Narrative Approach." *Journal of Social Psychology* 143, no. 6 (2003): 707–26. doi:10.1080/00224540309600426.

Pike, Gary R., and George D. Kuh. "Relationships among Structural Diversity, Informal Peer Interactions and Perceptions of the Campus Environment." *Review of Higher Education* 29, no. 4 (2006): 425–50. doi:10.1353/rhe.2006.0037.

Pippert, Timothy D., Laura J. Essenburg, and Edward J. Matchett. "We've Got Minorities, Yes We Do: Visual Representations of Racial and Ethnic Diversity in College Recruitment Materials." *Journal of Marketing for Higher Education* 23, no. 2 (2013): 258–82. doi:10.1080/08841241.2013.867920.

Porter, Christa J., and Laura A. Dean. "Making Meaning: Identity Development of Black Undergraduate Women." *NASPA Journal about Women in Higher Education* 8, no. 2 (2015): 125–39. doi:10.1080/19407882.2015.1057164.

Pries, Ludger. "Ambiguities of Global and Transnational Collective Identities." *Global Networks* 13, no. 1 (2013): 22–40. doi:10.1111/j.1471–0374.2012.00368.x.

Pritchard, Mary W., and Gregory S. Wilson. "Using Emotional and Social Factors to Predict Student Success." *Journal of College Student Development* 44, no. 1 (2003): 18–28. doi:10.1353/csd.2003.0008.

Purdie-Vaughns, Valerie, Claude M. Steele, Paul G. Davies, Ruth Ditlmann, and Jennifer Randall Crosby. "Social Identity Contingencies: How Diversity Cues Signal Threat or Safety for African Americans in Mainstream Institutions." *Journal of Personality and Social Psychology* 94, no. 4 (2008): 615. doi:10.1037/0022–3514.94.4.615.

Ratcliffe, Caroline, and Signe Mary McKernan. *Forever in Your Debt: Who Has Student Loan Debt, and Who's Worried?* Washington, DC: Urban Institute, 2013.

Ravji, Beber. Resolution draft on University Residence Housing. Sponsored by Culture and Minority Student Affairs, Illinois Student Senate Resolution (11-03-2008-01), November 2008.

Rawls, Anne W. "'Race' as an Interaction Order Phenomenon: W. E. B. Du Bois's 'Double Consciousness' Thesis Revisited." *Sociological Theory* 18, no. 2 (2000): 241–74. doi:10.1111/0735–2751.00097.

Read, Barbara, Louise Archer, and Carole Leathwood. "Challenging Cultures? Student Conceptions of Belonging and Isolation at a Post-1992 University." *Studies in Higher Education* 28, no. 3 (2003): 261–77. doi:10.1080/03075070309290.

Reardon, Sean F., Joseph P. Robinson, and Ericka S. Weathers. "Patterns and Trends in Racial/Ethnic and Socioeconomic Academic Achievement Gaps." In *Handbook of Research in Education Finance and Policy*, 2nd ed., edited by H. A. Ladd and E. B. Fiske, 497–516. New York: Lawrence Erlbaum, 2012.

Reason, Robert D., and Nancy J. Evans. "The Complicated Realities of Whiteness: From Color Blind to Racially Cognizant." *New Directions for Student Services*, no. 120 (2007): 67–75. doi:10.1002/ss.258.

Redden, Elizabeth. "Reaching Black Men." *Inside Higher Ed*, July 14, 2009. https://www.insidehighered.com/news/2009/07/14/blackmale.

Reid, Jeanne M., and James L. Moore III. "College Readiness and Academic Preparation for Postsecondary Education: Oral Histories of First-Generation Urban College Students." *Urban Education* 43, no. 2 (2008): 240–61. doi:10.1177/0042085907312346.

Rendon, Laura I. "From the Barrio to the Academy: Revelations of a Mexican American 'Scholarship Girl,'" *New Directions for Community Colleges* 80 (1992): 55–64. doi:10.1002/cc.36819928007.

——. "Validating Culturally Diverse Students: Toward a New Model of Learning and Student Development." *Innovative Higher Education* 19, no. 1 (1994): 33–51. doi:10.1007/BF01191156.

Renn, Kristen. "Creating and Re-creating Race: The Emergence of Racial Identity as a Critical Element in Psychological, Sociological, and Ecological Perspectives on Human Development." In *New Perspectives on Racial Identity Development: Integrating Emerging Frameworks*, edited by C. L. Wijeyesinghe and B. W. Jackson, 11–32. New York: NYU Press, 2012.

Rhoads, Robert A. *Freedom's Web: Student Activism in an Age of Cultural Diversity*. Baltimore: Johns Hopkins University Press, 1998.

Richardson, Richard C., Jr., and Elizabeth F. Skinner. "Helping First-Generation Minority Students Achieve Degrees." *New Directions for Community Colleges*, no. 80 (1992): 29–43. doi:10.1002/cc.36819928005.

Richardson, Michelle, Charles Abraham, and Rod Bond. "Psychological Correlates of University Students' Academic Performance: A Systematic Review and Meta-Analysis." *Psychological Bulletin* 138, no. 2 (2012). doi:10.1037/a0026838.

Robbins, Stephen B., Kristy Lauver, Huy Le, Daniel Davis, Ronelle Langley, and Aaron Carlstrom. "Do Psychosocial and Study Skill Factors Predict College Outcomes? A Meta-analysis." *Psychological Bulletin* 130, no. 2 (2004). doi:10.1037/0033–2909.130.2.261.

Rodriguez, Norma, Consuelo Bingham Mira, Hector Myers, and Julie K. Morris. "Family or Friends: Who Plays a Greater Supportive Role for Latino College Students?" *Cultural Diversity and Ethnic Minority Psychology* 9, no. 3 (2003): 236–50. doi:10.1037/1099–9809.9.3.236.

Rodriguez, Richard. "Going Home Again: The New American Scholarship Boy." *American Scholar* 44, no. 1 (1974): 15–28.

Roksa, Josipa, Cindy Ann Kilgo, Teniell L. Trolian, Ernest T. Pascarella, Charles Blaich, and Kathleen S. Wise. "Engaging with Diversity: How Positive and Negative Diversity Interactions Influence Students' Cognitive Outcomes." *Journal of Higher Education* 88, no. 3 (2017): 297–322. doi:10.1080/00221546.2016.1271690.

Rosenbaum, James E. "The Complexities of College for All: Beyond Fairy-Tale Dreams." *Sociology of Education* 84, no. 2 (2011): 113–17. doi:10.1177/0038040711401809.

Rosenbaum, James E., Shazia Rafiullah Miller, and Melinda Scott Krei. "Gatekeeping in an Era of More Open Gates: High School Counselors' Views of Their Influence on Students' College Plans." *American Journal of Education* 104, no. 4 (1996): 257–79. doi:10.1086/444135.

Rothman, Stanley, Seymour Martin Lipset, and Neil Nevitte. "Does Enrollment Diversity Improve University Education?" *International Journal of Public Opinion Research* 15 (2002): 8–26. doi:10.1093/ijpor/15.1.8.

Sáenz, Victor B., and Beth E. Bukoski. "Masculinity: Through a Latino Male Lens." In *Men of Color in Higher Education: New Foundations for Developing Models for Success*, edited by R. A. Williams, 85–115. Sterling: VA, Stylus, 2014.

Sáenz, Victor B., Hoi Ning Ngai, and Sylvia Hurtado. "Factors Influencing Positive Interactions across Race for African American, Asian American, Latino, and White College Students." *Research in Higher Education* 48, no. 1 (2007): 1–38. doi:10.1007/s11162-006-9026-3.

Sáenz, Victor B., and Luis Ponjuan. "The Vanishing Latino Male in Higher Education." *Journal of Hispanic Higher Education* 8, no. 1 (2009): 54–89. doi:10.1177/1538192708326995.

Samuels, Alexandra. "Leaked Emails from U. of Chicago Fraternity Go after Blacks, Muslims." *USA Today*, February 3, 2016. http://college.usatoday.com/2016/02/03/leaked-emails-from-u-of-chicago-fraternity-go-after-blacks-muslims/.

Samura, Michelle. "Remaking Selves, Repositioning Selves, or Remaking Space: An Examination of Asian American College Students' Processes of" Belonging." *Journal of College Student Development* 57, no. 2 (2016): 135–50. doi:10.1353/csd.2016.0016.

Santos, Silvia J., Anna M. Ortiz, Alejandro Morales, and Monica Rosales. "The Relationship between Campus Diversity, Students' Ethnic Identity and College Adjustment: A Qualitative Study." *Cultural Diversity and Ethnic Minority Psychology* 13, no. 2 (2007): 104–10. doi:10.1037/1099–9809.13.2.104.

Scheurich, James J., and Michelle D. Young. "White Racism among White Faculty: From Critical Understanding to Antiracist Activism." In *The Racial Crisis in American Higher Education: Continuing Challenges for the Twenty-First Century*, edited by W. A. Smith, P. G. Altbach, and K. Lomotey, 221–42. New York: SUNY Press, 2002.

Schlesinger, Arthur M. *The Disuniting of America: Reflections on a Multicultural Society*. New York: W. W. Norton, 1998.

Seidman, Irving. *Interviewing as Qualitative Research: A Guide for Researchers in Education and the Social Sciences*. New York: Teachers College Press, 2013.

Sellers, Robert, M. A. Smith, J. N. Shelton, S. A. J. Rowley, and T. M. Chavous. "The Multidimensional Model of Racial Identity: A Reconceptualization of African American Racial Identity." *Personality and Social Psychology Review* 2, no. 1 (1998): 18–39.

Shulevitz, Judith. "In College and Hiding from Scary Ideas." *New York Times*, March 21, 2015. https://www.nytimes.com/2015/03/22/opinion/sunday/judith-shulevitz-hiding-from-scary-ideas.html.

Sidanius, James, Shana Levin, Colette van Laar, and David O. Sears. *The Diversity Challenge: Social Identity and Intergroup Relations on the College Campus*. New York: Russell Sage Foundation, 2008.

Sidanius James, Colette van Laar, and Stacey A. Sinclair. "Ethnic Enclaves and the Dynamics of Social Identity on the College Campus: The Good, the Bad, and the Ugly." *Journal of Personality and Social Psychology* 87, no. 1 (2004): 96. doi:10.1037/0022–3514.87.1.96.

Sidanius, James, Shana Levin, Colette van Laar, and David O. Sears. "Ethnic Organizations and Ethnic Attitudes on Campus." In *The Diversity Challenge: Social Identity and Intergroup Relations on the College Campus*. New York: Russell Sage Foundation, 2008, 228–49.

Simmons-Duffin, Selena. "For Millions of Millennials, Some College, No Degree, Lots of Debt." National Public Radio, November 19, 2014. http://www.npr.org/2014/11/19/362802610/for-millions-of-millennials-some-college-no-degree-lots-of-debt.

Smith, Jonathan A., Paul Flowers, and Michael Larkin. *Interpretative Phenomenological Analysis: Theory, Method and Research*. Los Angeles: Sage, 2009.

Smith, William A., Walter R. Allen, and Lynette L. Danley. "'Assume the Position . . . You Fit the Description': Psychosocial Experiences and Racial Battle Fatigue among African American Male College Students." *American Behavioral Scientist* 51, no. 4 (2007): 551–78. doi:10.1177/0002764207307742.

Snyder, Thomas D., Cristobal de Brey, and Sally A. Dillow. *Digest of Education Statistics 2014, NCES 2016–006*. Washington, DC: National Center for Education Statistics, 2015.

Solberg, V. Scott, and Pete Villareal. "Examination of Self-Efficacy, Social Support, and Stress as Predictors of Psychological and Physical Distress among Hispanic College Students." *Hispanic Journal of Behavioral Sciences* 19, no. 2 (1997): 182–201. doi:10.1177/07399863970192006.

Solórzano, Daniel, Miguel Ceja, and Tara Yosso. "Critical Race Theory, Racial Microaggressions, and Campus Racial Climate: The Experiences of African American College Students." *Journal of Negro Education* 69, nos. 1–2 (2000): 60–73. https://journalnegroed.org.

Solórzano, Daniel, and Tara Yosso. "Critical Race Methodology: Counter-Storytelling as an Analytical Framework for Education Research." *Qualitative Inquiry* 8, no. 1 (2002): 23–44. doi:10.1177/107780040200800103.

Spencer, Margaret B., and Carol Markstrom-Adams. "Identity Processes among Racial and Ethnic Minority Children in America." *Child Development* 61, no. 2 (1990): 290–310. doi:10.1111/j.1467–8624.1990.tb02780.x.

Springer, Kristen W., Brenda K. Parker, and Catherine Leviten-Reid. "Making Space for Graduate Student Parents: Practice and Politics." *Journal of Family Issues* 30, no. 4 (2009): 435–57. doi:10.1177/0192513X08329293.

Stephens, Nicole M., Tiffany N. Brannon, Hazel Rose Markus, and Jessica E. Nelson. "Feeling at Home in College: Fortifying School-Relevant Selves to Reduce Social Class Disparities in Higher Education." *Social Issues and Policy Review* 9, no. 1 (2015): 1–24. doi:10.111/sipr.12008.

Stephens, Nicole M., Stephanie A. Fryberg, Hazel Rose Markus, Camille S. Johnson, and Rebecca Covarrubias. "Unseen Disadvantage: How American Universities' Focus on Independence Undermines the Academic Performance of First-Generation College Students." *Journal of Personality and Social Psychology* 102, no. 6 (2012): 1178–97. doi:10.1037/a0027143.

Stephens, Nicole M., MarYam G. Hamedani, and Mesmin Destin. "Closing the Social-Class Achievement Gap: A Difference-Education Intervention Improves First-Generation Students' Academic Performance and All Students' College Transition." *Psychological Science* 25, no. 4 (2014): 943–53. doi:10.1177/0956797613518349.

St. John, Edward P., Shouping Hu, and Tina Tuttle. "Persistence by Undergraduates in an Urban Public University: Understanding the Effects of Financial Aid." *Journal of Student Financial Aid* 30, no. 2 (2000): 23–37. https://www.nasfaa.org/journal_of_student_financial_aid.

Strayhorn, Terrell L. "When Race and Gender Collide: Social and Cultural Capital's Influence on the Academic Achievement of African American and Latino Males." *Review of Higher Education* 33, no. 3 (2010): 307–32. doi:10.1353/rhe.0.0147.

Stryker, Sheldon, and Peter J. Burke. "The Past, Present, and Future of an Identity Theory." *Social Psychology Quarterly* 63, no. 4 (2000): 284–97. doi:10.2307/2695840.

Stuber, Jenny M. *Inside the College Gates: How Class and Culture Matter in Higher Education*. Lanham, MD: Lexington Books, 2011.

Derald W. Sue, ed. *Microaggressions and Marginality: Manifestation, Dynamics, and Impact*. Hoboken, NJ: Wiley, 2010.

——. *Microaggressions in Everyday Life: Race, Gender, and Sexual Orientation*. New York: John Wiley & Sons, 2010.

——. *Overcoming Our Racism: The Journey to Liberation*. San Francisco: Jossey-Bass, 2003.

Sue, Derald W., Christina M. Capodilupo, and Aisha Holder, "Racial Microaggressions in the Life Experience of Black Americans." *Professional Psychology: Research and Practice* 39, no. 3 (2008): 329. doi:10.1037/0735–7028.39.3.329

Sue, Derald W., Christina M. Capodilupo, Gina C. Torino, Jennifer M. Bucceri, Aisha M. B. Holder, Kevin L. Nadal, and Marta Esquilin. "Racial Microaggressions in Everyday Life: Implications for Clinical Practice." *American Psychologist* 62, no. 4 (2007): 271–86. doi:10.1037/0003–066X.62.4.271.

Sue, Derald W., Annie I. Lin, Gina C. Torino, Christina M. Capodilupo, and David P. Rivera. "Racial Microaggressions and Difficult Dialogues on Race in the Classroom." *Cultural Diversity and Ethnic Minority Psychology* 15, no. 2 (2009): 183–90. doi:10.1037/a0014191.

Svrluga, Susan. "OU: Frat Members Learned Racist Chant at National SAE Leadership Event." *Washington Post*, March 27, 2015. https://www.washingtonpost.com/news/grade-point/wp/2015/03/27/ou-investigation-sae-members-learned-racist-chant-at-national-leadership-event/?utm_term=.8031c791bdc4.

Sy, Susan R. "Family and Work Influences on the Transition to College among Latina Adolescents." *Hispanic Journal of Behavioral Development* 28, no. 3 (2006): 368–86. doi:10.1177/0739986306290372.

Szymanski, Dawn M., and Jioni A. Lewis. "Gendered Racism, Coping, Identity Centrality, and African American College Women's Psychological Distress." *Psychology of Women Quarterly* 40, no. 2 (2016): 229–43. doi:10.1177/0361684315616113.

Tajfel, Henri, ed. *Social Identity and Intergroup Relations*. Cambridge: Cambridge University Press, 2010.

Tajfel, Henri, and John Turner. "An Integrative Theory of Intergroup Conflict." In *The Social Psychology of Intergroup Relations* 33, no. 47 (1979): 56–65.

Tatum, Beverly D. *Why Are All the Black Kids Sitting Together in the Cafeteria? And Other Conversations about Race*. New York: Basic Books, 2017.

Tavory, Iddo, and Stefan Timmermans. *Abductive Analysis: Theorizing Qualitative Research*. Chicago: University of Chicago Press, 2014.

Tinto, Vincent. "Building Community." *Liberal Education* 79, no. 4 (1993): 16–21. https://www.aacu.org/liberaleducation.

——. *Leaving College: Rethinking the Causes and Cures of Student Attrition*. 2nd ed. Chicago: University of Chicago Press, 1993.

——. "Taking Retention Seriously: Rethinking the First Year of College." *NACADA Journal* 19, no. 2: 5–10. http://www.nacadajournal.org.

Tompor, Susan. "College Students' Nightmare: Loan Debt and No Degree." *USA Today*, June 7, 2015. https://www.usatoday.com/story/money/columnist/tompor/tompor/2015/06/07/student-loans-repay-delinquency-federal-reserve/28562447/.

Towles-Schwen, Tamara, and Russell H. Fazio. "Automatically Activated Racial Attitudes as Predictors of the Success of Interracial Roommate Relationships."

Journal of Experimental Social Psychology 42, no. 5 (2006): 698–705. doi:10.1016/j.jesp.2005.11.003.

Tyson, Karolyn, ed. *Integration Interrupted: Tracking, Black Students, and Acting White after Brown*. New York: Oxford University Press, 2011.

Ulriksen, Lars, Lene M. Madsen, and Henriette T. Holmegaard. "What Do We Know about Explanations for Drop Out / Opt Out among Young People from STM Higher Education Programmes?" *Studies in Science Education* 46, no. 2 (2010): 209–44. doi:10.1080/03057267.2010.504549.

Vaccaro, Annemarie, and Melissa J. Camba-Kelsay. *Centering Women of Color in Academic Counterspaces: A Critical Race Analysis of Teaching, Learning, and Classroom Dynamics*. Lanham, MD: Rowman & Littlefield, 2016.

Valdes, Francisco. "Latina/o Ethnicities, Critical Race Theory, and Post-Identity Politics in Postmodern Legal Culture: From Practices to Possibilities." *La Raza Law Journal* 9, no. 1 (1996): 1–31.

Valenzuela, Sebastián. "Unpacking the Use of Social Media for Protest Behavior: The Roles of Information, Opinion Expression, and Activism." *American Behavioral Scientist*, 57, no. 7 (2013): 920–42. doi:10.1177/0002764213479375.

Varsity Tutors. "7 Extracurricular Activities That Can Enhance Your College Experience." *USA Today*, September 5, 2014. http://college.usatoday.com/2014/09/05/7-extracurricular-activities-that-can-enhance-your-college-experience/.

Vasquez-Salgado, Yolanda, Patricia M. Greenfield, and Rocio Burgos-Cienfuegos. "Exploring Home-School Value Conflicts: Implications for Academic Achievement and Well-Being among Latino First-Generation College Students." *Journal of Adolescent Research* 30, no. 3 (2015): 271–305. doi:10.1177/0743558414561297.

Villalpando, Octavio. "Practical Considerations of Critical Race Theory and Latino Critical Theory for Latino College Students. *New Directions for Student Services*, no. 105 (2004): 41–50. doi:10.1002/ss.115.

——. "Self-Segregation or Self-Preservation? A Critical Race Theory and Latina/o Critical Theory Analysis of a Study of Chicana/o College Students." *Qualitative Studies in Education* 16, no. 5 (2003): 619–46. doi:10.1080/095183903200 0142922.

Waddell, Glenn, and Larry Singell Jr. "Do No-Loan Policies Change the Matriculation Patterns of Low-Income Students?" *Economics of Education Review* 30, no. 2 (2011): 203–14. doi:10.1016/j.econedurev.2010.10.004.

Wallenborn, Manfred, and Stephen P. Heyneman. "Should Vocational Education Be Part of Secondary Education?" *Journal of Educational Change* 10, no. 4 (2009): 405–13. doi:10.1007/s10833–009–9117-y.

Walton, Gregory M., and Geoffrey L. Cohen. "A Brief Social-Belonging Intervention Improves Academic and Health Outcomes of Minority Students." *Science* 331 (2011): 1447–51. doi:10.1126/science.1198364.

Warnock, Deborah M., and A. L. Hurst. "'The Poor Kids' Table': Organizing around an Invisible and Stigmatized Identity in Flux." *Journal of Diversity in Higher Education* 9, no. 3 (2016): 261–76. doi:10.1037/dhe0000029.

Watkins, Nicole, Theressa L. LaBarrie, and Lauren M. Appio. "Black Undergraduates' Experience with Perceived Racial Microaggressions in Predominantly White Colleges and Universities." In *Microaggressions and Marginality: Manifestation, Dynamics, and Impact*, edited by D. W. Sue, 25–58. Hoboken, NJ: John Wiley & Sons, 2010.

Watts, Roderick J., and Omar Guessous. "Sociopolitical Development: The Missing Link in Research and Policy on Adolescents." In *Beyond Resistance! Youth Activism and Community Change: New Democratic Possibilities for Practice and Policy for America's Youth*, edited by S. Ginwright, P. Noguera, and J. Cammarota, 59–80. New York: Routledge, 2006.

Watts, Roderick J., Matthew A. Diemer, and Adam M. Voight. "Critical Consciousness: Current Status and Future Directions." *New Directions for Child and Adolescent Development*, no. 134 (2011): 43–57. doi:10.1002/cd.310.

Williams, Joanna L., and Tanya M. Nichols. "Black Women's Experiences with Racial Microaggressions in College: Making Meaning at the Crossroads of Race and Gender." In *Black Female Undergraduates on Campus: Successes and Challenges*, edited by C. Chambers and R. Sharpe, 75–95. Bingley, UK: Emerald Group, 2012.

Williamson, Joy A. "In Defense of Themselves: The Black Student Struggle for Success and Recognition at Predominantly White Colleges and Universities." *Journal of Negro Education* 68, no. 1 (1999): 92–105. doi:10.2307/2668212.

Willie, Sarah. *Acting Black: College, Identity, and the Performance of Race*. New York: Routledge, 2003.

Winkle-Wagner, Rachelle. *The Unchosen Me: Race, Gender, and Identity among Black Women in College*. Baltimore: Johns Hopkins University Press, 2010.

Wirt, John, et al. "Financing for Postsecondary Education: Debt Burden of College Graduates." In *The Condition of Education 2004* (Washington, DC: National Center for Education Statistics, 2004).

Wolniak, Gregory C., and Mark E. Engberg. "Academic Achievement in the First Year of College: Evidence of the Pervasive Effects of the High School Context." *Research in Higher Education* 51, no. 5 (2010): 451–67. doi:10.1007/s11162-010-9165-4.

Wong, Gloria, Annie O. Derthick, E. J. R. David, Anne Saw, and Sumie Okazaki. "The What, the Why, and the How: A Review of Racial Microaggressions Research in Psychology." *Race and Social Problems* 6, no. 2 (2014): 181–200. doi:10.1007/s12552-013-9107-9.

Yosso, Tara, and Corina B. Lopez. "Counterspaces in a Hostile Place." In *Culture Centers in Higher Education: Perspectives on Identity, Theory, and Practice*, edited by L. D. Patton, 83–104. Sterling, VA: Stylus, 2010.

Young, Iris M. *Justice and the Politics of Difference*. Princeton, NJ: Princeton University Press, 1990.

Index

CPSIA information can be obtained
at www.ICGtesting.com
Printed in the USA
LVHW030456230222
711732LV00008B/1417

9 781501 747908